Howard,
    You made the right move. I'm not far behind.
        Tom Pleisner
        1984

THE RISE AND FALL OF THE CONGLOMERATE KINGS

Also by Robert Sobel:

The Origins of Interventionism
The Big Board: A History of the New York Stock Market
The Great Bull Market: Wall Street in the 1920s
Panic on Wall Street: A History of America's Great Financial Disasters
The Curbstone Brokers: The Origins of the American Stock Exchange
Conquest and Conscience: The United States in the 1840s
The Age of Giant Corporations
Amex: A History of the American Stock Exchange
Machines and Morality: The United States in the 1850s
Money Manias: Eras of Great Speculation in American History
For Want of a Nail . . . .: If Burgoyne Had Won at Saratoga
The Entrepreneurs: Explorations Within the American Business Tradition
Herbert Hoover at the Onset of the Great Depression
N.Y.S.E.: A History of the New York Stock Exchange
The Manipulators: America in Media Age
Inside Wall Street
The Fallen Colossus: The Crash of the Penn Central
They Satisfy: The Cigarette in American Life
The Last Bull Market: Wall Street in the 1960s
The Worldly Economists
IBM: Colossus in Transition
ITT: The Management of Opportunity

THE RISE AND FALL OF THE CONGLOMERATE KINGS

ROBERT SOBEL

STEIN AND DAY/*Publishers*/New York

First published in 1984
Copyright © 1984 by Robert Sobel
All rights reserved, Stein and Day, Incorporated
Designed by Louis A. Ditizio
Printed in the United States of America
STEIN AND DAY/*Publishers*
Scarborough House
Briarcliff Manor, N.Y. 10510

Library of Congress Cataloging in Publication Data

Sobel, Robert, 1931 Feb. 19-
  The rise and fall of the conglomerate kings.

  Bibliography: p.
  Includes index.
  1. Conglomerate corporations—United States—History.
2. Consolidation and merger of corporations—United
States—History.   3. Directors of corporations—United
States—History.   I. Title.
HD 2756.S62   1984   338.8'042   83-40358
ISBN 0-8128-2961-1

For Marvin, Gail, Ilisa,
and Adam Schaffer

CONTENTS

THE
RISE
AND
FALL
OF THE
CONGLOMERATE
KINGS

1

Origins

———————•◆•———————

Conglomerates were the rage on Wall Street in the late 1960s, and their managers among the most visible businessmen in that high noon of post-World War II American capitalism. Scarcely a week passed without reports that at least one old line, familiar corporation was being raided by what some euphemistically termed a "multiform company," which didn't even exist prior to the war and which now was high on *Fortune*'s list of 500 largest corporations. Conglomerates were the most exciting corporate form to appear in more than a generation, and they shook up the business scene as no other phenomenon had since the era of trust creation at the turn of the century. They seemed to have come out of nowhere, these new firms and the men who led them. In fact, such diversification arguably was the most unanticipated development in American business during our time.

The movement flourished for little more than a decade, and then swiftly declined. Even now students of the phenomenon disagree as to its origins, quarrel over its accomplishments (and lack of same), and aren't quite sure we have seen the last of the breed.

For a while it was fashionable to claim that the conglomerators were direct descendants of those sedentary merchants whose shops and offices lined Wall Street more than two centuries ago. These men dealt in such paper as insurance contracts and lottery tickets. They sold shares in private land companies that they had organized to purchase sections in undeveloped parts of the colony north of the city. These shares were to be liquidated at higher prices once settlers (and potential buyers) appeared. Wall Street's shopkeepers supervised commercial voyages to Europe, Africa, and the Far East, chartering ships, hiring captains and crews, raising the necessary capital, and providing insurance. Afterward, should the enterprise prove successful, they would preside over the distribution of profits.

These were only a few of their more important activities. In fact, such men—and their counterparts in Boston, Philadelphia, Charleston, and other seaports—were opportunists in the best sense of the term. All they had were business and family contacts, some capital, and their wits. Uncommitted to any single business, they positioned themselves to react to shifts in the economic and business scene.

Individuals like these, it was argued, would not have had much trouble understanding the machinations of Royal Little, Harold Geneen, and Jimmy Ling in the late 1950s and the 1960s. The resemblance didn't go much beyond the surface, however. The conglomerators were innovators who broke new ground in management, organization, and finance. Not so the sedentary merchants, who were traditionalists to the core, and whose counterparts had existed since the beginnings of commerce. The Polos of Venice were of this breed, and one of the family, the famous Marco, reported on similar businessmen in China. Free-form merchants might have been located without difficulty in Rome and Greece at the height of their power. They were the backbone of the commercial establishments in ancient Egypt, Mesopotamia, and Persia. Discussions of their activities may be found in the Old Testament. Some of the money changers Jesus expelled from the Temple doubtless were sedentary merchants, and his indignation at their activities probably was similar to criticisms of this kind of businessman heard in every civilization of which we have knowledge. In fact, the antitrusters of the 1960s felt somewhat the same way about conglomerates such as International Telephone & Telegraph, Ling-Temco-Vought, Gulf + Western, and Litton Industries.

However, there is no direct link between the sedentary merchants and the conglomerators. Concentration and specialization, not diversification, had been the tendency of American business during the century prior to the arrival of the first conglomerates. The name of a corporation told you its business: United States Steel, General Motors, Dow Chemical, General Foods, American Tobacco, American Sugar Refining, and so on. To be an executive at Continental Can meant to be devoted to the container industry—not land development, electronics, fast foods, and underwear, but cans. As recently as the mid-1940s, no serious student of American capitalism expected this situation to change.

Nonetheless it happened. Just as the specialists had replaced the generalists, so the conglomerators would challenge, often successfully, the leviathan corporations of mid-century, industrial America. One might claim the conglomerators represented a return to the ancient tradition of sedentary merchants, though it does seem implausible. But they surely weren't in the direct line of descent from the sedentary merchants of a pre-industrial age.

In 1948 the Federal Trade Commission undertook a major study of the new merger movement then gathering force. At the time this appeared a prelude to an important antitrust crusade, an attempt to gather materials, create a rationale, and provide a springboard for the Justice Department's lawyers. In the report were the usual warnings regarding the increase in vertical takeovers—in which companies acquired suppliers or distributors—and concern about horizontal ones—when a firm purchased a competitor producing similar items. These were both familiar to the FTC and might be dealt with through the application of antitrust experience gathered over the past half century. Corporations like Standard Oil of New Jersey had become expert at vertical takeovers, while General Motors had developed through horizontal ones. Most companies—the classic case being American Tobacco—tried their hands at both varieties. No second-year law student would have had trouble sniffing out candidates for antitrust prosecution. Similarly, corporation lawyers knew just how to erect defenses when attacked by competitors or the government. There were few surprises here.

The FTC was troubled, however, about conglomerate mergers, which sometimes were referred to as "circular" in nature. This appeared to be something new, and one can almost sense the confusion felt by the author of the FTC report. "Of all the types of mergers," he observed, "the reasons for this particular form of acquisition are the most difficult to ascertain." The rationale wasn't at all clear, and he was at a loss as how best to characterize and categorize such takeovers. One can almost feel him struggling with the concept, attempting to make sense of it, and ultimately failing to do so. "The motives underlying conglomerate acquisitions appear to include such diverse incentives as desires to spread risks, to invest large sums of idle liquid capital, to add products which can be handled with existing sales and distribution personnel, to increase the number of products which can be grouped together in the company's advertisements, etc." All of which were far off the mark. Of these motives only the first, the hope of spreading risks, played any role at all in the conglomerate philosophy of the period, and then it was only of peripheral importance. Moreover, the writer was referring here to acquisitions of the kind made by conventional corporations for many decades. Nowhere does he discuss any true conglomerates. But this is not surprising, since in 1948 the first of the modern breed—Textron Inc.—was yet to be born; its founder, Royal Little, was still intent on creating a textile empire. In fact, the FTC was able to locate only one firm that it labeled a conglomerate, but quickly conceded it was unique and not likely to be imitated—certainly this was not the progenitor of the movement that followed.

The company was American Home Products, which was founded in 1926 by a group of faceless and half-forgotten businessmen and which was supposed to turn out manufactured items used by families. It started out as a small company, but it grew rapidly through acquisitions. In itself, this growth was hardly unusual; as will be seen, the 1920s saw the second of the three great waves of takeovers in American business history. What set AHP apart from the others was its continued acquisition of new firms even after the movement came to an abrupt halt with the arrival of the Great Depression. Also, almost all the takeovers were of companies in nonrelated areas.

Ever tight-lipped regarding such matters, AHP will not say just who it was who thought up the idea, but in the next two decades the company acquired, in an apparently random fashion, sixty firms in such diverse product areas as ethical and proprietary drugs, floor wax, coffee, Italian foods, lubricating oil, cheese products, insecticides, and beauty preparations. American Home was a rapidly growing and highly profitable corporation, which by 1948 was posting revenues of more than $140 million and showed a net income of $9.1 million. Yet while many of its products were widely used throughout the country and overseas, AHP itself was relatively unknown except within the industry and on Wall Street and was content to remain so.

Antitrusters who monitored such companies as General Foods, Quaker Oats, General Mills, Procter & Gamble, Pillsbury, Bristol-Myers, and Colgate Palmolive variously categorized AHP as a food company, a drug-based operation, or an industrial concern. But clearly each definition excluded some of its units. American Home was an anomaly, an enterprise that defied the conventional cubbyholes, and one that the Federal Trade Commission and other regulatory agencies did not understand.

This was more than simply irksome. Without understanding there could be no policy, especially when it came to antitrust prosecutions. The low-keyed leaders of AHP understood this. They refused to cooperate with business writers seeking stories, advertised their products rather than the base company itself, and were content to see revenues and earnings rise steadily. Such people were not the prototypes of the splashy conglomerators of the 1950s and 1960s.

The FTC appreciated this. At the same time, however, some at the agency wondered what might happen if a corporation embarked upon a program of haphazardly gobbling up other firms. The author of the 1948 FTC report seemed to view such growth as akin to cancer—uncontrolled, unregulated, and dangerous, perhaps fatal to the orderly progression of American business. "There is present in most conglomerate acquisitions a simple drive for power," he concluded. Without much in the way of evidence, and using his imagination to the fullest, he tried to sketch an outline of an almost autonomous business empire of the future, and here too demonstrated an incapacity to appreciate the full potential of the conglomerate form, concentrating instead upon peripheral matters.

With the economic power which it secures through its operations in many diverse fields, the giant conglomerate corporation
may attain an almost impregnable economic position. Threatened with competition in any one of its various activities, it
may sell below cost in that field, offsetting its losses through
profits made in other lines—a practice which is frequently
explained as one of meeting competition. The conglomerate
corporation is thus in a position to strike out with great force
against smaller businesses in a variety of different industries.[1]

A flimsy rationale indeed—such criticism could be leveled against
almost any large corporation, and the fact that conglomerates might
expand in many product areas instead of one or two hardly made them
more dangerous. Actually, price cutting never became a hallmark of
conglomerate operations, as evinced by an investigation of American
Home Products. While marketing dozens of products, that company
never became a leader in any single industry—nor would LTV, Litton,
ITT, Gulf + Western, and other conglomerates a decade and more later.

One should not be too harsh on the FTC writer, who was only trying to
offer analysis and recommendations at a time when the movement had
not really begun. A generation later, when the Justice Department
started moving against these firms, the government still lacked a rationale, and had to substitute hyperbole for law.

Although it concentrated on vertical takeovers, then considered the
obvious method by which corporations would expand, the FTC report
was significant as the first important attempt on the part of Washington
to explore the developing movement. The report does not explore the
origins of the conglomerate philosophy—because there was none at the
time. What was occurring was the beginning of what one publication
termed "the conglomerate commotion," which emerged from an unusual
complex of economic, political, social, and psychological factors, all of
which came together after World War II. There were no precedents for
such a movement; the conglomerators were more than willing to rethink
almost every important stricture by which Big Business had been guided
during the past century.

In order to appreciate just why and how the conglomerate movement
originated, one first must consider the social, economic, and political
atmosphere of the post-World War II period, the backdrop against which
the drama was played.

During the war newspapers and magazines carried stories about what
to expect after peace returned. While many of these publications were
naturally optimistic, a vein of uncertainty and fear ran through others.

In different words they asked the same question: "Would the arrival of peace result in a return to the miseries of the Great Depression?"

Most mainstream economists seemed to think so. Their reasoning was clear and convincing:

The underlying American economy had never truly recovered from the depression. Rather, war-related demands had provided it with what amounted to a temporary "hype," and the bad times would return when it was removed. They pointed out that in 1940, when the United States was already gearing up for war, the gross national product came to a shade under $100 billion, almost twice what it had been at the bottom of the depression seven years earlier, but still below the $103 billion mark set in 1929. The GNP for 1944 was $210 billion, the result of the creation of an arsenal economy. What would happen when the war-related orders came to an end? Economists observed that the GNP fell by almost a quarter in the aftermath of World War I. This time, they predicted, the falloff would be even more severe.

The unemployment rate in 1940 had been 14.6 percent; more than 8 million Americans were classified as being out of work. Not once in the 1930s had the United States experienced single digit unemployment. By 1944 the rate had come down to 1.2 percent, which meant that, allowing for those who were changing jobs or entering or leaving the work force, the nation really had no unemployment. Moreover, in this period millions of women entered the labor pool, and many considered remaining at their jobs after the wartime emergency ended. What would happen when the armed forces returned to their prewar level? In 1945 the various services had more than 12 million personnel, up sharply from less than half a million in 1940. The dumping of some 11 million servicemen onto an economy in which military procurement had come to an end would lead to tremendous dislocations.

The economists predicted disaster. Seymour Harris wrote and spoke of an unemployment rate exceeding 20 percent. Alvin Hansen wondered whether a combination of continued wartime controls and a massive public works program might keep the economy steady, and concluded it would not. Wesley Clair Mitchell observed that there had been slumps after all wars, and saw no reason why it should be different this time. As early as 1943, a young Paul Samuelson, in an essay entitled "Full Employment After the War," concluded this could not be. Assuming rapid demobilization and the liquidation of controls, "there would be ushered in the greatest period of unemployment and industrial dislocation which any economy has ever faced," and along with the others he reiterated the thought in 1945. By then General Frank Hines of the Veterans' Administration was warning of the creation of a native fascism if these millions of discharged servicemen were unable to find work. Demoralized by an ailing economy and frustrated by broken promises, "drifting aimlessly about the country," they might easily become radicalized. Demagogue Gerald L. K. Smith embraced this notion. While conceding that his cause could expect little support in the 1944 election, Smith looked forward to the campaign of 1948, when he expected to support a disgruntled former serviceman for the presidency.

Some of the problems predicted during conversion to a peacetime economy did develop, but there was no significant slump. The gross national product declined slightly in 1946, and then surged ahead, crossing the $257 billion mark in 1948. Much of this strength came from the consumer sector. The economists had expected the public to enter the marketplace to make up for years of hardship during the depression and war, but not to this extent. After some hesitation businessmen geared up to meet the demands, which involved beefing up labor forces and competing for scarce resources. There was to be no important postwar depression; instead, the nation experienced a major inflationary spiral in 1946 and 1947. The strong economy was able to absorb all of the veterans, so that the unemployment rate was a low 3.8 percent in 1948, by which time inflation had declined to an uncomfortable but manageable 2.7 percent. Profits soared, as virtually every major industry (the most important exception being defense) posted new records. Total corporate profits, which prior to the imposition of new war taxes had reached a peak of $12.1 billion in 1943, rose to $16.3 billion in 1946 and then went to $22.5 billion in 1948. By then most of the earlier uncertainties were gone, and were replaced by a growing conviction that the boom would continue.

ECONOMIC PERFORMANCE OF SELECTED CORPORATIONS, 1945, 1946, and 1947
(in millions of dollars)

Corporation	Revenues			Profits		
	1945	1946	1947	1945	1946	1947
American Can	243	258	338	22	14	36
American Woolen	163	171	175	24	35	26
Boeing	421	14	22	23	(8)	(1)
Curtiss Wright	1198	72	83	91	(35)	(11)
General Electric	1466	911	1525	58	44	101
General Motors	3128	1963	3815	188	88	288
International Tel & Tel	95	27	143	13	(5)	4
Michigan Bumper	1	3	4	0	0.2	0.4
Raytheon	173	106	66	3	0	(0.1)
Textron	47	113	125	4	17	14
United Aircraft	484	20	208	25	(5)	15
U.S. Steel	1740	1486	2117	84	86	217

Source: *Moody's Industrial Index*, 1948

Not even the most confirmed pessimist could deny that the American economy was the strongest in the world. Emblematic of this was the strength of the dollar, the supreme currency of the postwar period. Its central role in world business was ratified by the Allied powers even while the war continued. Under the terms of the Bretton Woods agreements of 1944 the other nations agreed to fix the price of their currencies in terms of dollars and to intervene in the money markets should their prices rise above or fall below certain limits. In turn the United States was obliged to tie the dollar to gold at $35 an ounce, and stand willing to buy or sell at that price to any central bank. Not even at the high noon of the empire in the late nineteenth century had the pound sterling enjoyed such status and recognition. The strong, central role of the dollar was yet another reason for the growing confidence of American businessmen in the late 1940s and early 1950s, and they looked with fresh interest at the possibilities of expanding overseas.

This optimism was furthered by a government in Washington dedicated to growth and stability, though its virtues and accomplishments weren't fully recognized at the time. Although it had a shaky start, Harry Truman's stewardship of the economy should have been praised by the business community, but such wasn't the case and most leaders of large corporations supported Republican Thomas Dewey for the presidency in 1948.

Dewey's unexpected defeat shocked the nation and may have contributed to the gloom that helped bring about an economic slump the following year. The decline was ending in 1950 when North Korea attacked South Korea, resulting in American intervention and a sharp increase in military spending. Defense expenditures, which came to over $74 billion in 1944, the last full year of World War II, had declined to $12 billion by 1948. In 1952 close to $39 billion went for military purposes. The figure declined somewhat after the war, but in no year of the 1950s would it fall below $35 billion.

The Korean War boosted the economy and demonstrated once again how wartime spending could take up the slack should the market for civilian goods falter. The economy revived, and in 1952, Truman's last full year in office, the gross national product came to $345 billion and corporate profits to $19.5 billion. During his seven years in office the GNP had grown by more than 60 percent and profits nearly doubled. In 1952 the unemployment rate was 3 percent and the Consumer Price Index advanced by less than one percent. An impressive accomplishment, but one unappreciated on Wall Street, where stock prices failed to reflect this new prosperity. While the Dow Jones Industrials did advance by slightly more than 80 percent in the Truman era, it did so from a depressed base, and there was none of the exuberance one might have expected from such an economic performance.

While the economy boomed during the last years of Truman's second term, there was a political and social malaise in the land. Senator Joseph McCarthy and other Republicans accused the administration of being "soft on communism," and McCarthy often referred to "twenty years of treason." At the same time there were scandals within the administration itself, mostly involving the Bureau of Internal Revenue and the Reconstruction Finance Corporation. And there were clear indications that members of the White House staff had accepted bribes from businessmen. Senator Estes Kefauver, a Tennessee Democrat who had announced his intention of challenging Truman for the nomination, uncovered corruption in several of the nation's largest cities, all of which were controlled by Democrats. Finally, the Korean War peace talks dragged on, with the President apparently incapable of concluding them satisfactorily. Public opinion polls indicated that Truman's popularity was at an all-time low. Trust in political institutions had eroded badly. Not since 1932 had the time seemed so ripe for a "savior."

Commentators in both parties cast Dwight Eisenhower in that role. *The New Republic* called him "one of the country's precious national assets." Democratic Senator Paul Douglas seriously suggested the general be given the nomination of both parties in 1952. There even is evidence that Truman offered to support Eisenhower on several occasions. Clearly Eisenhower was the most popular person in the nation, and after he won the Republican nomination, his victory was never really in doubt.

American business craved confidence in and support from Washington. With the inauguration of Eisenhower they received both. The last ingredient for a bold transformation of the scene was now in place. Looking back on the 1950s, some historians have concluded that it was a period of relative tranquility, a pause between the often hectic and exhilarating reformism of the New and Fair Deals, John Kennedy's New Frontier, and Lyndon Johnson's Great Society.

Perhaps it was a tranquil time in most social and political matters, and of course Eisenhower did end the Korean War and managed to avoid other foreign entanglements of that sort. In many respects this was indeed a "silent generation." But not in business, where there was more innovation and expansion than had been seen in any peacetime period since the late 1920s. Given the secure and confident atmosphere provided by a benevolent government, many of the nation's big businessmen abandoned some of their old conservatism and experimented more than they had in over two decades. Low and stable interest rates, together with a higher stock market, enabled them to raise capital with relative ease, and so they did. Such was the kind of soil and climate in which the seeds of diversification germinated.

With all of this the conglomerators might not have acted when and how they did were it not for the postwar presence of the final, elusive ingredients—a sense of mission; a somewhat naive optimism; a craving for challenges, adventure, and success; and finally, a belief in and identification with the American Dream, ill-defined, experienced rather than intellectualized, well understood by those who embraced it, and more alluring to outsiders than to those already a part of the nation's elite.

Almost to a man, the major conglomerators were classic outsiders. Some were foreign born, most were Jewish or Catholic, and many came from areas of the country not known for producing major businessmen, namely the South and Far West. Their education was scanty, and these men were poorly connected with the old establishments, which in some cases rejected them out of hand, and considered them somewhat barbaric. Unable or unwilling to work within the traditional constraints, they threw them off and drew up their own rules, which in turn were often discarded. Like most of the famed "robber barons" of the late nineteenth century to whom they occasionally were compared, the conglomerators were regarded with mistrust and incredulous wonder by the more conventional businessmen of their times, many of whom would be shunted aside and consigned to the corporate scrap heap. At the time the conglomerators were alternately portrayed as revivers of a dormant capitalism and barbarians out to destroy the essentials of the system, vampires leaching the vitality from productive enterprises.[2]

The fashioning of a new business form, especially one as audacious as the conglomerate, requires as much imagination and ingenuity as the creation of great works of art. Powerful individuals whose accomplishments inspired lesser men may have been brutal and heavy-handed, but rarely did their efforts derive from a narrow cynicism and a mere craving for wealth. Businessmen interested solely in piling up profits to the exclusion of all else seldom innovate. The great movers and shakers of previous generations—individuals like E. H. Harriman, John D. Rockefeller, Henry Ford, David Sarnoff, and above all, Andrew Carnegie and Thomas Edison—had an almost poetic view of their work. That they craved power and were not above bending or breaking conventions and laws cannot be denied, but each also sought the satisfactions that came with realizing their creative impulses.

The impulse surfaced at different times for each of the great conglomerators. For Royal Little it came when he decided to abandon earlier plans to create his textile giant and to concentrate upon turning managements around at a wide variety of companies. It arrived slowly for

Jimmy Ling, when in the early 1950s he came to understand that it was possible to raise hard cash and purchase producing assets by printing and peddling stock certificates. Around that time Tex Thornton learned there was more to life than electronics, and it was simpler, cheaper, and faster to buy research and product lines than work at them himself. Harold Geneen tried to convince his superiors at American Can and then at Jones & Laughlin that diversification could bring beneficial changes, and he failed. He then had the same experience at Raytheon. By the time he arrived at ITT, Geneen was well prepared to transform that firm into a conglomerate. Charles Bluhdorn, Ben Heineman, and a score of others had similar experiences.

Except for Little, these men were of a new generation. None had much in the way of corporate experience during the Great Depression. A few worked at second-and third-level jobs through World War II, while others were in the armed forces. Most were financially and managerially oriented; only a few had any clear idea of the new technologies and inventions spawned by the military procurement programs. They were opportunists, seeking the main chance.

They came along at the right time.

2

Royal Little: The Pioneer

It would be nice to assert that Royal Little knew what he was up to when he started transforming Textron Inc. from a medium-sized, somewhat flabby textile corporation into the first of the modern conglomerates. Students of American business might then claim that the movement had a coherent base set down by a master strategist, a firm ideological substructure upon which he and others erected their businesses. Were this so Little might be set beside the likes of J. P. Morgan who, seated in the opulent study of his Park Avenue mansion, brought order out of what he considered the chaos of several industries while playing endless games of solitaire. Or of Alfred Sloan, assiduously poring over organizational charts in the enormous board room at General Motors' Detroit headquarters in the early 1920s, as he established lines of responsibility that have been widely imitated and have been studied in every respectable graduate school of business in the world. But this was not to be.

After it was all over—when he stepped down as Textron's chairman and CEO—Little set down on paper his beliefs regarding structure, strategy, tactics, organization, and the like, and did so in a rambling, sketchy, and disorganized fashion. What emerges from his memoir is a picture of an amiable eccentric, an original who, while clearly intelligent and shrewd, innovative and thoughtful, had an almost playful attitude toward business. Perhaps these were desirable, even necessary traits for success in such enterprises, but they appear jarring to those familiar with the personalities of such as Morgan and Sloan, who were virtually humorless. Trust creation at the turn of the century and the organization of giant industrial corporations in the 1920s demanded a studied approach and a flair for subjects like logic and geometry. This would not do for the conglomerate movement, which possessed a measure of randomness and demanded more imagination than any of its predecessors. For example, the scope and power of several of Morgan's greatest creations, such as United States Steel, filled his contemporaries with a sense of awe. In contrast, some of James Ling's takeovers and spin-offs seemed absurd. When the time came for Sloan to compose his memoirs he called upon the talents of John McDonald, one of the best business writers of his day, and entitled his book *My Years With General Motors*. Little's memoir, written by himself with the assistance of some Harvard Business School students, was entitled *How to Lose $100,000,000 and Other Valuable Advice*.

Little was born in Wakefield, Massachusetts, in 1896, into a middle-class family, a member of which was Royal's soon-to-become famous uncle, Arthur D., founder of the prominent consulting firm which bore his name. Four years later his father died, and two years after that his mother remarried. Little rarely spoke of his stepfather—we don't even know his name—but Little's memoir notes indicate that his stepfather was the outcast of a prominent Boston family, the head of which ran a large printing operation, and that he too was a printer. He was not a particularly good one, with absolutely no talent for business.

Yearning for success, Little's stepfather took his new family to Buffalo, where he opened, struggled to maintain, and finally shut down a small print shop. Slipping out of town to avoid his creditors, he hopscotched his way westward, the family in tow, and repeated the experience in Cleveland, Chicago, Sioux City, Denver, Salt Lake City, and finally, in 1910, San Francisco. By then Royal was fourteen years old and about to enter high school, having already attended more than a dozen schools.

It was then what Little later called "the most important thing in my life" occurred. His Uncle Arthur was establishing himself in Boston and had married, but there were no children. Always having had a fatherly interest in Royal and knowing of his sister-in-law's circumstances, Arthur proposed that the boy come east to live with him in Brookline, attend private schools, and then enter Harvard to study chemical engineering, after which he would take a post at his firm. Royal's mother knew there was little hope for her son in San Francisco and consented. He arrived in Brookline in January 1911, and after four years at Noble and Greenough entered Harvard as a member of the class of 1919.

Royal wasn't much of a student, flitting on and off probation, and demonstrating no talent for or interest in engineering. It was with some relief that he entered the Army when the United States declared war on Germany in 1917, and after a half year of training went overseas as an infantry first lieutenant.

Little was discharged in 1919, at which time Arthur urged him to return to Harvard, complete his studies there, and then go on to M.I.T. By now Royal was 23 years old, and his early disinterest in academia had been reinforced by experiences in France and Germany. He did not want to be an engineer, and in any case had no intention of spending the next four or five years in classrooms. While he did manage to obtain what was known as a "war degree" from Harvard in 1919 by passing a few inconsequential exams, Little did so more in recognition of the prestige value of the B.A. than anything else.

Little told his uncle he wanted to go into business, and although Arthur was dismayed at Royal's decision, he did all he could to place him in a good firm in a promising industry. Arthur had been one of the chemists who had developed rayon, the miracle fabric of its day. This so-called "artificial silk" appeared capable of reviving the moribund New England textile industry by placing it upon a new base. He spoke of these ideas, and Royal seemed impressed. Arthur then introduced him to two old friends already in the business, Eliot Farley of Lustron Corporation and Bradley Dewey, the founder of Dewey & Almy, and each offered him a job.

But Royal was not quite ready to take the plunge. Instead he signed on as an apprentice at the Cheney Brothers Silk Company, where the real thing was turned into filament yarn. There he learned how to operate the machines, studied management techniques, but above all, absorbed as much as he could about the textile industry and the relative merits of silk and rayon. A half year later, fairly certain rayon had a bright future, he left Cheney Brothers to join Lustron as a salesman. As an indication of his new confidence, Little invested his entire savings, $2,500, in company stock.

As it turned out Lustron was underfinanced, Farley was not a particularly good manager, and rayon met with resistance from a public that still preferred silk. The postwar recession didn't help matters either. Finally, Lustron could not compete with several larger and more efficient companies. In the end Farley sold out to one of them, Celanese. Nothing was left after the creditors and preferred stockholders were paid off. Now Little was both out of work and out of money.

But the interest in rayon had grown, and Little sought new opportunities in the field, preferably as head of his own company. Together with some friends he borrowed $10,000, part of which was used to purchase the corporate shell of a defunct firm, the Chemical Products Corporation. He then transformed one of its divisions, Special Yarns, into an operating unit and used the rest of the money to purchase equipment and start operations. The recession had ended by then and the nation was in the first stage of a major economic boom. Rayon had become more acceptable; slightly more than 10 million pounds of packaged rayon and acetate were produced in America in 1920, the year Lustron failed. This figure was to expand tenfold during the 1920s, as demand for rayon often outran production. While Special Yarns had to struggle against such giants as Celanese and Du Pont, there was room for all. Little not only survived but prospered, to the point where he dreamed of using Special Yarns as a base upon which to erect a major textile corporation. Seeking power through size, he merged his company with Franklin Rayon Dyeing in 1928 to form the Franklin Rayon Corporation. Now he tried to interest several investment bankers in underwriting a stock issue. It was the height of the great bull market, but even then, Franklin was too chancy. No Wall Street or Boston house would touch it.

Rayon consumption increased sharply in the early 1930s, even while the nation suffered through the early stages of the Great Depression. Franklin's profits expanded by $42,000 in 1930 to peak at $285,000 in 1933 before leveling off. Little acquired several mills in this period, following accepted industry practice during times of economic malaise: when small units went under they would be gobbled up by survivors at distress prices. As late as 1937 it seemed Franklin would emerge as one of the more important factors in the rayon field.

It was then that Little decided to take a sabbatical. An old friend offered him a partnership in the respected Wall Street investment banking firm of Herrick Berg, at the reasonable price of $200,000. Perhaps a trifle bored with textiles, Little accepted, and moved to Manhattan. He could not have picked a worse time to enter this field. The 1937 slump was to be even more severe than that of 1929, and many of Herrick Berg's positions were wiped out. Little lost his entire investment, and had to return, badly bruised, to Franklin, where conditions were hardly better. Due to the slump, sales and profits declined. In 1938—when the company's name was changed to Atlantic Rayon—it posted a $72,000 loss. To further complicate Little's problems, the Internal Revenue Service ruled that his wipeout at Herrick Berg was a short-term capital loss, not a business expense, and so was subject to unfavorable tax consequences. Reflecting upon this more than three decades later, Little was able to discern "two silver linings" in that dark cloud.

> First, my short experience as an underwriter gave me a tremendous advantage in the future in dealing with the investment banking firms that underwrote the many public offerings that I was later to be involved with. Second, I was so burned up by the arbitrary way that the IRS had treated me in the business expense case that I decided to learn something about the tax laws. If the government could take advantage of a technicality in the law perhaps I could do the same to them in return. Every technicality that I have ever taken advantage of since then has been completely legal—no cheating, no iffy cases. What the IRS

gained by treating me unfairly in 1937 has cost them many, many millions of dollars since.[1]

Thus, two of the attributes so necessary to the future conglomerator were set in place.

Atlantic was solidly in the black for 1939, but showed a small deficit the following year, when the industry was plagued by price cutting. By then it was a medium-sized factor in what had become a highly cyclical industry. Revenues that year came to $7.5 million, and the firm's net worth, after 18 years in operation, was only $1.8 million.

Like many other companies of its size, Atlantic was saved from stagnation by war-related events. With the coming of World War II workers in defense industries had regular and large paychecks, and they came to market for new clothes, which resulted in better and firmer prices for rayon. More important were government orders for uniforms, tenting, and the like. Mill operators like Little went to Washington seeking contracts and returned with larger orders than they could handle. Successful manufacturers did well, but the real bonanza was for those who had struggled through the depression with excess capacity.

Little was one of these. Casting about for ideas, he soon decided to enter the parachute market. His old friends at Cheney owned a moribund operation called Pioneer Parachute, which was badly in need of reorganization and refinancing. Although Atlantic Rayon was desperately short of cash itself, Little decided to make an offer for Pioneer. He would provide management and refinancing, in return for 60 percent of the company. Cheney agreed, and out of this came Atlantic Parachute.

The new company did well at first. Little got his orders, put on extra shifts, and sought out old, abandoned factories to acquire. In 1943 he took over Suncook Mills, a New Hampshire competitor, as part of his plan to become the nation's leading parachute manufacturer. It seemed a sensible move. The war was going badly, and it appeared the production boom would continue for the foreseeable future. That year Atlantic Rayon showed sales of $23.8 million and an after tax profit of more than half a million dollars. The factories in Lowell, Massachusetts, and Manchester, New Hampshire, were running full out.

This is not to say Little hadn't any problems. Unwilling to enter into what amounted to a "sweetheart deal" with two underhanded government purchasing agents, he lost parachute orders. Bouncing back, he obtained a variety of new contracts for military products, among them several for the manufacture of hammocks to be used by soldiers in the Pacific war.

For the first time since the 1920s, Little enjoyed the luxury of having extra cash in his treasury. More was obtained through the sale in 1944 of two small divisions for $1.5 million, and another $2 million was raised by selling an issue of debentures. This was in preparation for a renewed campaign to become a dominant figure in the textile industry, even to the point of challenging the chemical companies that had taken leadership in artificial fabrics. As though to signal his ambitions, in 1943 Little changed the name of his company to Textron Inc.[2]

What would happen to textile sales once the war ended? This question was uppermost in the minds of New England's mill owners. Some of them, flush with profits for the first time in their lives and understanding that there would be tremendous overcapacity throughout the industry when the wartime orders stopped, hoped to sell out before hit by a new slump. Bolder than most, Little planned to buy out some of the best of them in the process of fashioning his new Textron. And he would do so in such a way as to have the government bear a large portion of the costs.

Little had become an ardent student of tax laws ever since clashing with the IRS over the Herrick Berg losses. Along with other businessmen he had developed a keen appreciation of several interesting segments of the wartime excess profits statutes. These provided for virtually confiscatory tax rates for all profits above a certain percentage of revenues, with the proviso that they might be set against losses incurred during the reconversion period. There was a wide and deep loophole in the law. A company with excess profits might buy out one that had losses, and then submit a consolidated tax report, one in which the profits of one company were offset by the deficits of the other. This would result in sizable refunds—often enough to pay for most, if not all, of the purchase price.

Textron had reported excess profits during the war, and Little meant to take full advantage of the statutes. "It's the only time in my lifetime that I'll ever have a situation like that," he later said. "You have to have a war that makes marginal operations profit-heavy, a tax situation plus large family holders that want to get out. And you have an insurance policy from the government if you're wrong."[3]

Little's problem, which apparently he didn't recognize at the time, was that his professed objective couldn't easily be reached by this strategy. Most of the truly desirable textile firms were in positions similar to that of Textron, in that they too had paid excess profits taxes. Little was on the prowl for losers which could be purchased for knocked down prices, and there were precious few of these in the industry.

Occasionally he would come across a firm with a large tax loss on its books, its stock selling near or at the recent low, and whose managers were eager to join Textron. Such a firm might be purchased through a bank loan, and then parts of its operations disposed of through resales, these often providing sufficient cash with which to pay off a large part of the borrowed money. On the other hand, the company's products might not have a place in Little's plans for Textron. He was put into the position of either rejecting a bargain or abandoning his plans to create an integrated textile firm. This situation had to be faced on several occasions in the postwar period, and upon the choice hinged Textron's future and Little's place in entrepreneurial history. In the end he rejected the goal and concentrated upon the strategy. Instead of becoming just another CEO in a declining industry, Little emerged as the pioneer conglomerator.

For the moment, however, plans for the textile giant were put into action. In 1944 Little organized a new company, American Associates, which was to serve as his prime vehicle in takeovers. Then he opened negotiations for the acquisition of Manville-Jenckes, a run-down manufacturer of greige (unfinished) cloth, with a book value of $6.5 million and a long string of deficits. Little paid $5.5 million for Manville-Jenckes, most of which came from a loan from the First National Bank of Boston. Then he sold off several facilities for $2.2 million, and this sum, together with Manville-Jenkes' liquid assets and tax loss carry-forwards, came to more than the original purchase price. In effect, Little had acquired for nothing an operating company which, once turned around, would be capable of earning upward of half a million dollars a year.

It had been a fine deal, with only one flaw: there was no connection between Textron's main business and that of Manville-Jenckes. While it was true that both were in textiles, the market for synthetics was wholly different from that for greige. Some saw in this a horizontal expansion, but this had not been the reason for the takeover. Rather, it had been dictated by sheer expediency. The conglomerate philosophy was taking shape, due more to IRS regulations than anything else. Without realizing it, Little had started relinquishing his goal of creating a textile giant in his search for higher profits and beneficial tax treatments.

Little scoured the industry for other likely candidates, while at the same time devising new strategies to use in his operations. In October 1945, he acquired the Lonsdale Company, a firm that had fallen upon hard times and whose line complemented Textron's. Two months later he took a position in a much larger company, Nashua Manufacturing, which had an indifferent sales and earnings record, and later Textron acquired all of the common stock. Nashua, one of the nation's oldest textile companies, manufactured a full line of blankets and sheets and had 1945 revenues of more than $33 million and assets of $17 million. Unlike Lonsdale, its products were quite dissimilar from those turned out by Textron's other plants, but this did not bother Little; it was just too good a deal to pass up, since under the worst circumstances Nashua might be liquidated for more than its selling price.

These two companies cost Little $16 million, most of which was raised through the sale of debentures. Without waiting to absorb these firms, Little purchased twelve textile plants in the Carolinas from Gossett Mills and Hoskins for more than $12 million, shaping them into a new holding company called Textron Southern.

As a result of these whirlwind transactions Textron had two major subdivisions—and a debt of $14.3 million owed to several banks, along with a $6 million commitment to Textron Southern. Little removed part of the pressure by selling some of Nashua's assets and then transferring the cash and other assets to Textron Southern, after which the banks were paid off. This financial byplay resulted in Nashua being relieved of $9.5 million—only $1 million less than its purchase price—and emerging a stronger firm than before. By the end of the year Textron's debt had been reduced to $7 million, and this was halved over the first three months of 1947. That year Textron reported sales of $125 million and a net profit of $6.3 million. The dividend was doubled to a dollar per share. By these measures Textron was a success, and Little became accustomed to being hailed as a financial wonder.

However, his manipulations troubled some investors while delighting others. What exactly was he up to? No one—not even Little himself—seemed to know the answer, and this uncertainty was reflected on Wall Street. The company's common stock fell to below ten in late 1946, at which point it was going for less than one and a half times earnings. Then, in a period of less than three months, the price doubled, only to fall back to twelve by midyear. Later on, when Little tried to purchase companies with stock rather than cash, he chafed at the relatively low price afforded it at the marketplace, and he wooed the financial press and the investment advisory services. To little avail. Rarely would Textron command a premium price, and even in the late 1960s, when some high technology issues and a handful of the more glamorous conglomerates were going for more than 70 times earnings, Textron was available at below 20. This was due, in part at least, to the reputation Little had acquired in the postwar period as the junkman of American industry, casting about for underpriced and ailing firms he might turn around.

Textron was supposed to become a textile giant. At least this was Little's professed objective in the late 1940s and early 1950s. In this period, however, the parts simply were not coming together. Instead, he had put together a mixed bag of unrelated or barely related textile companies, almost all of which were saddled with antiquated facilities badly in need of modernization. One mill would overproduce, while another would be forced to the open market for purchases. Little hadn't acquired or developed either retail outlets or clothing production facilities. The reason was obvious: there were no bargain companies in these fields, and Little had concentrated more on seeking bargains and loopholes in the tax laws than in putting together a viable, integrated firm.

The long-anticipated textile glut finally arrived in 1948, complicated by the move by many manufacturers out of their antiquated New England facilities to new ones in the union-free South. Now it appeared that those who had sold out to Textron, often at high prices, had outfoxed Little. He admitted as much by trying to close down Nashua Mills. This proved a messy affair, with Little being branded as antilabor. Textile Workers Union President Emil Rieve called him "a blight upon Nashua," while Senator Charles Tobey characterized some of his dealings as "tax dodges."[4] That year Textron's sales fell below $100 million; in 1949 they were $68 million. Now profits were replaced by a deficit of almost $1 million. By then the bottom had fallen out of the textile market, and there was some doubt about Textron's ability to remain a significant factor in many of its old markets, much less to expand into new ones. Hopes of using stock to make new purchases were now dashed, as Textron common sold at around eight in the summer of 1949.

Little emerged from the 1948–49 slump badly bruised, but he had learned two important lessons. First, textiles would remain a highly cyclical market. He still hoped to master it, but he had not appreciated the difficulties along the way more than he had earlier in his career. Equally important, Little felt that while there was nothing wrong with expansion through acquisitions, he had gone about it the wrong way, and he had sought the wrong firms. Textron would continue to seek merger candidates, but not necessarily in textiles. Rather, whenever the situation called for it, Little would separate objectives from strategies and tactics.

In sum, he would continue to build Textron into a corporate giant in textiles, which would be supported by an acquisitions program in diverse areas. Profits from nontextile operations might be plowed back into the fabric business. Thus, one branch of the corporation would function as a "cash cow" for the other, a fairly common practice in a wide variety of industries. Furthermore, this diversification would serve to dampen the effects of the boom-and-bust cycle in textiles, providing profits to tide the corporation over during any future slumps.

Finally, Little intended to keep expansion in existing textile mills to a minimum, and so avoid the problem of overcapacity which had plagued the industry for more than a century. Instead, excess capital would be used to acquire ongoing operations at low prices at the bottom of recessions. Some would be in textiles, but others might be in any of several declining industries or suffering from mismanagement. Textron would move in, sell off part of the business, and restructure what remained. This approach had worked out well at Manville-Jenckes, to that point

Little's greatest triumph, and he saw no reason why the process wouldn't be repeated again and again.[5]

His initial move in this direction would be the acquisition of Cleveland Pneumatic Tool Company, the nation's leading manufacturer of aircraft landing struts, and as such a beneficiary of World War II spending programs. Cleveland Pneumatic's profits were high from 1942 to 1945, so the firm was vulnerable under the terms of the excess profits tax. The Schott brothers, who controlled the company, thought this presented no major problem. After all, like most manufacturers of military hardware they anticipated large deficits in the immediate postwar period, which would eat up those excess profits while Cleveland Pneumatic geared up in a reconversion effort. This is precisely what happened—but only briefly. With the onset of the Cold War in the late 1940s, military spending programs accelerated, bringing new prosperity to Cleveland Pneumatic. Awash in orders, the Schotts were borrowing money to finance plant expansion. In the midst of this they were informed by their accountant and treasurer that unless they soon showed large deficits, the tax credits would run out. In addition, the company would have to pay a special dividend of $1.5 million to its stockholders, or become subject to another creature of the IRS code, the undistributed profits tax. President Harold Schott was irate. It now appeared that due to the workings of the tax code, his firm could succeed only by losing money, while profits were a source of worry. "To hell with that," he was supposed to have said. "I'm going to sell the business."[6]

The company could not be disposed of that easily. Other aircraft companies either refused to consider a takeover for fear of antitrust prosecution or did not require additional capacity. Nor were they eager to merge with a company like Cleveland Pneumatic if it meant taking Harold Schott as its CEO. Schott had a fiery temper and a penchant for power. He would not be easy to get along with.

Textron was interested. Little knew Textron would have a deficit in 1949 as a result of the textile glut and write-offs for Nashua. Other segments might be liquidated later on, if need be, to produce more red ink. Thus, Textron would make an ideal merger partner for Cleveland Pneumatic—in financial terms, if nothing else.

The more Little investigated the tax situation, the more he became convinced he would turn a large profit by purchasing Cleveland Pneumatic. Schott would not be that much of a problem for him. Little felt he could work with the man, who, after all, would have a large degree of independence insofar as operations were concerned since no one at Textron had any experience with such products as landing gear. In other words, no attempt would be made to integrate Cleveland Pneumatic into the rest of Textron unless Harold Schott agreed, which hardly seemed likely.

There was one minor technicality, the solution to which would bring Little additional criticism. Under the terms of its charter Textron could not acquire a company outside the textile field. Little got around this by purchasing Cleveland Pneumatic (for $6.8 million) through the Sixty Trust, Textron's pension fund. Now Little was charged with misusing pension fund assets. He denied this, noting somewhat disingenuously that he had abstained from the vote.

In 1950, by which time textile operations were picking up, the Trust purchased Pathe Industries, Inc., a newsreel and real estate operation that owned some of the defunct Van Sweringen interests in Cleveland. Losses might be incurred there to offset profits at Textron and Cleveland Pneumatic, and so they were. As it turned out, Pathe's major asset was a loss-ridden balance sheet. Once again Little was criticized for misuse of the pension fund. By then he was deemed not much more than a corporate scavenger, more concerned with financial manipulations than anything else. He still hadn't cast aside the idea of becoming a textile tycoon and had to defend—usually lamely—forays into other fields.

Conglomeration as a viable concept and philosophy was still to be born in 1952; Little was an opportunist in this period, and he seemed to know it. But failures in textiles had taken a toll of his spirit, while the growth at Cleveland Pneumatic must have set him to thinking along new lines. "I recalled that back in the middle twenties Eliot Farley, who had endorsed the original note to get Special Yarns started, had told me he thought there was a great opportunity to put together a lot of completely unrelated businesses in one corporation and even suggested a name—Disassociated Industries."[7] Perhaps this would prove the way out of the dead end in textiles. It might have been what prompted him to alter Textron's charter in 1952 to permit the corporation to acquire nontextile businesses, and that year both Cleveland Pneumatic and Pathe were transferred to the parent firm—with the Sixty Trust realizing a nice profit. Still, Little's reputation on Wall Street remained that of a not-quite-respectable manipulator, and it would be years before he could alter this perception.

Textron faired poorly in 1952, due in large part to Little's misreading of political machinations in Washington regarding price controls on textiles. On revenues of $99 million the corporation posted a loss of $6.5 million. While the use of tax loss carry-forwards reduced this to $3.5 million, it still was the worst year of the postwar period for the firm. Little was 56 years old by then, less than a decade before the age at which most chief executives retired. Perhaps there could be one last major push in textiles, but not much more than that. He decided to take the plunge, perhaps thinking to turn elsewhere if he failed this time.

Little's unlikely objective was American Woolen—the old Wool Trust, which had been organized in 1899 through a combination of 27 mills, and which for a while had dominated the industry. But the growth of competitors and the rise of artificial fabrics had crippled the firm, which also suffered from indifferent leadership. During World War II and the immediate postwar period, demand for products masked management errors. Still, profits remained high through the Korean War, and as late as 1952 it was considered a quasi-blue chip, its stock still in the portfolios of several trust funds.

Then everything fell apart. The company posted a major deficit in the 1953 recession, losing nearly one quarter of its working capital. The once large and wealthy firm now was only a bloated giant. But it did have some $26 million in cash and equivalents as well as a tax loss carryforward of $30 million. In Little's view its major liability was Francis White, American Woolen's CEO, an old fashioned conservative who had done a poor job even allowing for factors beyond his control. Each man knew of the other, at least by reputation. White thought Little a buccaneer, and Little considered White a fossil.

This would not be a friendly takeover.

In preparation for the American Woolen campaign, Little set his own house in order. As a first step he liquidated several peripheral and profitless units—a list of which seemed a catalogue of his postwar failures. Atlantic Parachute, Manville Fabrics, Nashua, Posees, Textron of Delaware, Textron of New York, Textron Mills, Textron Southern, and Textron Mississippi—all were written off. The elimination of Textron Southern was particularly painful, since at one time this was meant to become the nucleus of the firm. Then, in February 1953, Little spun off Indian Head Mills, which had come in with Nashua, by distributing its stock to the Textron shareholders.

Textron was a much smaller firm as a result of these liquidations. Sales declined from $99 million in 1952 to $71 million the following year. Once again there was a net loss for the year, but as a result of the divestitures it came to less than $900,000, or $171,000 after the use of tax loss carry-forwards. This was to be the last red ink year for Textron. By acting ruthlessly and disregarding sentiment, Little had saved that part of the corporation that had a chance of being profitable. Now he was free to turn to American Woolen.

The plan was simple enough. Little would obtain control of the company through open market purchases and then a tender offer for the rest of the stock. At the same time he would acquire Bachmann-Uxbridge, a small firm headed by Harold Walter, considered to be an excellent manager by those in the industry. Little would then combine the three companies—Textron's remaining textile operations, American Woolen, and Bachmann-Uxbridge—with the B-U management team, headed by Walter, in charge. Walter would run the company on a day-to-day basis, while Little would concentrate on acquiring additional textile companies as well as firms in other areas. He would also close down several antiquated American Woolen plants (and so gain additional tax losses) and open new ones in the South, thus repeating the kind of procedure he had developed with Nashua.

As expected, White opposed the plan, and in late 1953 promulgated a plan of his own. He would use American Woolen's not inconsiderable assets to gain control of companies in related fields, in this way attempting to form a major textile giant of his own. White's counterattack included wooing and winning Bachmann-Uxbridge to his side.

Had he been of a mind to do so, White might have short-circuited Little with a tender offer of his own—for a majority of Textron common, which at the time was fluctuating between 13 and 18. Textron had 1.2 million shares outstanding, and a bid for, say, 700,000 of them at 20, would have cost slightly more than $14 million. At the time American Woolen had cash items alone of $11.8 million, and a line of credit for $5 million more. Yet White didn't mount this flanking attack. As will be seen, three decades later the likes of Mobil, Du Pont, Seagram, and Bendix would enter into such contests with a panache and funds which would have astonished the players of the early 1950s.

The battle was on and lasted more than a year. In the process Little and White shook New England's textile establishment, with the major mills taking turns supporting one or the other. In the end, though, Little won control of the company, and White continued the struggle and finally had to be ejected from office.

By then Little had identified another takeover candidate. Robbins Mills was a medium-sized manufacturer of synthetics and wool blends and a perfect complement for American Woolen. At the time it was controlled by one of the industry's giants, J. P. Stevens. All of Robbins' factories were in the South, and quite modern by most standards. Like others in the field, it had suffered through the industry-wide glut of 1952–53; it came close to bankruptcy in 1954, having lost $10 million during the previous three years. Little liked the company, approved of its management, and was lured by the large tax loss carry-forward. He believed Robbins could be had for a reasonable price, and he was correct. Little took control of it later that year for $5.1 million, with $1 million down and the rest due over two years. In 1955 he purchased the remainder of the stock for Textron convertible preferred shares and common shares.[8] Then he set about uniting American Woolen, Robbins, and other Textron textile operations.

The result was a new company—Textron American—which received its form and name in February 1955. This was the giant Little had planned for since the end of World War II. The company had a large debt but a huge tax loss carry-forward, most of which came from American Woolen and Robbins. Textron American's facilities were scattered across the country, and there was some duplication of effort and overlapping of product lines. In other words, it bore some resemblance to the hodgepodge of textile firms Little had brought together in the late 1940s and early 1950s, and which fell apart in 1952–53. But he appeared to have learned a lesson from these failures. Little formed a management operation, known as Amerotron, which also engaged in sales and purchasing, and whose task it would be to coordinate Textron's textile units.[9]

This was to be a major assignment, for the corporation now was large and amorphous, badly in need of a strong coordination effort. Little devoted most of his energies to this task, but the turnabout in Textron's fortunes in 1955 was more the result of improving industry conditions than anything else. That year the corporation reported revenues of $192 million, nearly twice that of 1954. Profits soared now that the recession had ended and Textron had a fresh source of tax loss carry-forwards. In 1954 Textron had earnings of $1.3 million; in 1955 they came to $9.5 million. The dividend had been cut to $0.10 per share in 1954; the 1955 payout was $0.60, and at the end of the year Little put Textron on a $1.60 basis. As might have been expected, Textron common performed well, more than doubling in 1955 to close at above 25, a new high for the stock—which now became a more attractive vehicle with which to make new acquisitions.

Still, Textron American hadn't jelled, and never would become the viable, vigorous corporation Little had predicted it would be. Part of this was due to management failures, and part to the chronic ailments of a declining industry. But other firms in various segments of the textile business performed far better and more consistently than Textron American. Major firms like M. Lowenstein & Sons and J. P. Stevens, and smaller units like Graniteville and Dan River, racked up impressive records at different times during the postwar period. Perhaps the major reason for Textron American's mediocre record was Little's refusal to acquire well-run, profitable firms and lure top managers with high salaries and effective support. He remained the bargain hunter in textiles, and while this approach might produce fine results in good times, it could be disastrous in bad years. Moreover, it was not a valuable long-term strategy.

Clearly Little was not destined for textile greatness. The ailments of

1952-53, the anguish of the American Woolen merger, bad feelings at Nashua, and Textron American's inability to overcome the industry's boom-and-bust pattern, were signs of this. Textron American never would become more than a bloated, inefficient collection of heterogeneous junk, within which there were a few decent units. Even after successfully putting it together, Little seemed to realize this. Perhaps the struggles of 1954-55 had soured him on textiles. Was the merger worth it? The prospect of running American Woolen and Robbins wasn't that alluring. Nor did he relish directing the coordination effort. How much simpler it would be to leave them apart, to have intercompany sales but retain separate managements at each firm. In other words, run the entire operation without the intercession of Amerotron.

Little had proven himself remarkably adept at acquiring new firms at low prices and in some cases turning moribund properties into money makers. In effect, Textron was a fairly competent management company when it came to overseeing intercompany relations, but mediocre at best in integrating them and providing day-to-day leadership.

Little may have taken stock of his assets and liabilities in this fashion sometime late in the American Woolen contest. Further consideration to these matters might have been given when Textron American encountered difficulties the following year, and when Amerotron proved incapable of resolving them. After having won the prize Little seemed to have concluded that it had not been worth the effort. At the age of 59, he decided to set out in a new direction, one presaged by the Cleveland Pneumatic takeover. Textron would not be a textile giant after all. Rather, Little would turn it into a conglomerate, larger and more profitable than any textile firm. Or so he hoped.

There wasn't anything mysterious about the new Textron strategy. Little had decided to take his critics seriously and abandon some of his earlier practices. There would be no more acquisitions based upon tax loss carry-forwards, and the era of unfriendly takeovers had ended. Little's career as the junkman of American industry was over, and never again would he undergo the searing experiences of rejection and humiliation suffered in the Nashua and American Woolen situations. The alteration in Little's image was startling. Soon after abandoning the textile-based strategy for conglomeratization he was being hailed as "the wonder man of American business" and "one of the more innovative entrepreneurs on the scene today."[10] "That is where Little's heart really lies today," wrote *Fortune* after the American Woolen deal was completed, "in acquiring, both for profitability and diversification, companies outside the textile field; for there his incredible talents as a deal maker can be exercised to the fullest."[11]

Over the years Little had thought he was learning about textiles and then applying that knowledge to the creation and management of a corporation in that industry, while in reality he was honing and perfecting his talents as a wheeler-dealer.

It was to his credit that Little recognized the difference between strategy and objectives and was able to make the switch so late in his career—to concentrate upon the former and reject the latter. In effect, the takeover strategy became the new objective—but toward what end? Years later, in his memoir, Little claimed that as early as 1953 he had established several goals in the area of conglomerization. This is doubtful; there was nothing in his statement or actions at that time to indicate that. Rationalization, rather than experience, had led him along this new path. However, in 1979 what he said about his "conversion" a quarter of a century earlier was, "Our basic concept of unrelated diversification at that time was to accomplish these objectives:

1. Eliminate the effect of business cycles on the parent company by having many divisions in unrelated fields.

2. Eliminate any Justice Department monopoly problems by avoiding acquisitions in related businesses.

3. Eliminate single industry's temptation to overexpand at the wrong time. Finance the growth of only those divisions which show the greatest return on capital at risk. Rather than overexpand any division, use surplus funds to buy another business.

4. Confine acquisitions to leading companies in relatively small industries. Never buy a small company in the $5 to $10 billion industry. One of my particular 'No-No's'—never buy a company that manufactures a product with an electric wire attached—no radios, televisions, washing machines, driers, electric stoves, or refrigerators.

5. Having made a complete analysis of all major manufacturing companies' return on net worth and found that only about twenty-five in 1952 earned over 20 percent on common stock equity, I set that rate of return in 1953 as Textron's goal for the future."[12]

There was no evidence that Little feared the Justice Department in 1953, and in fact no sign that Justice was considering antitrust prosecutions, least of all against Textron. Nor would it do so for the immediate future. Little's continuation of efforts in textiles during the next two years indicate a continuing desire to grow in that highly cyclical field. On occasion he would expand at the wrong time—the height of the cycle rather than its bottom. As for his fifth point, one of Little's most successful takeovers would be in the giant defense industry, which didn't meet its requirements. In Little's later years, Textron rarely achieved the desired return on equity that he had set as its goal.

Little's new approach was perhaps better exemplified by the five criteria for acquisitions he set down in 1955, the year after Textron embarked upon its merger rampage:

1. Company should be privately owned for ease of acquisition.
2. Company should have pre-tax earnings of over $1 million.
3. Company should have a broad product line.
4. Company should have long range potential.
5. Company should have young, competent, hungry management.[13]

Needless to say, such firms wouldn't come cheap, or be easy to locate. In time Little would settle for an accepted product line, a decent balance sheet, and most of all, superior management that would mesh well with Textron's leaders. He summed it up this way: "All I ever did as a businessman was to bring men and money together. I was just extremely fortunate in some of the men I picked."[14]

In fact, the raider of the American Woolen war had been transformed into the conglomerator most concerned with the sensibilities of leaders of potential takeover candidates. This was the one "secret" Little rarely discussed in any great detail. Several of his more successful acquisitions came when managers of medium-sized prospering enterprises sought him out, asking to be taken over when some other, less friendly, conglomerator started to nibble at their company.

From 1955 to 1962, at which time he retired from Textron, Little concentrated on four objectives. First, he created a corporate structure to handle Textron's operations. He kept the management team small and his office staff modest. Presidents of operating companies were given a great deal of leeway; Little was a believer in the adage that a wise CEO selected the right manager and then permitted him freedom in achieving agreed upon objectives.

Next, Little continued to acquire additional firms, adding them at the rate of one every two months. He did so in an apparently serendipitous fashion, without much of a plan at the start. Always more a master of finance than anything else, he increased Textron's debt from $4 million in 1954 to $92 million in 1961, using the funds to make these purchases and improve productivity once the companies came under the Textron banner. In the same period, the number of Textron shares outstanding rose from 1.3 million to 4.9 million, with most going to acquire new companies.

Little's third objective was to liquidate Textron's marginal and unprofitable operations, most of which were in the textile business, the residue of the old Textron. He did dispose of several of the new companies added after 1954, but only when they failed to meet objectives established at the time of their takeovers. Little developed a fascination with plywood and veneer, and purchased several small entities in the field. He had hoped to integrate backward by taking over a forest company, but gave up on the idea when unable to buy one at a low price. Then he sold off the plywood and veneer units, most at losses, and deployed his assets elsewhere.

Finally, Little wanted to create a semi-independent "glamour company" which in time might be able to acquire firms in advanced technology industries with high price/earnings ratios. Perhaps he did so in order to answer critics who claimed that even while a conglomerator, he remained the quintessential junkman.

It all began with Dalmo Victor, the largest supplier of airborne radar antennas to the federal government. The owners, headed by Tim Moseley, were to receive $3 million in cash under an elaborate program worked out by Little. Only $300,000 changed hands in January 1954, when the deal was consummated, with another $1.2 million to come in monthly installments over the next four years, and the rest of the money payable in or before 1964. In effect, Moseley and the others were being paid out of Dalmo Victor's earnings. And to make certain these continued, the old management team remained in place. Thus, Textron acquired a growing company for virtually nothing. This made more sense than picking up antiquated or stagnant textile companies for their tax loss carry-forwards.

A few months later Textron purchased MB Manufacturing, which turned out a line of vibration eliminators for piston engine aircraft, and some testing equipment. On this occasion Little's yearning for bargains led him into trouble. MB had a good balance sheet and the previous year had earned $1 million before taxes. It had a backlog of $6 million and a capable management team led by Rollin Mettler, who were asking $2 million for the company. Little leaped at the chance and the price. As it turned out, he had been outfoxed by Mettler, who understood that piston engines soon would be replaced by jets, making most of the MB line obsolete.

Little said this taught him a valuable lesson: never again would he undertake an acquisition without having first acquired detailed knowledge of the industry. This did not mean he would refuse to purchase firms with troubled product lines, especially if they could be had at low prices. Rather, in the future he would better understand the nature of the risks he was taking.

In 1955 and 1956 Little acquired a wide variety of small companies in an apparently haphazard fashion. Into Textron came Kordite (plastic clotheslines and polyethelene film), Ryan Industries (electromechanical equipment), Homelite (chain saws), Camcar Screw and Manufacturing, Coquille Plywood, General Cement Manufacturing (which, despite the name, was in radio, television, and electronics parts), Benada Aluminum (extruded products), and in April 1956, Myrtle Point Veneer. These and several other smaller units cost Textron some $37 million in cash in addition to common and preferred stock. As in the case of Dalmo Victor, Textron paid relatively small sums up front for most of the companies, with the rest to come later through earnings. Managements stayed on, perhaps to make certain they would get all their money.

Little was becoming something of a celebrity. As the putative founder of a new corporate form his opinion was sought on a wide variety of matters. While in a semi-euphoric haze during the spring of 1956, he predicted conglomerates would come to dominate the business scene. Insofar as Textron was concerned, he said the firm would turn in record earnings for the year, with acquisitions alone providing more than $9 million in profits before taxes. As it turned out he was too optimistic; in fact, net income for the entire corporation came to $6.5 million, against $9.5 million the previous year. But Textron's revenues were nearly a quarter of a billion dollars, two and a half times what they had been in 1954, when Little had begun its transition from textiles to conglomerate. Textron might not have turned in a stellar earnings record, but at least it was getting bigger, which pleased Little no end. Two years later the corporation would enter the ranks of the 100 largest American corporations, as the result of a continued program of acquisitions.

Without stopping to digest this initial batch of takeovers Little added Bandon Veneer, Carolina Bagging, Hall Mack (which manufactured bathroom accessories), and Federal Leather. Then came Campbell, Wyant, and Cannon, the nation's largest independent grey iron foundry and an important supplier to the automobile industry; it cost $15.5 million in cash. How this fit in with the other companies eluded analysts, who by now had become accustomed to Little's maneuvers, but still could not discern any pattern to them. He even purchased an old troop ship, the S.S. *LaGuardia,* for $3.8 million, and after extensive renovations renamed it the S.S. *Leilani* and put it on the Hawaii tourist run. This quixotic venture never panned out. Little could not even sell many berths to Textron shareholders by offering substantial discounts. In the end, the ship was disposed of at a loss.

Textron's revenues and earnings advanced, along with the acquisitions. In 1959 they were $309 million and $16.6 million respectively. But the stock failed to take off, never rising above 30 during the Little chairmanship. That year Textron's price/earnings ratio, at its peak, came to less than nine, at a time when many other conglomerates commanded double digit P/Es, with Litton Industries leading the pack at 37.

Most of the other conglomerators acknowledged Little as the father of the movement, but while he could lead them to the promised land, he himself was not permitted to enter. Still dubious regarding the viability of Textron's structure, and aware of Little's tendency to blunder, Wall Street analysts held back from making the kinds of recommendations needed to boost the stock.

But there was another, more important reason for their lack of enthusiasm. For all of his panache, Little was an old fashioned character, a product of the prewar period who could not come to terms with the flash and glitter of the late 1950s. His last venture into anything new was with rayon, and that was in 1920. His character had been toughened by the Great Depression, which had taught a generation of businessmen the need to husband resources and to make certain they got value for their money. All of the companies he acquired in the postwar period were involved with technologies and markets quite familiar to businessmen of his generation. He purchased American Woolen and Carolina Bagging at a time when Wall Street was becoming enchanted with firms with prefixes of "electro-" and suffixes like "onics," and containing such buzz words as "digital," "piezo," and "data." Textron was acquiring firms whose names actually provided a clue as to their businesses, when the style was to employ letters which signified nothing.

As has been seen, Little delighted in purchasing assets for fifty cents on the dollar from firms that had tax loss carry-forwards. He did this at a time when companies started by a handful of brash M.I.T. scientists with no more than $10,000 among them were capitalized at millions of dollars. Such was alien to Little's experience and temperament, as he showed in 1959, when he finally created his own "glamour company," Textron Electronics. This company turned out to be an unhappy amalgam of MB Electronics, GC Electronics, and Schafer Custom Engineering, all of which came from the mother company in a stock transfer operation. Later, Textron Electronics also acquired Globe Electronics from Textron. While Wall Street afforded TE a higher price/earnings multiple than Textron's, the company simply dragged along, and never amounted to much.

Yet there was another side to all this. If Textron became a family of rather conventional companies, at least they were well run and, for the most part, allowing for the business cycle, profitable. For all his manipulations and convoluted dealings, Little never could be accused of cooking the books or presenting a false face to the investing public. Textron was one of the more straightforward and honest conglomerates, but also a stodgy example of the breed, the spinster aunt in this exciting new family of companies.

Little departed the conglomerate scene in pretty much the same way he had entered it: by acquiring fistfuls of mundane companies at low prices, usually with cash. During the next three years he took over a variety of firms for a total of slightly more than $40 million in cash plus a small amount of stock. These were in such businesses as steel castings (Pittsburgh Steel Foundry), furnaces (Ansler Corporation), optical products (Shuron), and fasteners (Townsend). The most expensive of the lot was Fanner Manufacturing, which turned out foundry equipment, and cost Textron $9.2 million in cash. Except for California Technical, a small manufacturer of electrical testing equipment, none were in fields considered pioneering or novel. Little also established Textron Pharmaceutical and Photek, Inc., the latter company having what Little termed "a secret process" for photocopying and thermocopying papers. In fact, these were inadequate and feeble attempts to enter glamorous industries on the cheap. Both companies failed. In early 1960, as he planned to retire, Little purchased Albert H. Wienbrenner (which produced work shoes), E-Z Go Car (a medium-sized factor in golf carts), and Dorsett Marine (which manufactured sail and power boats). Little later conceded that these, too, were "disasters."[15]

However, his final acquisition turned out quite well, though this was more the result of good fortune than anything else. For $32 million (half in cash, the rest borrowed at low cost from the parent of the acquired company) Textron purchased the defense business of Bell Aircraft. *Forbes* magazine wondered whether Little had been "hornswoggled," and *Fortune* was certain he had been.

Once a major manufacturer of fighter and attack planes, Bell had fallen on bad times after the war and had been obliged to leave prime contracting in these areas to others. It remained a factor in helicopters, but lacked a substantial backlog of orders. In 1959 the defense business had come to slightly more than $100 million, on which Bell earned after tax profits of only $1.9 million. Prospects were bleak, but Little believed he had yet another of his now familiar bargains. Bell was acquired for less than its net asset value. Even should everything fall apart Little might break the company down to its components and then sell them off individually for a small profit.

As it turned out Bell became a major beneficiary of the Kennedy administration's new procurement program. By 1963 it was accounting for $160 million of Textron's revenues, more than a quarter of the total, while profits doubled. It would do even better later, as its helicopters became ubiquitous during the Vietnam War.[16] Thus, Bell became one of the fastest growing segments of the conglomerate—an indication of just how unglamorous the other parts were.

Before his departure Little made a stab at providing Textron with a structural rationale. He said the corporation functioned in four major areas: Aerospace, Metal Products, Industrial Products, and Consumer Products. The original textile business fell under the last group. But not for long. Two years later, with Little's approval, Textron sold Amerotron to Deering-Milliken for $45 million, thus taking itself completely out of textiles.

Rupert C. Thompson Jr. succeeded Little as chairman and CEO. Little stayed on briefly as a member of the board and chairman of the executive committee, but generally kept out of Thompson's way. The two men got along well together, though their personalities and approaches were quite different. Thompson, who had arrived in 1956 to take charge of the nontextile businesses, was a meticulous, careful, well-ordered, and somewhat somber individual, who was once described by Little as "a conservative New England banker." While respecting his predecessor, Thompson clearly thought him a trifle racy, observing that Little "operated out of a hat" and was "never much for committees and meetings." Thompson strongly implied there would be a new order at Textron. "We are more concerned with increasing profit margins and sales volume than with the feverish search for new acquisitions," he said in early 1962. "We will make more money by attending to the business we already have."[17]

Thus, the new CEO attempted to signal that in the future most of Textron's growth would come internally, and that unlike Little he would not go on the prowl for takeovers.

Thompson didn't have to; they came to him. He became chairman at a time when the conglomerate craze was heating up. During the early 1950s less than half of all mergers were of the conglomerate variety. From 1961 to 1965 they accounted for 60 percent of mergers and rose to 82 percent from 1966 to 1969. In the midst of this merger-mania many medium-sized firms feared for their very survival. Hoping to elude one or more of the predatory conglomerates, they approached Textron, which under Little had assiduously cultivated the image of a "friendly company." Not only would they cooperate with Thompson on the acquisition—they now were willing to accept stock, for along with the equity of other conglomerates, that of Textron rose sharply in this phase of the great bull market of the 1960s. The shares finally went above 40 in 1965, split two for one, continued to advance, and two years later had another two-for-one distribution. A share of Textron common purchased at 20 in 1960 would have become four shares at 55 each in 1968. And Thompson was able to use this paper to acquire additional companies. Several well-known firms were taken over, among them Speidel (watchbands), W. A. Sheaffer (pens and pencils), and Gorham Silverware. By 1968 Textron had revenues of $1.7 billion and earnings of $76 million. It stood at 47 on the Fortune 500 list, behind such conglomerates as ITT, Ling-Temco-Vought, and Litton Industries, but ahead of Gulf + Western, Teledyne, and U.S. Industries.

Royal Little watched all of this from semiretirement. He played golf, went on several camera safaris to Africa, served as chairman of the board at Indian Head Mills (a job that required less time and effort than its title indicated and had no connection with Textron), and submitted to dozens of interviews conducted by journalists and others eager to learn how he decided to make the switch from textiles to conglomeration. What was his secret? How did he come upon the idea of creating a multi-industry corporation?

They never found out, probably because Little himself was not really sure of the answers. He simply went where opportunities beckoned. An inveterate dabbler, Little loved juggling several ideas at a time, devoting full attention to no one of them. Even in retirement he helped create a new small business investment company, known as Narragansett Capital, which purchased equity in many emerging enterprises. He enjoyed his work immensely. Other businessmen tended to concentrate upon a single company, or at most an industry. In his early fifties, after repeated frustrations in textiles, Little discovered he really preferred to spread himself thin.

It was the mark of the conglomerator.

3

Tex Thornton: The Illusionist

Textron always seemed to be poking around in the scrap heaps of American industry; Litton's eyes were on the stars. Based in Beverly Hills, where Litton's headquarters complex was only minutes away from the Hollywood studios, and its managers could mingle with rhinestoned motion picture personalities, it seemed quite natural for the most glamorous leaders of corporate America to live side by side with the darlings of the screen, for they too inhabited a make-believe world.

In time other conglomerates would eclipse Litton in performance, but none in sheer razzle-dazzle or hype. There was a tinsel quality at Litton that would remain long after it was discovered that undergirding it all was a flimsy and makeshift foundation.

During most of the 1960s, that golden age for conglomerates, Litton's leaders mesmerized securities analysts, charmed trust company portfolio managers, and delighted their shareholders. Revenues rose from $187 million in 1960 to $1.8 billion in 1968, the last of the truly good years, and in the same period reported earnings went from $7.5 million to $58.4 million. Those who had purchased Litton shares in 1960 and held on to them saw their net worth increase tenfold. None had reason to complain. Any doubts regarding the quality of Litton's earnings, the value of some of the companies acquired, or the somewhat casual managerial style at headquarters and in the field, were dissolved in the glow of America's greatest bull market.

Each spring shareholders would receive a thick annual report, printed on highly polished paper, containing elegant photos and art reproductions, and a commentary that might be described as breathlessly optimistic. The body of the annual reports bore a greater resemblance to first rate auction gallery catalogues than the accountings of major corporations.

This is not to suggest that they lacked any of the necessary statistics and figures. They were all there, along with graphs and charts, and made for pleasant reading. Litton had a clean balance sheet, and per share earnings climbed steadily. And if the returns on equity and sales were somewhat low, and a good deal of the profit increases due to takeovers rather than ongoing operations, this was either lost on or ignored by a majority of stockholders. In the back of the "book" were lengthy footnotes, written in the usual careful jargon employed by lawyers and accountants. The story was there to see; Litton hid nothing. Still more could be uncovered in the 10-K reports submitted for the Securities and Exchange Commission, available on request.

What these documents showed was that Litton had become a fair-to-middling military supplier, had expertise in several areas of electronics, and ran a fine seismic operation. But much of the rest of the corporation was bland, flabby, starved for capital, and mismanaged. The firm's leaders were far more adept at wooing Wall Streeters, acquiring small and medium-sized companies, and pasting together statistics in attempts to present a favorable picture to analysts than in turning out superior goods and services at competitive prices. It was as though a bowl of thin gruel dotted with a handful of raisins was being passed off as plum pudding. The wonder was that so many intelligent and sophisticated brokers, businessmen, bankers, and investors could be made believers, and cling to their convictions for so long.

Charles "Tex" Thornton was not only Litton's creator and long-time chairman, but also the firm's image maker, the de facto chief of its public relations arm, and largely responsible for the patina of glamour. This is not to suggest that Thornton was a trickster, or that he set out to deceive and obfuscate. Nor was he lacking in entrepreneurial skills and imagination, and he certainly knew how to inspire and motivate his staff and other coworkers. Rather, Thornton was a capable executive who had the good fortune to come onto the scene at a time when a person with his talents could exploit them to the hilt. The electronics age had begun at a time when military procurement was high, civilian markets growing rapidly, money rates low, and the stock market soaring. No other conglomerator—not James Ling, Charles Bluhdorn, or even Harold Geneen—could put all of these elements together so neatly and with so much style and grace as did Thornton. No one was more articulate regarding the "new age of free-form management" which had dawned, and Thornton's visions of the opportunities that abounded were more vivid and imaginative if not as realistic and practical as those painted by the others. It mattered little that accounting experts openly criticized both Litton's method of reporting assets and earnings, and also the distorted comparisons with earlier years, slanted to make the record more appealing to investors. Thornton was ever so much more convincing, especially when talking about "concepts" rather than concrete performance. In a *Barron's* article of February 5, 1968 entitled, "Want to Get Rich Quick? An Expert Gives Some Friendly Advice on Conglomerates," financial analyst John Wall, apparently inspired by Thornton and Litton, wrote:

> Get hold of the speeches and annual reports of the really savvy swingers, who know the lingo and make it sing. . . . You have to project the right image to the analysts so they realize you're the new breed of entrepreneur. Talk about the synergy of the free-form company and its interface with change and technology. Tell them you have a windowless room full of researchers . . . scrutinizing the future so your corporation will be opportunity-technology oriented. . . . Analysts and investors want conceptually oriented (as opposed to opportunist) conglomerates, preferably in high-technology areas. That's what they pay the high price-earnings ratios for, and life is a lot less sweaty with a high multiple.[1]

Which is to say that while Royal Little was the master junkman, Thornton was a positive genius at the creation of illusions.

Thornton, whom most analysts credit with providing Litton with that multiple, was a medium-sized, somewhat portly man, with a craggily handsome face, who wouldn't have seemed out of place as a background character in a John Wayne western, and who bore a resemblance to latter-day Secretary of State Alexander Haig. He aged well. In 1953, when he put together the financial package to form Litton Industries, Thornton was a smooth-faced, pudgy, ebullient executive of 40, who, despite an impressive record in the Army and later at Ford Motor Co. and at Hughes Aircraft, appeared to have mismanaged his career. At a time when many others of his generation were firmly entrenched in middle management of large corporations and on their way upward, Thornton was at loose ends, unable to find a proper niche. That he was not quite conventional in background, style, and interests was obvious. Like Little, he possessed the temperament and scope of a conglomerator, not of an ordinary businessman.

Charles Bates Thornton was born on July 22, 1913 in the minuscule Texas town of Goree. The Thorntons were an old, occasionally distinguished American family—one of Tex's ancestors, Matthew, signed the Declaration of Independence, and another, William, designed the Capitol building in Washington. How they arrived in Texas is not known. John Thornton, the town veterinarian in the late nineteenth century, had seven children, one of whom was Thornton's father (also known as Tex), who in his time was the nation's most famous extinguisher of oil and natural gas field fires. Charles's mother was Sarah Alice Bates, whose father probably ran a small farm near Goree. Their marriage was short and stormy. The elder Tex spent most of the year traveling around the country, putting out fires, and he and Sarah soon became estranged. Slightly more than three years after the child's birth they were divorced. The father moved out, remarried someone more in tune with the way he lived, and rarely returned to that part of the state to see his son.[2]

Sarah Alice Thornton tried to remain in Goree for a few years, but there was little she could do there to earn a living. In 1921 a younger married sister invited her and young Tex to come to live with her in the larger nearby town of Haskell. Sarah Alice accepted, and found work as a salesperson in a millinery store. Shortly thereafter she met and married A. J. Lewis, like her former father-in-law a veterinarian, by whom she was to have two boys and a girl. Although Lewis was not wealthy, he was able to support his family well. Tex attended the local schools and at the bottom of the depression, in 1931, he graduated from Haskell High School with what he described as average grades. At that time the Lewises moved to Lubbock, where Tex entered the Texas Technological College, expecting to major in engineering. But he had little talent and less interest in the subject, and soon switched to economics, a far less demanding course of study at Texas Tech. Tex dropped out of college at the end of his sophomore year, and after spending the summer in Haskell working at several jobs, trying to raise a stake, he went to Washington to seek a job in the one great growth area in the economy in 1934, the federal bureaucracy.

After casting about in several agencies, Thornton managed to find employment as an "under clerk" in the Agricultural Adjustment Administration with an annual salary of $1,260. Dissatisfied with both the work and the money, he immediately set about looking for a better post. In late December the New Deal established the Federal Surplus Relief Corporation, designed to help farmers by purchasing surplus commodities and storing them. Thornton immediately applied for a position, and was hired as a junior clerk at $1,440. This set a pattern for the rest of the decade. Thornton hopscotched across the federal landscape, going from the FSRC to the Works Progress Administration to the Public Works Administration, and by 1937 was at the United States Housing Authority, working in the statistical section, with a salary of $1,800. At night he attended college, first George Washington and then Columbus University, where he took business courses and from which he received a bachelor's degree in commercial science. Thornton married the former Flora Laney, whom he first had met while both were students at Texas Tech.

In 1938 Thornton was promoted to assistant statistician at the Housing Authority, and by late 1940 was in an executive post there. At the age of 28 he had become a quintessential bureaucrat. It was a comfortable life, especially during a depression. Thornton had security and a salary of $4,600 a year. He did not seem to want much more than that—safety and a slowing increasing pay check. He was firmly entrenched in government work, with no real experience or apparent interest in anything else. Were it not for the coming of World War II, Thornton might have remained in Washington until retirement in 1978, by which time he perhaps might have risen to head an agency or serve on the staff of a cabinet member.

In 1940 Thornton wrote a report on methods of financing low-cost housing that interested Assistant Secretary of War for Air Robert Lovett, at the time occupied with bolstering his staff in preparation for hostilities. Lovett was impressed with the way Thornton was able to extract essential information from complex statistics and formulate programs to deal with problems. He needed someone with these talents, and at his urging Thornton transferred to the War Department in March of 1941.

The United States entered the war nine months later, and shortly thereafter Thornton was commissioned a second lieutenant in the Army Air Forces, charged with helping plan for expansion and development. This was a hectic period, during which talented individuals with the right specialty in the right place advanced rapidly, and so it was with Thornton. Within a year he became a colonel and headed the Statistical Control Division, which, operating out of Harvard, helped plan for and manage the Army Air Forces. It was then that Thornton received an additional education in managerial problems. When asked to describe just what it was that he did, Thornton replied, "Statistical control is just a fancy name for finding out what the hell we had by way of resources and when and where it was going to be required."

At the age of 28 Thornton was directing the efforts of some 2,800 officers and specialists, hobnobbing with generals and members of the Cabinet, and accumulating valuable experience in heading a large enterprise. He cultivated contacts with dozens of officers who would return to executive posts at major corporations after the war. Most of all, Thornton became accustomed to exercising power. When the war ended in 1945 he had no intention of returning to the federal bureaucracy.

Instead he sought a top management position at a large corporation, where the knowledge obtained in the military might be applied to solving problems in the private sector. Assembling a "team" of six (later expanded to nine) former officers with similar qualifications, Thornton tried to sell it as a package to several major companies. He had nibbles from some, including an offer from Alleghany Corporation, but in late

1945 the team, which included such men as Robert McNamara, Arjay Miller, George Moore, and James Wright, decided to go to Ford Motor Company, then in the process of a thorough revamping.

Ford was in shambles at the time, losing close to $10 million per month. Henry Ford II had just taken over, with little industrial experience. Thornton might have dreamed of becoming the de facto leader of the corporation, for even then he believed a good manager could quickly acquire the necessary expertise to adjust to any industry. Ford disagreed and selected General Motors executive Ernest Breech for the top position. Along with him came a cadre of veterans from that organization. Thornton became director of planning, while his team—now known as the "Whiz Kids"—scattered through the corporation. In time both McNamara and Miller would become "automobile men," and move up to the presidency. Had he remained there, and made the necessary adjustments, Thornton might have preceded them to that office. Unwilling to wait, impatient with his progress, and more interested in other industries—such as military electronics—he decided to move on. The switch was well timed, since by 1948 he had clashed repeatedly with Henry II and knew he had to leave before being fired.

There was an opening at Hughes Aircraft, a recently formed and out-of-control subsidiary of Hughes Tool, all of which was owned by the eccentric and flamboyant Howard Hughes. Hughes Aircraft had few contracts, a reputation for mismanagement and failures to deliver as promised, and a bleak future in aviation. But the corporation did have a talented engineering staff, which included Simon Ramo and Dean Wooldridge, and a rapidly developing expertise in electronics. Howard Hughes was involved with running RKO Studios and Hughes Tool, and in addition had a majority interest in Trans World Airlines. Already a semirecluse who soon would sink deeply into a psychological haze, he left much of the day-to-day operations to his chief aide, Noah Dietrich, who wanted to dissolve the aircraft company. Both men agreed that the company needed a strong leader. Hughes offered Thornton the position, along with a vice-presidency in the parent organization. Even though it meant a slight reduction in salary Thornton accepted, and he arrived in Houston in the summer of 1949 to take over.

Much to Dietrich's seeming chagrin, Thornton set about pulling the company together. To do this he needed a new staff, more committed to growth than salvage, which had been the prime concern of the old-timers. None of the Whiz Kids would leave Ford, so Thornton turned to other men he had met while in the Air Force and afterward. One of these was Roy Ash, the new assistant controller, who had been through the war with Thornton and later became a statistician at the Bank of America. "Thornton took all the bright guys in the Air Force to Ford and when he went to Hughes, scraped around the bottom of the barrel and found me," said Ash later. This was not the case, of course, and Ash was to become Thornton's second in command in the 1950s and 1960s.[3]

Thornton was to remain at Hughes for nearly five years, during which he reconstructed the company, underwent a crash course in top management procedures and military electronics, developed scores of contacts in Washington (and became adept at hiring former officers who could provide others), and battled constantly with Dietrich and occasionally with Hughes himself. Aided by military orders during the Korean War he managed to turn Hughes into a profitable operation. By virtually any measure—revenues, profits, assets, and backlog—Thornton had done a fine job. Research and development picked up under his leadership, and Ramo and Wooldridge turned out a stream of new products, the most important of which was a novel fire control system for military aircraft. Revenues the year Thornton arrived came to $8.5 million, and that year Hughes had a deficit. In 1954 revenues totaled $600 million, and profits $8 million.[4]

Despite all of this, Hughes Aircraft remained a troubled company, in large part due to personality and policy differences between it and the parent organization. At a critical moment in the summer of 1953, Hughes sided with Dietrich (and the group at Hughes Tool) against the management and scientific teams at Hughes Aircraft. According to Thornton, the final break occurred in September, when without consulting with anyone Dietrich notified Ash of his displacement. Now Thornton, Ash, Ramo, Wooldridge, and others submitted their resignations. Thoroughly alarmed, Hughes tried to halt the exodus, but there was no way to heal the breach.[5] Ramo and Wooldridge went off to form their own company, Ramo-Wooldridge, which specialized in military electronics.[6] Thornton, Ash, and others also intended to enter the electronics industry on their own.

In late September, Thornton, Ash, and a former Hughes research scientist, Hugh Jamieson, set about organizing a firm that was to be known as Electro Dynamics Corporation. Jamieson was supposed to become staff engineer and Ash secretary-treasurer. Thornton would become chief executive and operating officer as well as president. After serving for more than seven years under such imperious and often arbitrary men as Ford and Hughes he never again would place himself in a subordinate position.

While only a paper organization, Electro Dynamics possessed individuals with management and scientific skills, as well as a certain expertise at obtaining contracts. No one at the company knew how to start from scratch, however, and none had even had to raise operating funds. Thornton's first task, then, was to locate a company—preferably small, with good products and a customer base—which could be purchased for a low price, and then find the money with which to buy it.

Thornton investigated several firms, most of them in the Southwest and Far West, suppliers and manufacturers of electronic components and units to Hughes, before deciding upon Litton Industries. A San Carlos, California, manufacturer of magnetrons and other tubes, most of which were sold to military-oriented companies, Litton had revenues of less than $3 million in 1953, but it was growing rapidly. Like many other small electronics firms, Litton suffered from lack of capital and from indifferent management. The company's founder, president, and general manager was Charles V. Litton, an electronics engineer more adept at invention and inspiration of his workers than in operations and long-term planning. Litton recognized his deficiencies and was prepared to sell out and use the money to start another business. His price, arrived at after some dickering, was set at $1,050,000 in cash, with $300,000 as a down payment.

Thornton hadn't a fraction of that amount, and since no one at Electro Dynamics had much experience in finance, he had to improvise. The initial $300,000 was obtained from the Wells Fargo Bank, the collatoral being personal notes signed by Thornton and Ash. They next approached several venture capitalists, but those who were interested wanted too large a slice of the company or, as in the case of Joe Kennedy, insisted upon financial and operational control.

In the end, Thornton and Ash got the money from the investment banking firms of Lehman Brothers and Clark Dodge. At a meeting in New York they sketched ideas as to how Litton might become a $100 million corporation in five years, mainly through acquisitions made possible by the exchange of paper for assets. There really was no other way to succeed in military electronics, said Thornton. Given a bouyant stock market and a high price/earnings ratio for Litton common, such an approach could prove feasible. The high P/E would be obtained by concentrating on glamorous operations considered fast growing at the time. As Thornton later recalled, "I told them that I wanted to start a company that would become a strong blue chip in the scientific and technological environment of the future. It would be a balanced company—not just engineering, not just manufacturing, not just financial."[7]

Now events moved swiftly. The underwriters created 50 "units," each consisting of 20 bonds, 50 shares of convertible preferred stock, and 2,000 shares of common. These units were offered at $29,200 each, to bring in a total of $1,460,000 before deductions for commissions and expenses. The money was raised by early December 1953, enabling Thornton to redeem the Wells Fargo notes and pay off Charles Litton, leaving less than $400,000 for operation expenses. Then Electro Dynamics absorbed Litton and took its name. Once it appeared that the underwriting would be a success Thornton searched for a new corporate headquarters, found one in a somewhat shabby art deco office building in Beverly Hills, moved in, and began operations.

Under ordinary circumstances, with a different, capable, conventional management, Litton might have grown internally, and within a few years emerged as a medium-sized subcontractor in the field of defense electronics. Other companies had done so in the past and more would appear in the future. Not tied to any single prime contractor, a firm might turn in outstanding performances in good years to balance the bad ones—when military appropriations were cut, or the firm experienced failures in biddings. Certainly there was little hope any subcontractor could rise much above this, if not due to the lack of capital, then to thinness of management and labor forces. Whether Thornton ever hoped to achieve this status and enjoy the satisfaction of successfully outmaneuvering such companies as Hughes in a bidding contest is not known. Thornton had always claimed that initially he expected to create an important subcontracting operation at Litton, and to achieve this objective through acquisitions made possible by exchanges of Litton common stock for assets.

In early 1954 Thornton made one of his most important acquisitions, Myles Mace of the Harvard Graduate School of Business, the author of a book on boards of directors at small companies and an expert on takeovers. As was the case with many who worked with Thornton, Mace had met him while both served in the armed forces. Now they came together to develop an overall corporate strategy, seek out potential merger candidates, and develop tactics to bring them into the fold; Thornton's major task was to convince the sought-after companies of the rewards awaiting them as part of Litton.

Ash increasingly assumed managerial responsibilities at the plant, but from the first there was no clear demarcation of duties and responsibilities between him and Thornton. The style at headquarters was open and informal, and this suited both men. It became one of several Litton hallmarks, and soon was celebrated in business journals as "free-form management." But it wasn't arrived at deliberately. Rather, Thornton's personality and interests led him to simultaneous efforts in several directions, leaving details to others once projects were well underway or close to completion. More often than not he would initiate a program and then entrust its implementation to Ash or someone else at headquarters.

Litton gave its leading executives a great deal of freedom, and encouraged them to use their imaginations in dealing with problems. Publicity releases stressed the existence of a "new breed" of business leader at Litton, and this enhanced the corporation's glamour, eventually helping boost stock prices. This aura of freshness, vigor, competence, and youth tended to create a revolving door at headquarters, as dozens of Litton executives remained there for a few years only to move on and become CEOs of other conglomerates. Almost from the first Litton was to become a "school for conglomerators," and within the industry these men even had a name—"LIDOS"—which was the acronym for "Litton Industries Drop Outs." Rather than being discouraged by this, Thornton considered the growing roster of Lidos a sign of success. "We not only accept the idea that some executives will leave," said Ash, "but we recognize it as a way of revitalizing the organization."[8]

From the beginning, Litton exhibited that familiar "urge to merge" that characterizes all conglomerates, but nothing Thornton acquired during the first four years caused any great stir. It simply was another case of a small electronics company becoming larger through vertical and horizontal mergers. Into Litton came such regional operations as West Coast Electronics, which manufactured tubes, and Ahrendt Instruments, a defense electronics supplier. They were joined by U.S. Engineering (terminals and terminal boards), Automatic Seriograph (seriograph machines), Triad Transformer (transformers and transducers), Chromatic TV Laboratories (components), Digital Controls (meters), Maryland Electronics (radar antennas), and Roger White Electron Devices (traveling wave tubes). Some of these takeovers didn't work out—the businesses of West Coast Electronics, Ahrendt Instruments, and Chromatic TV were discontinued, though the facilities and work forces were utilized for other Litton products. For the most part, however, the companies meshed well enough with one another to enable Litton to bid on ever larger government defense contracts. Eventually most became part of a major Litton division, the Component Group, which for many years not only was the heart of the corporation, but its most innovative and successful business. Even those who later criticized Thornton, claiming he proved incapable of running a conglomerate, conceded his expertise in putting together and operating a military electronics firm.

Litton's first important product was the 4J52 magnetron, a tube developed by Charles Litton; it already had achieved wide acceptance when Thornton took over. Now Myles Mace took charge of the new Electronics Equipment Division (actually the only one in the firm at that time) and sought new product areas that could utilize the expertise of companies then being acquired. Mace also sought out additional ones that might complement any promising ongoing research. He assembled a talented team of scientists, the most prominent of whom was Henry Singleton, formerly of M.I.T., who then moved on to North American Aviation, where he had worked on inertial guidance systems. Singleton continued these efforts at Electronics Equipment, and out of his work came an advanced product that won immediate acceptance from the military. Singleton's inertial guidance efforts became the cornerstone for another Litton division, Guidance and Control Systems, which would become the largest and most profitable in the corporation.

The next step was a textbook example of how Litton expanded in its early years. Seeking new applications for knowledge and patents obtained from work on inertial guidance systems, Mace, Jamieson, and Singleton decided to enter the field of small, military-related computers utilized for electronic controls. Litton lacked facilities, personnel, and scientists, however, and Thornton set about obtaining all three. From Hughes came scientist George Kozmetsky and others, who had some experience in this area. Thornton then arranged for a line of credit and sold additional shares through Lehman Brothers to bring in additional capital. Then he purchased—for stock—Digital Controls, whose scientist-president, George Steele, was anxious to leave administration and return to the laboratories. Within a few months Steele had developed a small airborne computer that enabled Litton to win yet another important subcontract. Soon this product became the nucleus of another division, Data Systems, and Thornton was on the lookout for other ways to expand into new areas.

Litton was not a conglomerate in 1957, but rather a rapidly growing, solidly based specialist in military electronics, characterized as such by *Moody's, Financial World,* and other Wall Street-oriented publications.[9] That year Litton reported revenues of $28.1 million and a net income of $1.6 million, and Thornton trumpeted the news at meetings of financial analysts throughout the country, part of a publicity campaign begun in 1955. Rarely had a corporation of this size engaged so fully in or expended so much energy on image-making, and few could match Thornton when it came to salesmanship. It worked. Litton common, which had sold at ten in 1955, peaked at a fraction under 57 in 1957, lofty even by electronics industry standards.

Thornton used this stock to pay for acquisitions, something Royal Little rarely could manage and always hoped he might. Textron was a relatively stodgy firm whose stock usually sold for a low price/earnings multiple since the atmosphere on Wall Street in the late 1950s put the accent on glamour, not assets or tax loss carry-forwards. Textron was a grab bag of firms, a company still trying to shuck off its old image as a textile company, while Litton was fresh, new, exciting, and adventuresome—or so it appeared when sketched by Thornton and others who made the pitch to financial analysts and writers.

But the stock could not remain at such a level without a continuous flow of favorable news and excellent earnings reports. Thornton meant to keep both coming. Some of the expansion would derive from ongoing operations; Singleton and Kozmetsky had shown themselves capable of turning out a steady stream of technologically advanced products. More would come through the acquisitions process, at which Thornton and Mace had become expert.

There wasn't anything secret about the technique or its mathematics; others had utilized it in the past, but none as well as Thornton would. Stated simply, when a corporation whose stock commanded a high price/earnings ratio took over one with a low P/E, earnings per share would rise.

For example, consider the case of Glamour, Inc., a rapidly growing concern with earnings of $4 million and 2 million shares of common outstanding, which means that earnings per share come to $2.00. Since it is involved with exciting products in growing markets Glamour is in great demand among investors and speculators, so the price of its shares is 80, or 40 times earnings.

Now look at Oldtime Co., which also reported earnings of $4 million and has a capitalization of 2 million shares, for identical earnings of $2.00 per share. But it is a poor performer in an unpromising industry, and Oldtime common is selling for 30, or 15 times earnings.

In what might appear to outsiders and the uninitiated as a burst of generosity, Glamour offered one of its shares (worth $80 at current quotations) for every two of Oldtime's ($60 at the market price). Properly courted, the management of Oldtime supports the deal, as do the stockholders. Thus, the 2 million shares of Oldtime are transformed into 1 million of Glamour.

There now are 3 million shares of Glamour outstanding on a consolidated basis, while the merged earnings of the two firms come to $8 million, which means earnings per share now are $2.67—again, on a consolidated basis. Those glancing quickly at financial reports, and others who had only a passing knowledge of them and ignored footnotes, might conclude that Glamour's earnings had risen by one-third, and rush to purchase the stock. Even if Glamour common remained at the old P/E of 40, the price would rise to over 106, but chances are, in a buoyant market, it would go higher. Now management could use this richly priced stock to purchase more firms whose shares carried low P/Es.

The process might be repeated indefinitely. Or at least so it would appear in the great bull market that began in the late 1950s and lasted through the 1960s. Those companies that purchased others with cash had to utilize borrowings or retained earnings, or like Little find loopholes in the tax laws. CEOs like Thornton, able to buy firms in exchange for their own company's stock, relied upon the market to inflate the price. Men such as Little had to be on good terms with bankers and make certain that operations were profitable, while Thornton and his ilk courted investors and speculators and remained in constant touch with investment bankers who specialized in seeking out suitable candidates for acquisition. Litton showed the way; many of the others merely imitated, or went out and hired a Lido who put into practice lessons learned from Thornton and Ash.

What was unusual about Litton, what distinguished it from the other conglomerates of the 1960s, was its seeming ability to project an aura of glamour and growth even after it had evolved from a medium-sized electronics firm into one involved in several industries, some of which were decidedly mundane. Certainly by middecade Litton was a full-fledged conglomerate with a record about on par with others in the category, and so its stock might have been expected to be valued as were others. That year, however, Litton's average P/E ratio was 33, while Textron's was 11, Gulf + Western's came in at 16, LTV's was 13, and ITT—every bit as much a growth operation and far more solidly based and better managed—was a shade below 17, or half that of Litton.

Much of this was due to Thornton's salesmanship and abilities at public relations. His ebullient manner, winning optimism, and vivid rhetoric, best seen when wooing Wall Streeters, remained intact even when several of his more ambitious acquisitions turned sour and when flaws in ongoing operations became apparent. In the end Litton was unable to transfer to other businesses its skills in electronics, some of which remained formidable. Thornton's often-repeated claim that a good manager could operate in almost any industry proved overstated, if not a clear case of self-deception. But the glow remained for a while even after the fire had died down, a tribute to Thornton the illusionist, in this respect the best of the breed.

As indicated, all of the early acquisitions were made for high P/E multiple Litton stock. For example, Maryland Electronics, which arrived in early 1958, cost 18,788 common shares, worth slightly less than a million dollars, and Roger White Electron, acquired a few months later, cost 7,371 shares, less than half a million dollars worth. While Litton's capitalization doubled from 1954 to 1957, earnings per share rose by more than sixfold. Some of the increase was due to consolidation of earnings, but more to internal growth. In its early years, Litton had been a successful electronics firm; it didn't have to resort to that kind of gimmickry.

The switch occurred in 1958, after the Maryland Electronics takeover and before Roger White was acquired. Seeking a way to utilize Litton's expertise beyond the military markets, Thornton came across Monroe Calculating Machine Co. In its industry Monroe was dwarfed by the likes of Burroughs and National Cash Register, and was equivalent to Friden, a competitor in a very narrow segment of the market, in this case small mechanical adding, calculating, billing, and check-writing machines. The company had marked time in the early 1950s, failing to come up with new lines of electromechanical devices, nor did it move into electronics. Earnings and revenues were on a plateau and Monroe's leaders, many of whom were relatives of the founder, weren't doing much to alter the situation. While scanting research and development, officers received fat salaries and paid themselves large dividends. They were willing to sell out at a high price.

This situation was altered somewhat in 1953, when Fred Sullivan moved into the presidency from the comptroller's office. A young, aggressive executive, Sullivan saw no hope of prying research and development funds out of the board of directors, and so set about finding a company willing to purchase Monroe and then reinvigorate it.

Thornton probably thought Monroe a perfect takeover candidate. So what if its product lines were outdated and the old leadership flabby and weary? At least the family wouldn't require much persuasion to step down, and since Monroe admittedly was stagnant the majority shareholders would accept a lower price than might otherwise have been the case. Problems at the top might be solved by the infusion of some of the Litton magic—bright young executives, the next generation of Whiz Kids. Then there was Sullivan, who would fit in well at Litton, and who in time might become the central figure in a new division, as had Singleton and Kozmetsky before him.

Monroe could benefit from Litton's know-how in electronics; the research program to catch up with the competition wouldn't have to be costly. Or so it appeared. Finally, Monroe was willing to accept payment in Litton securities, and since its 1957 earnings came to $6.00 per share while Litton's were $1.51, the parent's figures would be boosted substantially when reported on a consolidated basis.

Litton was by far the smaller of the two firms; in 1957 it reported revenues of $28.1 million and had a book value of $6.71 per share. In contrast, Monroe's sales came to $44.9 million, and its book was $42.71. Both had virtually the same earnings, $1.8 million, but Monroe had a stronger cash position and better financial ratios. This was the classic case of a small, glamorous firm gobbling up a larger, somewhat flawed operation, and as a result appearing much bigger and stronger than it actually was.

SELECTED STATISTICS FOR LITTON INDUSTRIES
1954–1958

Year	Revenues (millions of dollars)	Earnings	Shares Outstanding	Earnings Per Share
1954	3.0	0.2	525,000	$0.28
1955	8.9	0.4	967,000	0.44
1956	14.9	1.0	1,047,000	0.97
1957	28.1	1.8	1,194,000	1.51
1958	83.2	3.7	1,691,000	2.13

Source: *Moody's Handbook of Common Stocks, 1958*

Litton paid 27,747 shares of convertible preferred and 366,759 of common for Monroe, which worked out to one and a half of its shares for every one of the acquired company. What this meant was that Thornton was exchanging one bundle of paper for another, and what he received had more than twice the earnings and four times the book value—at a time when Litton had less than 1.3 million shares of common outstanding. Thus the dilution was considerable, but the positive impact of the Monroe takeover on Litton's earnings and book was even greater. From Thornton's point of view, the takeover was admirable.

Later on analysts would realize that in fact Monroe would require huge sums to be made a competitor once again, and that Litton lacked the will and even the funds to make such expenditures. But for the moment the Monroe deal was hailed as Thornton's greatest coup and a preview of more to come.

Had the Monroe takeover transformed Litton from an electronics company into a conglomerate? Strictly speaking the answer was "no." There was a "fit" in this merger that was lacking, for example, in Textron's acquisition of Cleveland Pneumatic, and this was an important indication of the essential difference between these two corporations. Little would roam all over the industrial map, picking up whatever bargain or interesting situation that came his way, while all of Litton's takeovers meshed with at least one and often several existing operations. Lehman Brothers, which brought many candidates to Thornton's attention and acted as matchmaker for the company, understood this, as did the firms which lined up seeking to exchange their assets for Litton's paper.

Much of this had to do with Thornton's personality and his conception of what Litton should become. Where Little was almost playful, Thornton was deadly serious, with a deep craving for order. Randomness and opportunism rarely played a role in takeover strategy at Litton. When on one occasion Thornton gave fleeting thought to the idea of purchasing the ailing American Motors, he mused that the firm might become profitable if all of Litton's subsidiaries purchased its automobiles, providing AM with what amounted to a captive market. Thornton did not pursue the matter, perhaps because the price wasn't right or in recognition of the problems of that industry, but also because there really wasn't anything in Litton with which the auto maker could "connect." In time Litton would resemble a giant complex molecule, in which each atom is connected with, but often quite far from, another.

Which is to say that Thornton wanted a theme at Litton of high technology, electronics in particular. He rarely strayed from it, in part because he knew this industry better than any other, but perhaps also due to an inner suspicion that managerial expertise *couldn't* be as easily transferred as the conglomerators imagined. Moreover, the core of high technology at Litton provided its stock with that high multiple, without which few of the takeovers would have been possible. The price would remain high so long as investors perceived Litton that way.

Ever-increasing earnings per share, made possible through consolidation practices, masked the fact that several of the takeovers did not work out well, occasionally because of management failures or industry conditions, but also due to an unwillingness to make important commitments to research and development. Thornton preferred to purchase research rather than fund it himself. He could do so by paying for it with inflated stock, which also eliminated the risk of failure. But once they were part of the Litton team researchers often found their budgets cut. When the need arose for new products, Thornton was as likely to buy a small firm as to pour cash into existing laboratories. He boasted of never acquiring a firm with assets of more than $50 million, and this was so, but more a reflection of the desire to obtain inexpensive research than anything else.[10] Thus, in his own way, Thornton was as much of an opportunist as was Little. Both men were obliged to purchase inferior firms, but the gaps in product lines and operations were all the more apparent at Litton than at Textron, since Litton always claimed it was more unified, and indeed that was the case. Textron's individual free-standing companies were more capable of weathering adversity and embarking upon independent actions than were the more integrated operations at Litton, so that weaknesses in one segment of the latter could damage others.[11]

In the end Litton would be recognized as a hodgepodge of small-to-medium sized high-technology firms, none of which were truly outstanding, with a sprinkling of units in peripheral industries. Far too many were second or third rate, with only a handful capable of turning in sustained superior performances. By the early 1970s Wall Street would recognize that most of the components of Little's Textron were stronger and performing better than those of Thornton's Litton, but even prior to that time analysts concluded that Litton had become a conglomerate, though the specific moment of the transformation remained a matter for debate.

Two more firms were acquired in late 1958. The first was Airtron, a manufacturer of a variety of radar and microwave equipment which soon would report record revenues of $10 million a year, and which, as the others, was purchased for stock. The second, Westrex, represented an expansion out of the existing base, and for the first time Litton bought a significant unit for cash.

Westrex was a particularly attractive property. A subsidiary of Western Electric, it specialized in communications and sound equipment. Westrex's products could be found in all Hollywood studios, and most phonograph recording companies utilized them as well. It had offices and representatives in some 40 countries, affording Litton its first entry into most of them. The company was well managed, soundly financed, and had advanced technology. The only reason Western Electric was willing to sell was fear of antitrust prosecution.

Thornton wanted Westrex as another vehicle through which to deploy existing technology. Not only did he claim that Westrex's overall performance would improve once it became part of Litton, but also that the "mix" between it and other units would accelerate technological development. Along with other conglomerators, Thornton was a firm believer in the power of synergism—that the cooperative efforts of two or more operations would result in far greater effects than if each were to perform separately. Hence, two plus two could equal five, or even six, under the Litton umbrella.

While retaining most of Westrex's old management, Thornton brought in a new president, George Scharffenberger. Previously the leader of ITT's Kellogg division, Scharffenberger had hoped to become CEO of that corporation, and he left for Litton when the board turned to an outsider, Harold Geneen. Now he set about creating a new division around Westrex, which in time became known as Electronic Systems (and still later evolved into Professional Services and Equipment). At first the group was comprised of Westrex, Automatic Seriograph, and other small units. Then, in 1960, Thornton added the German medical electronics firm of Fritz Hellige, and Western Geophysical of America, which specialized in seismic exploration. Aero Service arrived two years later, augmenting Western Geophysical's know-how with its own in aerial mapping. Thus, Thornton had added yet another pearl to his string, and around it he created a new cluster of companies.

That same year, 1958, Harry Gray left the Greyvan subsidiary of Greyhound Corporation to take charge of Litton's Electronics Components Division. He began with seven companies, ranging from the original Litton to Roger White, and then added new ones—Poly-Scientific, Winchester Electronics, and Clifton Precision among others. Other pearls, other clusters.

With all of this, Litton's top personnel were stretched thin. The corporation's dynamism and the increasing momentum of change disturbed some while inspiring others, and Thornton's penchant for buying research rather than funding it internally dismayed several key scientists and technicians. The result was an acceleration of departures from the executive suites and laboratories.

Hugh Jamieson, one of the founders, started the "Lido exodus." He had urged Thornton to slow down and devote more time and energy to consolidating existing units rather than establishing new ones. Thornton insisted upon decentralization and free-form management, which unnerved the more conventional Jamieson, who resigned in 1958 to form Jamieson Industries, a minor factor in the electronic components market. The following year Singleton and Kozmetsky departed to start Teledyne, itself to become a major electronics-based conglomerate. In time Scharffenberger would go off to take command at City Investing while Harry Gray became CEO at United Technologies—two more conglomerates. Thornton and Ash told reporters that this was a sign of strength rather than weakness, and they took an almost missionary attitude toward the departures, as though the Lidos were going to spread the word to others. Ash suggested there was room for about half a dozen firms like Litton, each expanding rapidly into related areas and producing crops of executives who later would take up the banner at some other company. Moreover, Ash suggested that while the Lidos were talented, their replacements were equally so. But that wasn't true. Singleton and Kozmetsky (the latter later left for a life in academia) were sorely missed, and the magnitude of their loss would be recognized in the 1970s, when Teledyne grew rapidly and Litton ran into serious difficulties.

In early 1959 Litton acquired Times Facsimile from the New York Times Company through an exchange of stock, and this firm became part of the Defense and Space group, rather puzzling since it turned out gear utilized primarily by newspapers and others in the telecommunications field. As with its predecessors, Times Facsimile was supposed to augment several older Litton operations. By then Thornton had his line down pat; the press release announcing the takeover observed that "The increasing demand for high speed facsimile equipment makes the addition of Times Facsimile's capabilities and product line an effective supplement to Litton Industries' work in advanced electronics."[12]

Meanwhile Monroe was established as the core of the Business and

Equipment group, to which Svenska Dataregister, a Swedish manufacturer of a line of cash registers, was added later that year. The hope was that Svenska's products could be distributed in the United States by Monroe's sales force. This didn't work out well, and in time Svenska had to develop its own marketing program.

Once again, this was a case of Litton's trying to shave costs, an illustration of Thornton's unwillingness to provide sufficient funds for ongoing operations. Instead, six new firms (none of which were particularly exciting) were added to Business and Equipment during the next two years. They ranged from a company that serviced electronics products (Integrated Data Processing) to one that manufactured office furniture (Cole Steel Equipment). Others followed—there would be six additions to this group in 1964 and five more the following year, including Royal McBee, one of the world's leading manufacturers of typewriters. These firms varied from promising to moribund. Royal, which had reported $113.6 million in revenues in 1964, the year preceding acquisition, was barely holding its own in portable typewriters and had failed badly in office electrics, the most rapidly expanding part of the market. As with Monroe, the price was right—$29 million in inflated Litton common for a company whose net worth was far in excess of the understated book value of $18.4 million.

As with so many other acquisitions, Litton hoped to turn Royal around by shaking up and augmenting management. It didn't work any better there than it had at Monroe, which in mid-decade remained a poor performer in the rapidly growing office automation industry. In order to compete against the likes of IBM and Remington—or even with Underwood and Smith-Corona—Litton would have had to pour tens of millions of dollars into research and development, and even then might fail. Thornton was not prepared to make such a commitment. Instead, he resolved the matter in a typical fashion, by acquiring three foreign typewriter manufacturers—Imperial Typewriter Ltd. (of Great Britain), and Triumph-Werke and Adler-Werke, both of which were German—and then trying to meld their technologies and product lines with those of Royal to produce a coherent whole, an international entry to combat IBM. Not much came of this except a batch of favorable publicity, which deluded even the Federal Trade Commission into challenging the takeovers on the ground that the new entity would restrain trade. IBM and Remington knew better: the patched together Litton contestant would constitute no great challenge. Royal remained competitive in some areas of the market, and the firm did grow—but not as rapidly as the industry as a whole. Once again, Thornton had made a foray into a related territory; the tactic boosted earnings per share and book value, but further diluted Litton's major and best business, that of military-based electronics. What once had been a lean, tough competitor with fine, though limited, research facilities was suffering from bloat.

The key move toward conglomeration occurred in 1961, when Litton acquired Ingalls Shipbuilding. This move apparently was motivated by the kind of hubris that afflicted a number of conglomerators in the 1960s; by then Thornton and Ash had started believing their own press releases. Moreover, they had misbegotten notions about the future of shipbuilding, unrealistic assumptions about the navy's development program, little knowledge of the situation at Ingalls' Pasagoula, Mississippi, facility, and an implausible belief that in some convoluted fashion shipbuilding had become part of the electronics industry.

Ingalls made overtures to Litton in late 1960. This hardly was unusual; by then scarcely a week went by without one or more firms submitting themselves for inspection. But Ingalls was different. For one thing, it would not fit nicely into any existing division. Fred Mayo, who had assumed the presidency in 1959, took care of this by observing that the company was engaged in producing small, fast, attack submarines, each of which cost approximately $70 million. These would require a wide range of electronic gear, some of which Litton already manufactured, and more that might be developed under government contracts. As Ash later put it, "a submarine is the most expensive hotel in the world."[13] But under existing regulations—and provisions of the antitrust laws—Litton could not simply stock the Ingalls submarines with its electronics without first asking for bids for subcontracts. To do otherwise would be to violate strictures against "reciprocity," which held that corporations couldn't give "sweetheart contracts" to its own subsidiaries; it would have to permit outside competition. As a veteran of Hughes Aircraft, Thornton understood this, but he believed the rule might soon be altered. He thought that in the future, for the sake of efficiency, the navy would be permitted to contract entire systems to a single vendor. By then Ingalls would be integrated into Litton, which could take on the entire package. It was a delightful prospect.

Ingalls was the nation's third largest shipbuilder, but the Pasagoula yards were inefficient and plagued by labor difficulties. At best, shipbuilding is a highly cyclical industry, and in Ingalls' case this was compounded by the fact that virtually all of its business was tied to the defense establishment. The loss of an important contract, a major blunder in production, or simply rubbing powerful admirals and legislators the wrong way, could result in major deficits for years at a stretch. While Litton considered the takeover Thornton might have pondered the situation at the Martin Company. Once a significant manufacturer of planes for the armed forces, Martin had run afoul of navy brass, and had been all but frozen out of competition. At about the same time Thornton was acquiring Ingalls, Martin was reduced to subcontracting and merged with American Marietta, which had a diverse line of consumer products. Thus, Martin was leaving the prime contracting area just as Litton was about to enter. Where Martin's management knew the pitfalls, Thornton dreamed of opportunities. "We saw that here was something right under our noses that we should have been in before," said Ash, while Thornton noted that Ingalls would fit in well with Western Geophysical, and spoke glowingly of the future of oceanography, which he considered "as challenging as space."[14]

There was another kicker in the Ingalls takeover that might have clinched the deal. The founder's heirs had been quarreling for years, while the company declined. Although Fred Mayo had stopped the decay and instituted reforms, Ingalls bore a resemblance to Monroe Calculating at the time of that company's acquisition—a resemblance that later would also be seen in Royal. Here was a recognized industry name whose performance didn't match its reputation and which was available for a bargain price. In 1961 Ingalls was doing a $60 million business and had a backlog of some 250 million. For this Litton paid $8 million in its own stock while assuming an additional $9 million in debt.

At first everything went according to plan. The state of Mississippi constructed a $130 million shipbuilding facility across the river from the old Ingalls yards and leased it to Litton for a modest fee. Hoping to cash in on the demand for Great Lakes ore and grain carriers, Ingalls constructed a shipyard at Erie, paid for by Commonwealth of Pennsylvania bonds. These two were hailed as "state of the art" operations, incorporating the latest technologies developed not only in the United States, but Sweden and Japan as well. For once Litton spent lavishly; Thornton spoke of having "put millions into that [yard], all the R & D, all the new concepts of ship designs. The kind of ships that we are in are those that require a lot of technology." But virtually all the money came from those state bonds, and if the projects failed Litton could have walked away, dumping the mess on Mississippi and Pennsylvania. In fact only $3 million of Litton money went into this massive program, one calculated to transform Litton into the nation's premier shipbuilding concern.

Litton's failure with Ingalls is a classic case of corporate blundering. From the start nothing went well. There were delays in construction, cost overruns, errors in design, and mismanagement. The new labor force proved inept and worse, and even so the turnover rate was high by industry standards. Meanwhile Ingalls entered bidding wars with firms like Newport News and Bath and won many of them, but only by miscalculating and underestimating costs. As a result ships built for the U.S. Navy and for American President Lines-Farrell were delivered at losses. Furthermore, the snafus resulted in long delays and late deliveries—at one point Ingalls fell four years behind in a major contract for navy helicopter assault ships.

Ingalls became something of a joke within the industry, and its credibility with the government was irreparably harmed. The company and the navy traded verbal blows, there were lawsuits, claims, and counterclaims, which further damaged Litton's reputation. The yards worked their way through a succession of managers, winding up with Ellis Gardner in 1967, under whose leadership the company finally started coming out of its tailspin. By then Ingalls no longer placed bids on major contracts, in part because the logjam was still dangerous, but also due to its loss of stature in Washington, a factor that would plague the division through the 1970s. Yet Thornton continued speaking out about the great potential in marine construction, as if nothing had happened.[15]

The reasons were clear enough. The government paid for research and development performed on military projects, while Litton would have had to dig into its own treasury had it opted to concentrate on the civilian markets represented by such firms as Monroe, and later, Royal. Everything in Thornton's background prior to arriving at Litton prepared him for this kind of stance, and he would never change. The result was that Litton might perform well in military electronics, but little else. Furthermore, the government's standards, stringent as they might be in some areas, hardly came up to those demanded by civilian customers. As *Fortune* observed in 1968, "the requirements for profitability in government work are less exacting than those of the private marketplace. . . . Barring flagrant mismanagement, the company that can do the job can be reasonably sure of clearing a respectable profit."[16]

That was the situation at Litton. During the 1960s the corporation was able to report profits on government sales while demonstrating an almost uniform failure at cracking civilian markets. The Ingalls situation involved "flagrant mismanagement." In other areas, however, Litton performed more than adequately, at least insofar as the government was concerned.[17]

The Ingalls takeover took time to digest, and perhaps this was why Litton acquired relatively few firms during the next three years, and all of these in areas familiar to those who followed the corporation. Thornton brought in such companies as Emertron, Winchester Electronics, Adler Electronics, Clifton Precision, and Advanced Data Systems, which found niches in and complemented other units in the Defense and Space group and the Components group.

This pause resulted not from a lack of takeover candidates, but rather the military buildup of the Kennedy and early Johnson administrations. There was a 20 percent increase in military spending from 1960 to 1964, much of which went into procurement. Along with other defense-oriented companies, Litton scrambled for new contracts, a market in which Thornton was an acknowledged master; few corporation CEOs knew their way around Washington as well as he. Just as Ingalls won several navy competitions, so those Litton groups concentrating upon military electronics did quite well in subcontracts.

Whenever critics charged that Litton had grown primarily as a result of acquisitions, the corporation's defenders would point to the record from 1961 to 1964, when takeovers played a very small part in operations. In this period revenues rose from $250 million to $706 million (sizeable even when Ingalls is taken into account) and net income went from $10.1 million to $30.1 million. Thornton borrowed heavily to expand facilities, and for the first time was even willing to loosen the purse for research and development in nonmilitary areas. Litton's long-term debt rose from $49.2 million in 1961 to $134.7 million in 1964, but the corporation's balance sheet had never been stronger.

In this period the corporation was carried by the Components and the Defense and Space groups. The Business and Equipment group performed in a mediocre fashion, Professional Services and Equipment hardly was better, and Marine (a group whose sole member was Ingalls) was a disaster.

Was Litton primarily a conglomerate, an electronics company, or a defense contractor? Did the corporation bear a greater resemblance to Textron, Texas Instruments, or General Dynamics? In 1964 one might have supposed the latter firm to have been a closer analogy than the first two. Litton's basic business remained electronics, but Thornton's energies and imagination hardly could be contained to that spectrum. Forays into new fields seemed inevitable.

The expected move took place in 1965. Almost simultaneously with the purchase of Royal McBee; Litton announced the acquisition of Hewitt-Robins for $28.8 million, slightly less than half of which was paid in cash, the rest in convertible preferred stock. Hewitt-Robins was then a manufacturer of bulk conveying equipment and rubber products, mostly belting, for industrial uses. Like Royal McBee and other large Litton acquisitions, it was a troubled company, the difference being that in this case most of the difficulties had been or were in the process of being overcome. Seeking to expand into fields related to its basic business, management had entered the plastic foam and foam rubber markets, ventures that came to little and ended with a string of deficits that almost wrecked the corporation. These plants were sold off in the late 1950s, and with the money Hewitt-Robins purchased a minor entity in the materials handling industry, in effect entering a business to which it had been a long-term supplier. This subsidiary grew nicely through internal expansion and related acquisitions, to the point where it became Hewitt-Robins' major division. Now the corporation turned out lines of conveyers, gears, and similar products, most of which were well received. Revenues grew from $46.6 million in 1959 to $63.3 million in 1964, and in the same period earnings went from a deficit of $670,000 to a profit of $1 million.

Under ordinary circumstances Thornton might never have considered acquiring Hewitt-Robins. There was nothing in his background remotely connected with materials handling, and Thornton was a man to expand from an existing base, not leapfrog all over the industrial map as would a Royal Little. It was the Hewitt-Robins management that made the first move, approaching Litton in the summer of 1964 with the idea of effecting a takeover. The prospect was dazzling. Here was an industry still utilizing some of the technologies of the steam age, which only recently had come to terms with electrification and was now prepared to make the leap into electronics. Thornton visualized electronically controlled assembly lines utilizing Hewitt-Robins equipment, turning out precision parts rapidly and soundlessly in clinically clean environments. Conveyer belts could be designed to speed mail deliveries and facilitate warehousing. Computers united with such machinery might keep track of and retrieve inventories. And these were just some of the immediate prospects, as they appeared in the mid-1960s.

Thornton's growing interest in Hewitt-Robins was as much a tribute to and indication of his abilities at rationalizing takeovers as anything else. For all of its acknowledged expertise and even leadership in several product areas, this company was an integral part of the highly cyclical heavy machinery industry. Along with the other firms in it Hewitt-Robins experienced sales and earnings declines during the recessions of 1954 and 1958, and could count upon the same in future slumps. Management's attempts to diversify the product lines was largely the result of trying to break out of the cycle. Now Thornton hoped to do the same, by transforming Hewitt-Robins from a manufacturer of high quality but mundane machinery into a company that turned out complex, highly sophisticated electronic "delivery systems." Each system would be custom-designed for specific uses and would draw upon products and concepts from other Litton companies. Just as Ingalls was supposed to show the way for a new kind of shipbuilding enterprise, so Hewitt-Robins was to be in the vanguard of those who would remake the American factory.

Litton's planners got to work at Hewitt-Robins shortly after the takeover was completed. Going over the company with their usual precision, they came back with a report which sketched a somewhat run-down operation with several interesting programs and products. They were impressed with a mobile bridge operation about to come into production, and they believed that the markets for conveyer systems and gear speed reducers might be expanded somewhat. Competition in these fields was fierce, however, and progress would be slow. As the planners saw it, the core company might grow to the point where 1970 revenues would reach slightly more than $100 million.

Thornton would not have been so interested in Hewett-Robins were this all there was to it. Rather, he intended from the first to utilize Hewitt-Robins as the centerpiece for a new group, which would be known as Industrial Systems and Equipment. According to projections, companies with combined revenues of around $152 million were to be acquired within the next five years, making this a quarter of a billion dollar division by 1970.

The ambitious plan was outlined in a position paper drawn up shortly after Hewitt-Robins was acquired. Industrial Systems and Equipment was to enter such fields as construction and mining equipment by means of takeovers of both large and small firms in those industries. Among the possible acquisitions were such well-known companies as Bucyrus Erie, American Hoist and Derrick, Signode Steel Strapping, Dorr Oliver, and Hyster.

None of this came about. During the next five years Litton made overtures to more than 50 companies, most of which were not interested in being acquired by Industrial Systems and Equipment. But some did accept Litton paper for their assets. Alvey Ferguson, which produced handling equipment, arrived in 1966, and four more firms—Louis Allis, Chainveyor, Rust Engineering, and Von Gal Manufacturing—were added the following year. The largest of these was Rust, a comparatively minor entry in the specialized field of plant construction; it had sales of $77 million.[18]

Industrial Systems and Equipment was helped considerably by business generated as a result of the Vietnam War. Orders were relatively easy to come by, and several units actually had to reject would-be customers. By 1968 Litton was able to establish a related group, Machine Tool, which was composed of three medium-sized firms acquired that year: Landis Tool, New Britain Machine, and UTD. Together these two were among the fastest growing segments of the corporation's business.

The 1965 revenue projections for Industrial Systems and Equipment had to be scrapped; in fact sales for 1969 came to around $300 million, or half again what had been anticipated. Profits were low, however, slightly under $7 million. Margins were far below those of such competitors as Square D, Reliance Electric, and Rex Chainbelt. On the other hand Machine Tool, led by Landis, turned in a creditable performance, contributing $14 million to earnings on $200 million in sales. Taken as a whole, however, the situation in this part of the Litton complex was hardly encouraging. In 1965 Thornton had spoken of a "total systems approach to design solutions to industrial production problems." Nothing of the sort had been created. Industrial Systems and Equipment had become a hodgepodge of unrelated firms, incapable of leading the way to automation, a laggard that never lived up to expectations. Machine Tool remained profitable, but there were grave doubts it could keep up with the likes of Cincinnati Milling and Acme Cleveland once the war was over and conditions returned to normal.[19]

Litton managed to retain much of its old electronics-based glamour, even though the company had most of the trappings of a conglomerate by 1967. Acquisitions came in at the rate of one every three weeks. Some, like Louis Allis and Chainveyor, represented logical extensions of existing businesses, but others were jumps into unfamiliar territory, Thornton's always interesting rationalizations to the contrary notwithstanding.

For example, in 1967 Litton was the nation's largest manufacturer of microwave ovens, all of which were sold through its Atherton operation with that brand name. This hardly was a major business; only 10,300 units were sold that year, mostly to airlines and other commercial users, bringing in revenues of $7 million. Nor was Atherton an example of Litton's technological leadership. The original business came in via a takeover of Bruder & Co. four years earlier, while several major components were turned out under licenses from Raytheon, itself the second largest factor in the field. Microwave ovens were not in great demand, partly due to their high price, but also because homemakers were unfamiliar with their advantages, or simply didn't want them.

Hoping to increase sales by wedding Atherton to a familiar name, and also in order to enter the consumer field directly for the first time, Thornton tried to acquire Stouffer Food. Not particularly well considered in its industry, Stouffer had an indifferent record with its restaurants, inns, and food service businesses, and was best known for its line of frozen prepared foods. The company rejected Thornton's initial bids, holding out for a higher price, which it finally got in late 1967. Stouffer had assets of less than $40 million on which it produced sales of $95.1 million and turned a profit of $1.4 million, hardly an impressive performance. For this Thornton paid close to $100 million in Litton common, the most ever for a Litton acquisition.

During the next few months Litton's planners engaged in the same kind of projections that came after Hewitt-Robins had entered the corporation. Strategies were devised to make a major push into institutional feeding, expansion of hotels, and the franchising of Stouffer's Grog Shops. The nexus between Stouffer and Atherton was explored, but not in any great detail; Litton obviously was more excited about other aspects of the business. Plans were made for a Food Systems group, to be comprised initially of Atherton, an institutional division, and a management food systems design operation, the last two coming out of Stouffer. The planners mused about potential takeovers, with Servomation a prime target. All the while Thornton spoke with his usual enthusiasm about providing microwave ovens and frozen food to workers on oil drilling platforms, astronauts in space, and, in remote areas of the world, to servicemen who missed American food. Almost as an afterthought he observed that Stouffer enhanced Atherton's value to Litton. Far more enticing than the prospect of microwave ovens in American homes was that of dozens of units on every ship launched by Ingalls, each fitted with freezers carrying thousands of Stouffer frozen meals. Thornton had the good sense to restrict his visions to markets he could control, knowing perhaps that to mount an offensive in the consumer market would be very costly, and far too chancy a venture.[20]

American Book Company, another of the "class of '67," provided Thornton with another outlet for his imagination and a second new industry for Litton to explore. For several years Thornton had been intrigued with the technologies involved in data transmission, and of course Litton already was in the industry through Times Facsimile and several other small units. Now he sought to add audio-visual communications to the mix. Times Fascimile would provide the hardware, while American Book could contribute its software. Moreover, Litton had acquired Fitchburg Paper the previous year, and the fit between it and American Book was obvious. The takeover should not have surprised anyone familiar with the way Thornton's mind worked.

American Book was a typical Thornton acquisition, in that it was an old company recently fallen upon hard times, a secondary entry in a growth industry, but one that Thornton believed could be transformed by a generous helping of the Litton magic. Once a leader in the elementary and secondary text markets, American had come close to dissolution in 1960, at which time a new management team took over and halted the decline. Still, it was a small firm, with sales of $21.3 million and earnings of $1.9 million. American did have a small audio-visual unit that Thornton believed promising, and might have served as the nucleus for his high technology information ambitions. The Litton planners thought in terms of expansion into a wide variety of new areas, among them teaching machines, programmed instructional materials, and language laboratories. They weren't alone in this: prior to Litton's takeover of American Book such companies as IBM, ITT, RCA, Xerox, and Raytheon had acquired publishing operations, moves not unnoticed by the Litton people. Characteristically, however, they thought Litton could do it better.

"The technologies required by the current and immediate future audio-visual communications market have been developed and are readily available in a number of companies," read a corporation memo of the period. "What the market lacks is leadership based on the proper combination of creative business, marketing, and technical and financial techniques which Litton Industries is in a position to supply."[21]

Thus, American Book became the centerpiece for the new Educational group, to which were added the following year Chapman Reinhold and D. Van Nostrand. Like American Book, these were smallish companies of no particular distinction in a highly competitive industry. Here too, as in so many similar situations, Thornton demonstrated vision and imagination, while lacking the resources to implement them and the willingness to make a major commitment to a new venture. The Educational group went nowhere, with all units lagging in their fields.

This indeed had become a Litton trademark: bold, futuristic talk centering around new and emerging technologies combined with cautious investment policies. Was it because Litton had attempted to do too much too quickly with limited capital and human resources? Had top management sold itself a bill of goods instead of assessing possibilities in a cold, calculated fashion? Was this simply a case of good intentions gone wrong due to shallowness or some basic flaw in the design? Or was Thornton merely a super-salesman who fell for his own line, brought low by his own hubris? A more interesting and important question might be: how was it that so many supposedly astute Wall Streeters and other industry analysts failed to see through the rhetoric and discern the pattern of failures, miscalculations, and outright blunders? In 1968, as in 1954, Litton Industries was a company with genuine capabilities in some areas of military electronics, but little else. Monroe's new calculators were technologically inferior to those put out by Burroughs, NCR, and others in the business equipment field. Even with discounts Royal couldn't compete effectively against SCM in portable typewriters or with IBM in office models. An attempt to enter the copier market through a subsidiary, Royfax, was a disaster, as the machines captured no more than 1 percent of the business. Very little came out of Stouffer but talk. Ingalls remained a disaster area. Profits started to level off in 1967, but investors remained true to the vision—and the stock peaked at 118, slightly less than 60 times earnings, late that year.

Then came disillusionment and collapse. Within three months Litton common lost half its value, while Thornton and Ash appeared unable to reverse the decline at the conglomerate they had fashioned.

No single event or mistake brought Litton down. Rather, the corporation had never performed as well as Wall Street thought it had, and the magic was more in creative accounting than effective management. If one were to search for the best symbol of the decline, however, it might be found in Litton's ambitious plans to remake and manage entire societies in the late 1960s. Ash spoke confidently of Litton's intention to construct entire communities from the ground up, something he called the *de novo* city.

> Instead of trying to accommodate ten million more people a year in our present cities—and that's how many more we'll have each year toward the end of the century—we'll create new cities. All you have to do is fly over the country and see square mile after square mile where you could quite well set down a whole new city. There's no reason why you can't take 200 square miles some place that has the natural resources, which means primarily water—and even the water problem can be solved separately if it has to be—and create an ideal city with solutions for all these urban problems before it's even built.[22]

This wasn't an original concept. For nearly half a century planned communities had been constructed throughout the United States, the most famous being Levittown, New York, and Reston, Virginia, and even before then visionaries had put together suburban developments and utopian settlements. Some even considered Disney World such a project, with one observer noting that Walt Disney had proven himself the most original and successful urban planner American industry had ever produced. But these communities involved tens of thousands of people; Ash had something far more ambitious in mind.

Nothing ever came of such notions in the United States, but in 1967 Litton announced it would take charge of economic development on the island of Crete and in the western Peloponnesus, under contract from the Greek government. Over a twelve-year period, Litton International Development was supposed to attract some $800 million in new investments, to be used to construct port facilities, industrial plants, utilities, roads, and housing. They were, in fact, to take charge of planning and execution for those regions. For its efforts Litton was to receive a fee plus commissions which, if all went well, could come to more than $100 million. Ash announced the agreement with confidence and enthusiasm; "What we are attempting in Greece is putting together the think and the do." Thornton spoke of other countries interested in entering into such arrangements. Others at headquarters spoke of developing a new kind of political form, combining free enterprise capitalism with central planning. Early in 1968 there were rumors that Turkey might soon invite Litton to establish a pilot project, and that this could be a prelude to some kind of rapprochement between that country and Greece. Thus, Thornton and Ash might play diplomatic as well as business roles in the region. It was a heady vision even by Litton standards.

Once again the bold picture was just that: an image without much in the way of reality. During the first year Litton was able to attract less than $2 million in new capital to Greece, without much more in prospect. Such typical programs as "Litton Infrastructure Development Optimization" and "Litton Enterprise Optimizer" never got off the ground. Now Litton quietly folded its Greek operation, and nothing more was heard about *de novo* cities and the like from Thornton and Ash.[23]

In late January 1968, Litton announced that earnings for the first quarter of the year would be "substantially lower than planned for this period." In a letter to stockholders Thornton and Ash conceded the decline was due, "to a great extent," to "certain earlier deficiencies of management personnel," which were being corrected. Departures followed, and other executives were shuffled into vacated positions. Some of those leaving Litton spoke with reporters and told, with undisguised glee, of errors in judgment, plans that went astray, blunders, and the weaving of webs of fantasy by top management. "How can they talk about 'earlier deficiencies of management personnel' when Tex and Roy are still there?" asked one former executive. But both men remained optimistic. "There is no question in anybody's mind that Litton is going to be a successful large company," said Ash, at a time when that very question was being asked in all seriousness on Wall Street. "But our objective is to be a successful large *growth* company."[24]

In time Litton would be just that once again—but not in the 1970s. During that decade it did not grow at nearly the rate previously witnessed. Nor was Litton particularly successful. Thornton had run out of illusions. What remained was the need to preserve what already was at hand.

4

James Ling: The Magician

Of all the major conglomerators, none is more difficult to pigeonhole than James Ling. It requires no great stretch of the imagination to picture Tex Thornton sending scores of Lidos out into the world, each a clone of the master, intent upon propagating the gospel. Royal Little's roots went deep into the soil of pre-World War II American business, and of course he had his start in one of the oldest and most well-known of all industries, textiles. Wall Street's analysts found them familiar, even ingratiating figures—Thornton the new man of science and technology wrapped up in a soaring imagination, Little the elderly eccentric with a New Englander's eye for value. But Ling was different, and while students of American business were intrigued by his machinations and confused by their financial implications, they could not grasp his essential character and personality.

On the surface Ling appeared to have the financial adroitness of a young Joe Kennedy, the blunt power drive of a J. P. Morgan, the global vision of a John D. Rockefeller, the canny maneuvering abilities of an Andrew Carnegie, and the sheer imagination and inventiveness of a Samuel Insull. Yet on occasion he let the mask drop, and appeared a small-town boy suddenly grown up, finding himself in charge of an empire, and not certain what to do with it.

A decade after his fall from grace one commentator wrote that Ling might have provided the model for R. J. Ewing, the calculating villain of the television soap opera "Dallas," but this is far wide of the mark. If there is a single fictional character Ling resembled it was F. Scott Fitzgerald's Jay Gatsby, a man who was dazzled by the world of big business, often impressed by its leaders, and in the end brought down by forces he did not completely understand. Ling yearned for respectability, even though he was a far better businessman and appreciated the potential of financial leverage more than those he seemed to admire. He would never be accepted by the Establishment, which cheered when he stumbled in 1969. Fitzgerald understood what this meant much better than business analysts of the time. "Gatsby believed in the green light, the orgiastic future that year by year recedes before us. It eluded us then, but that's no matter—tomorrow we will run faster, stretch out our arms farther. . . ."

Little and Thornton left legacies, both in their companies and practices followed by others. No other conglomerator ever attempted to imitate Ling's stratagems; virtually none of his executives had much of a career at the firms they later joined, and even his firm, Ling-Temco-Vought, would alter its name to LTV, as though to dissociate itself from the founder. Ling has vanished from the main arena of American business life, like Gatsby, leaving no trace except in the memories of those who worked with him in his heyday. One has to go back to Insull to find an entrepreneur who rose to such a height so rapidly, and then plummeted to the depths in so dramatic a fashion.

Just how spectacular was his performance? In 1965 Ling-Temco-Vought was America's 204th largest industrial concern, and in the same year ITT was in the 30th slot, Litton was 72nd, and Textron, 81st. Four years later LTV ranked 14th, the second largest conglomerate behind ITT, then in the ninth position. Litton and Textron were far behind—39th and 57th respectively. There never had been anything quite like this in American business history, the closest parallel perhaps being J. P. Morgan's fashioning of the world's first billion dollar corporation, U.S. Steel, in 1901. Ling insisted he wasn't through conglomeratizing: insiders later claimed he intended to make Ling-Temco-Vought the largest American industrial corporation of them all and to accomplish this within a decade.

Bigger than Standard Oil of New Jersey, General Motors, or General Electric? Today such an ambition appears to have been hopelessly unrealistic. It did not seem all that farfetched at the time.

In common with most of the conglomerators (and all of the prominent ones), Ling is an outsider. He lacked the kind of breeding and credentials American business leaders at midcentury were expected to possess. Ling—his full name is James Joseph Ling—was born on New Year's Eve, 1922, in the small town of Hugo, Oklahoma, not far from the Texas state line. His father, Henry William Ling, was the son of Bavarian immigrants and a convert to Catholicism, while his mother, Mary Jones Ling, came from a family well entrenched in the area. Not much is known of either, except that Henry William was a fireman on a railroad, and that he suffered deeply from the anti-German and anti-Catholic bigotries epidemic in the region at the time. Taunted by fellow workers, he killed one of them. After being acquitted on grounds of self-defense, Henry William left the railroad, worked for a few years in the Oklahoma and

Texas oil fields and then, plagued with guilt, entered a Carmelite monastery in San Antonio.[1] Mary Ling tried to keep her six children together and succeeded in doing so for a while. But she died in 1933, and the family scattered, two younger brothers to Father Flanagan's Boys Town and the others to relatives. James went to live with an aunt, who owned a small boarding house in Shreveport, Louisiana, where he attended a local Catholic parochial school for a while. Restless and unhappy, he dropped out of school after a year, taking to the road as a hobo. This hardly was unusual; the Great Depression raged on, and there were tens of thousands of boys and young men like him drifting aimlessly from town to town, riding the rails when possible, taking whatever jobs they could find, and considering their futures bleak.

Ling finally wound up in Dallas, where he found work as an apprentice electrician, married, and had children. When World War II broke out he took a second job in the evening at Lockheed, which also involved electrical work. Granted a draft exemption as a result of his youth and his family status, Ling was able to obtain licenses as a master electrician and electrical contractor prior to entering the navy in 1944. Because of his credentials he was sent to electrical school and upon graduation shipped off to the Philippines where he helped string power lines and spent his spare time taking a correspondence course in electrical engineering. Mustered out of the service in 1946, he returned to Dallas, intending to go into business on his own as an electrical contractor.

Ling was 24 years old now, a tall, muscular man who bore more than a passing resemblance to mystery writer Mickey Spillane. Later he would take to Ivy League suits and subdued ties, and his broad, spadelike face would be softened by eyeglasses. When Ling started out in business, however, he looked more like a roustabout than an executive. Intensely ambitious and aware of his educational limitations, he was eager to learn all he could about running an operation, knowing that his experience in this area was deficient. And he intended to obtain the knowledge he needed through experience—throughout his life Ling felt he could learn little from merely studying the ways other businesses developed. Two decades later he told an interviewer, "I have some principles—a model perhaps—learned from observations and experience." Typically, when Ling felt the need to learn more about European banking methods he flew to the continent. "Over a period of six weeks I interviewed over 200 commercial and merchant bankers personally. I learned a lot about European finance. . . ." On another occasion Ling sketched a study of securities markets prices he once undertook. "I went back to the last day of 1922, the day I was born—I usually think that's far back enough for me to go."[2]

As a group the conglomerators would attempt to break new ground, and each did so in his own way. But none went as far as Ling. Little abandoned old practices once he found they wouldn't work, while Thornton began conventionally enough, altering Litton Industries only when he saw new opportunities. There was none of this with Ling, who rather than rejecting past methods simply ignored them. In his view contemporary business practices weren't right or wrong, but rather irrelevant. More than any other prominent businessman of his time, Ling attempted to start fresh, erecting a corporation on the basis of what made sense to him in the present and for the future as he imagined it, rather than recreating a firm on the model of what went before.

As much as anyone, Ling was an original.

He seemed conventional enough in the beginning, however. Ling Electric Company was organized in Dallas on January 1, 1947. As Ling tells it, it was housed in a small office, and all he had was a truck and some war surplus electrical equipment, paid for with money obtained from the sale of his house. For a while the Lings lived in rooms behind the office. Though the going must have been rough the experience was hardly unusual. Moreover, Ling knew his situation would quickly improve. Dallas was just starting to experience the postwar construction boom, and there was plenty of work for small electrical outfits. Ling soon was installing fixtures and wiring in new homes and small businesses, with most jobs leading to others. He took on helpers and planned for the inevitable expansion. Ling Electric grossed $70,000 in 1947; the following year revenues came to $200,000, and in 1949 it was a $400,000 company, well known in the Dallas area. The Lings had moved into a new home by then, but it was not ornate, since most of the earnings were plowed back into the business.

In the process Ling transformed himself from an electrician to a businessman. Learning to estimate costs and deal with suppliers and clients was easy enough. Along the way he discovered how to shave expenses, control costs, hire and fire workers, and keep books. By the early 1950s Ling Electric was bidding on large projects throughout the region and had construction units in New Orleans and San Diego. The company's backlog kept growing, and Ling himself was working longer hours than ever before. By then too he had come to believe that, given time and money, there was nothing he couldn't accomplish. Time became available as Ling learned how to delegate operational authority. Locating and marshalling capital was something else. By the mid-1950s he was discovering the intricacies of high finance, partly by associating with bankers and brokers at the country club he had joined. Ling now learned of wheeling and dealing Texas style from men who were experts at wildcatting, cattle futures, and insurance, at a time when Texas was growing rapidly and Dallas just starting to emerge as a regional financial center. All of which made electrical contracting seem rather mundane. Besides, although Ling Electric was doing $2 million a year in business it was vulnerable to recessions; moreover, his marriage was falling apart, and Ling was seeking new challenges.

Around this time Ling invested and lost some money in the stock of a newly formed insurance company. He later said this was one of the best investments of his life, for it taught him a few things about raising capital. "I had become acquainted with a prospectus," he recalled. Ling got in touch with the broker who had sold him the stock and said, "Thanks, you have just made me a million dollars."[3]

The basic idea was simple enough, and a plan carried through by thousands of other firms. Ling would sell off a portion of his wholly owned firm and use the money to expand operations. In 1955 he organized Ling Electric, Inc. with a capitalization of 1 million shares, 474,000 of which went to acquire the assets and business of the old Ling Electric. Then Ling had a prospectus drawn up and approved by the Texas Securities Commissioner, after which he set out to sell the rest of the shares. He distributed copies of the prospectus wherever he could find an audience, including the Texas State Fair. Within three months Ling had sold 450,000 shares at $2.25 each, providing the new Ling Electric with a treasury of some $800,000 (minus expenses). The next step seemed obvious: all he had to do now was expand the business, increase the earnings per share, and watch the stock rise in value, making him a multimillionaire. Others at the country club were doing it. Why not James Ling?

But it didn't happen, at least not at once. In spite of a strong stock market and a continuing mania for new issues, along with an outstanding performance by the business, Ling Electric's stock hardly budged. Ling even purchased a Glendale, California, electrical contracting business and indicated more would be added in the future, hoping this would boost the stock, but it didn't. By then he knew what was wrong. Electrical contracting was a solid but stodgy and familiar business. Investors and speculators were seeking high-technology stocks, especially those of companies deeply involved with electronics. Ling did not know a great deal about this field, but he knew enough to realize that expansion into it from his current base was possible.

From a Dallas friend Ling learned of L. M. Electronics, a California-based firm that turned out a line of testing equipment, and that was badly in need of capital. Ling looked the company over, liked what he saw, negotiated with founder Leon Mooradian, and purchased it for around $200,000 in cash and stock. L. M. was renamed Ling Electronics, taken in as a subsidiary of Ling Electric, and, when given additional funds, proved quite profitable.

Now "Electric" was both an operating and holding company, with "Electronics'" earnings fully consolidated into its own. The parent company's stock started to rise as earnings improved and the image was altered. Ling was gratified, and having learned the rudiments of takeovers set out to hone his newly acquired skills while adding some twists of his own.

Most of Ling's attention was devoted to "Electronics," which clearly was more glamorous than "Electric." He purchased a small, nearly bankrupt fabricator, Electronic Wire & Cable, for slightly more than $50,000, and set up Electron Corporation, a minuscule entry in the developing closed-circuit television industry; both became part of "Electronics." Then, in early 1957, he embarked on the first of the many convoluted maneuvers that would become his hallmark by the late 1960s.

Ling made a public offering of $1.3 million worth of Ling Electronics stock and convertible debentures, most of which was taken up by Ling Electric's shareholders. Then he renamed the parent firm Ling Industries, Inc., and set up another subsidiary, confusingly called Ling Electric. "Industries" then transferred all of the contracting business to "Electric" in return for all of its stock. The end result was that Ling Industries became a pure holding company, with all of the stock of Ling Electric and most of that of Ling Electronics. The reason for this shuffling of paper soon became obvious, as Ling set about creating additional operating companies to function under his banner. And of course there would be more changes to come. The creation of Ling Industries signaled the beginning of a new period in Ling's career. From that time on he showed little interest in running an operating company and concentrated on the financial end of the business.

Ling Industries' total sales for the fiscal year ending July 31, 1957 came to slightly less than $4 million, while net earnings were $308,000, or $0.35 for each of the corporation's 874,000 shares. Most of the revenues and almost all the earnings came from the contracting business, which was thriving, but Ling was turning ever more steadily toward electronics, which he was convinced had better prospects. As an indication of this, he regrouped his holdings for the second time in a year. Ling Industries was taken over by Ling Electronics, which now became the parent firm. Then Electronic Wire & Cable was merged into American Microwave, a company Ling had just acquired for less than $100,000 in stock and cash. The new entity was named Ling Systems, and placed under the control of Ling Electronics. Next, "Electronics" purchased United Electronics, a rapidly growing manufacturer of capacitors and tubes, for $750,000 plus 65,000 shares of "Electronics" common. For fiscal 1958 Ling's holdings reported revenues of close to $7 million, and the turn away from dependence upon electrical contracting and toward military electronics was well under way.

This continued during the next year, during which Ling exploded in a flurry of merger activity which earned him recognition on Wall Street as an up-and-coming tycoon. For $320,000 in cash and $922,000 in convertible debentures he acquired Calidyne, a well-regarded manufacturer of a line of electronic testing equipment, which despite its name was a Massachusetts-based concern. To balance his military sales with those in the civilian market (and because it came his way at a reasonable price) Ling went after the Altec Companies, an important manufacturer of audio equipment, for which he paid 335,000 shares of Ling Electronics common worth around $5 million. Shortly thereafter the corporation was once again renamed, this time Ling-Altec, which Ling felt would capitalize on the fame of Altec in its field. Then, to augment his new holding, he purchased University Loudspeaking for $2.3 million in cash, the money obtained through the issuance of short-term notes.

Next came Continental Electronics, which designed and produced radio transmitters for the military. Continental was an important factor in a narrow field, and with $25 million in sales the largest Ling takeover to that time. It cost Ling $3,250,000 in cash, $125,000 in short-term notes, and 10,000 common shares.

The additions of these companies enabled Ling-Altec to report revenues of $48.1 million and earnings of $1.9 million for 1959. Thus, within two years sales had increased twelvefold and earnings by more than 600 percent. But Ling-Altec now had nearly twice as many shares outstanding (1.6 million), while total long- and short-term obligations had ballooned to close to $8 million. Then, as later, long-term debt did not trouble Ling unduly; he was ready to exchange it for profitable assets. The short-term paper had to be paid off, however, so Ling set about transforming it into longer obligations.

First he floated an issue of ten-year debentures through the investment banking house of White, Weld, and then Ling obtained a 15-year loan from a group headed by the Mutual Life Insurance Company of New York. Interest charges on both were lowered by making the debentures convertible into common stock and attaching stock warrants to the loan. As long as the conversions were not made or the warrants exercised Ling-Altec's equity would not be diluted. As with the long-term debt, Ling would worry about that later.

Ling was always prepared to borrow in order to acquire new properties, and then use the additional earnings to pay the interest. He would buy a company with cash and short-term paper, and on the basis of the transaction sell longer-term obligations, the proceeds of which were to be used to wipe the balance sheet clean once again.

Ling now had completed his basic training in corporate finance, and had developed the rudiments of techniques that later would dazzle and confound congressional investigators and Wall Streeters. He had demonstrated how to restructure holdings so as to make them more pliable and attractive; he was quite willing to discard old forms when they no longer served his purposes. Ling had learned how to utilize borrowings to make large purchases and to delay payments. His new Ling-Altec was heavily in debt, but the service charges could easily be handled by the enlarged cash flow. And it was a true holding company, its leader concerned with overall strategy and financing, leaving operations to others.

More than any other conglomerator, Ling considered his holdings mere "properties," which could be disposed of when the price was right. Thornton, Little, and the others all demonstrated interest in management, and even developed enthusiasm toward the new industries they entered. Each of them was fascinated by operational practices. Not Ling, who remained indifferent to such matters throughout his career. Even in 1959 he was passionately involved with matters relating to capital—interest rates, Eurodollar accounts, bonds, stocks, and notes—and not matters concerned with the production of goods and services. He was more at home with bankers and accountants than with plant managers.

Those companies acquired by Ling would not be rejuvenated, as they were at Textron, or made part of an ever-growing entity, as was the case at Litton, but merely shuffled around, which could be seen as early as 1959. Whatever operational changes took place at Ling's companies resulted from the initiative of others, not of the CEO, who often continued to back inept and inadequate executives because he really did not know much about their activities or could not perceive the extent of their ineptitude. Ling cared little about details; all that mattered was the proverbial "bottom line," which could be doctored by skilled accountants. Ling had almost nothing original or interesting to say about actual production, which was why he left so vague a mark on the business scene, and a legacy only in the area of financial legerdemain.

Ling's next acquisition was conventional enough and surprised no one who knew the principals. In 1946, when most aircraft manufacturers were cutting back sharply due to the cancellation of military orders, Dallas businessman Robert McCulloch founded the Texas Engineering and Manufacturing Company, soon to be known simply as "Temco," and announced he would bid on prime contracts. The new firm had little capital and in fact only two important assets: McCulloch himself, an astute executive with extensive industry experience, and the support of the state's congressional delegation, practiced in the ways of bringing business to Texas.

At first the company struggled along, but aided by Harold Byrd, his financial backer, and Clyde Skeen, in charge of operations, McCulloch developed Temco into a major reoutfitter of military planes with a variety of significant subcontracts. By 1959 Temco was on the Fortune

500 list, and with revenues of close to $100 million was twice the size of Ling-Altec.

That year Byrd sought out Ling to explore the possibilities of a merger. Although McCulloch and Skeen weren't enthusiastic about the idea they eventually went along with it, and the deal was completed in July 1960.

At the time the Dallas business community wondered just who had taken over whom. The former Temco stockholders received nearly a million new Ling-Altec shares, with Byrd getting a substantial number of them. Together with others from Temco he now had sufficient stock to challenge Ling's leadership if he so desired. Byrd had never shown any inclination toward day-to-day management, but he might back a candidate—perhaps McCulloch or Skeen—if for some reason or other he became displeased with Ling. Both men knew this, but in 1960 there was no reason to suspect that a power struggle might develop. Still, Byrd must have rolled the idea around in his mind, while Ling appeared to have started to plan a way to divorce him from the firm.

Meanwhile, he again altered the name of his company, this time to Ling-Temco Electronics, the major division of which became Temco Electronics and Missiles. Whatever ambitions Ling once had entertained of balancing government sales with civilian sales were now discarded. For the time being at least, Ling-Temco would concentrate on military contracts. It was a natural and plausible strategy. Both Continental and Temco had wide experience with government work, and while the latter's backlog and prospects suffered when the navy cancelled its Corvus missile contract that summer, Ling was prepared to bid on new weapons procurement work.

Although Ling-Temco's 1960 revenues would come to $148.4 million, which was three times that of 1959, it was far from being the most important defense contractor in the area. Chance Vought was first in Dallas, with sales of more than a quarter of a billion dollars. Moreover it was one of the nation's oldest and best known manufacturers of navy planes, with excellent connections in Washington, a substantial backlog, and a strong balance sheet. C-V was an expansion-minded company branching into new fields as diverse as computer services, mobile homes, and financing. At a time when Temco was retrenching somewhat due to the loss of Corvus work, the talk around Dallas was that C-V would soon be expanding its facilities. What wasn't generally known was that the new businesses were unprofitable, and that C-V was having difficulties with some of its subcontracts and might be forced to take heavy write-offs.

That Ling eventually would think in terms of acquiring the company was perhaps inevitable. As it happened, the idea was broached by John Coughenour, a Denver broker who knew of a large block of stock for sale.

A takeover would be opposed by CEO Frederick Detweiler, who had no desire to work under Ling, but Coughenour observed that management owned or controlled only a small amount of C-V's shares.

Ling needed little convincing; almost at once he determined to make a stab at acquiring Chance Vought. Ling knew he couldn't make the purchase with Ling-Temco stock. Even in the unlikely circumstance that C-V's shareholders would go for the idea, this would more than double the equity base, and dilute Ling's own position even more than it had been by the Temco takeover. Thus, he would require another loan, which he tried to obtain from White, Weld and from Mutual Life, which had been his backers since the Altec deal.

Both companies balked at the idea of making the by now familiar short-term loans that would be converted into longer maturities after the merger was completed. Nor did they approve of so large a takeover less than a year after the Temco acquisition. Moreover, the prospect of a proxy fight with Chance Vought's management disturbed them. During the preceding year the somewhat conventional New Yorkers had become dismayed with Ling's wheeler-dealer approach. White, Weld and Mutual Life both severed their relationships with Ling after failing to dissuade him from making a tender offer for C-V. But he was able to retain the support of the Bank of America, which had taken a minor role in some of his earlier transactions. More important, Ling had the backing of Troy Post, a Dallas financier who had taken a fatherly interest in him. Among Post's several holdings was American Life Insurance Company, which made Ling a $6 million short-term loan, almost all of which was used to purchase Coughenour's block and more, bringing Ling-Temco's holdings to around 200,000 shares. Then Ling took on a new investment banker, Lehman Brothers, a house far better attuned to takeovers (in part by representing Litton) than was White, Weld.

Ling now made a tender offer for 150,000 shares at $43.50 per share, at a time when Chance Vought common was selling for $29. Detweiler promptly initiated a civil antitrust action, and there were indications that the Justice Department might do likewise. Indeed, the Antitrust Division came out against the takeover on the ground that it would lessen competition in the aerospace industry but Ling persisted and by March had around 400,000 shares, enough to take control. Reluctantly Detweiler ended his opposition, and although Ling had offered to let him stay on, he submitted his resignation. As for the Justice Department's suit, it was eventually decided in favor of Ling. But his troubles with the government weren't over; Ling later would claim that ever since the C-V takeover, he had been hounded by the Justice Department, which was out to destroy him—and eventually contributed importantly to his failure.

But he did have Chance Vought—along with an empty treasury, enlarged debts, and as a result of the bitter struggle, a board that wasn't certain it wanted more of the same and suspected that this time Ling had gone too far, perhaps beyond their control. While Ling celebrated the takeover by changing the name of his company for the last time—to Ling-Temco-Vought—the board prepared to take him down a notch.

What happened next is a matter of record, but none of the parties involved has ever disclosed the behind-the-scenes maneuverings which led to it. Simply stated, the board voted to make Robert McCulloch chairman and CEO, while Gifford Johnson, who replaced Detweiler at Chance Vought, was to be president and chief operating officer. As for Ling, he would step down to the newly created post of vice chairman and also serve as chairman of the executive committee. At the time it seemed that Ling had been deposed by an alliance of old hands from Temco and Chance Vought, and that his rule had ended. Perhaps that had been the intention, but it didn't work.

McCulloch and Johnson were not up to the demands of running a corporation as large and complex as Ling-Temco-Vought. Moreover, several units were in trouble. The problems at Chance Bought had surfaced, and Temco would have losses owing to the Corvus cancellation. Ling Electronics was in the red. All of this at a time when Ling-Temco-Vought itself had an empty treasury and short-term obligations about to come due. The new management did not know how to handle such problems, while Ling had proven himself a master at financial juggling. Even while in eclipse, he had the authority to deal with such matters.

Ling quickly sold off several C-V subsidiaries, taking large paper losses but gaining some money to pay part of the short-term loans. Vought Industries, which manufactured mobile homes, fetched $12 million, and a partial sale of Information Systems another $6.3 million. There were to be close to $34 million in write-offs in 1961, placing Ling in a rather strange position. On the one hand he was ridiculed for having purchased an ailing company at a high price, while on the other Ling impressed the Dallas financial community with his ability to save the firm. With Troy Post's help he managed to recycle the short-term debt and sell longer obligations. Total sales for the year came to $192.8 million, and there was a small operating profit. But owing to the write-offs, LTV reported a loss of $13.2 million, or $4.82 per share. The company had current assets of $123.6 million against current liabilities of $87.6 million, a ratio hardly indicative of a healthy operation. Investors took note of this reversal in fortunes. From a peak of 42 just prior to the Chance Vought takeover, LTV common fell to 23 by year's end, and the following spring hit bottom at 15.[4]

Yet Ling came through it all in fine style. Not only was he credited with having made the best of an admittedly bad situation, but in January 1963 he resumed the chairmanship, switching titles and jobs with McCulloch, while Clyde Skeen moved into the presidency replacing Johnson. There was remarkably little bitterness involved in these changes. McCulloch had always been more interested in production than management, and so was more than willing to take a post that called for this talent.

Ling's acquisition binge seemed at an end. Not only did he have to concentrate on improving the balance sheet and restoring both his and LTV's credibility with the financial community, but he no longer could use paper to purchase assets. So he continued paring down the corporation. Out went National Data Processing and Crusader Finance, both of which had come in with C-V. Ling sold LTV's industrial division, and even United Electronics. Supporters admired his sangfroid, the almost clinical way he carved companies like so much fat from LTV's carcass, while critics called him brutal and even flighty. There was always a suspicion that all wasn't what it seemed. Yet there can be little doubt that he saved the company in 1962 and started it upward once again. Revenues that year were $325.4 million and earnings, helped by a lower tax rate made possible by the write-offs and a revival at Chance Vought, were $8.6 million, or $3.03 per share, the highest in history.

Some said Ling had demonstrated that he was as adept at shrinking a firm as at building it. Others noted that had he not acquired so recklessly the pruning wouldn't have been necessary. One of the latter observed that he retained one company whose name said it all: Scam Instruments.

Internal growth, continued restructuring, and most of all, fiscal soundness, were the foremost objectives at LTV for 1963 and 1964. This was a period when LTV became more centralized, and Ling demonstrated some talents for if not an overwhelming interest in management. In part this was owed to the need for long overdue changes, but it was also because Ling had not given up on his acquisitions campaign. He realized that in order to renew it he would have to certify his financial credibility and get the price of his stock higher.

As was the case with Textron and Litton, LTV was helped along by the military procurement program that accompanied the Kennedy-Johnson arms buildup and the Vietnam War. Chance Vought received several important military and space contracts, and the electronics operations resumed their earlier growth. Thus, revenue advances in these areas more than compensated for the cuts resulting from the divestiture operations. Revenues for 1963 came to $331.3 million, only a shade higher than those of 1962, while the net income of $7.1 million was below that of the previous year, in part because of the absence of tax loss credits in 1963. For 1964 revenues and earnings were $324.2 million and $4.9 million respectively, hardly a spectacular or even impressive showing. But the balance sheet had been strengthened. Current liabilities were slashed from $87.6 million at the end of 1961 to $68.7 million two years later, and the long-term debt went from $57 million to $34.5 million, while cash on hand rose from $7.4 million to $12.1 million. In the same period, net stockholders' equity advanced to $32.8 million from $6.2 million. As part of his drive for a better image, Ling instituted a 12½ cent quarterly dividend policy in late 1963.

None of this had much of an impact on Wall Street, where LTV common continued in the doldrums, trading in a narrow range of 13-20 through 1963-64, a period during which the Dow Jones Industrials rose by more than 220 points, led by the drugs, electronics, and some conglomerates.

Ling understood why this was so, and just how to overcome the difficulties. In the first place, Temco had never fully recovered from the loss of the Corvus subcontracts, while Chance Vought had missed out on several competitions for navy work. Ling perceived the dangers in over-reliance upon government contracts, and later, speaking before a business group in 1969, said this was what motivated his move into new, unrelated areas, transforming LTV from a military supplier into a conglomerate.

> I made a vow that never again would any company for which I was responsible be dependent upon any one market, any one product, or any one technology. Our concept would be that we would continually and on a sustained basis seek diversification. We are a diversified company today, as the result of some rather unique experiences some six years ago. That's why.[5]

But this is not the whole story. To be sure, Ling sought diversification, but in a special way: he went after large, ailing enterprises that could be disassembled and sold to the public in pieces, on the assumption that the parts would be more highly valued than the whole. In this regard Ling was more a packager than a conglomerator. In other words, he took to conglomerization because this was the handiest rubric available to describe his highly original activities. Ling cheerfully admitted as much. "I guess you now would call us a conglomerate," he said in 1969, "although we did not know such a word existed in those days."[6]

Ling also realized that LTV would not be able to diversify unless its common stock became more valuable, for it (and debentures based upon the common) were to be his prime means of obtaining assets for paper. And the stock's price could not improve unless earnings per share increased. Such an advance could be brought about either by an increase in net earnings or a decrease in the number of shares outstanding. Ling planned to take both routes. He would break down his existing holdings, exchange parts of them to LTV stockholders for their common shares, and thus wind up with a lower total capitalization but control of the now independent subsidiaries. Thus, he would combine diversification with a radical restructuring of LTV, with the goal being growth for its own sake. Spectacular maneuverings such as this had been attempted before, but not on this scale, nor by anyone with Ling's boldness.

Ling began quietly, even conventionally, in 1964, by offering to exchange one share of a new convertible preferred stock that paid $3 in dividends plus $15 in cash for three shares of common turned in by shareholders. It was an attractive package, since the common then was paying 50 cents, and the preferred could be converted into 1.25 shares of common at the option of the owner. Thus, those who accepted the offer would have a bundle of cash, twice the dividend income, and still have a stake in LTV by means of the conversion provision. What would Ling gain from this? He would cut down on the number of common shares outstanding, in this way boosting his earnings per share. And it worked.

LTV was able to decrease its capitalization from 2.8 million shares to 1.9 million. The effect was dramatic. LTV's net income in 1963 came to $6.2 million, or $2.12 per share. Income for 1964 actually declined to $4.9 million, which were it not for the exchange would have worked out to $1.74 per share. But since the capitalization had shrunk so greatly, the per-share earnings came to $2.32, a small but respectable advance. And as Ling had anticipated, LTV's stock responded by staging a small rally on the New York Stock Exchange.

In late 1964 Ling announced what he called "Project Redeployment," an unusual plan to transform LTV into a pure holding company and divorce it from operating components to a degree unknown in American corporate history. The putative reason for this unusual procedure had almost nothing to do with efficiencies, management, or improvement of internal growth, though years later Ling would claim all of these had been involved. Rather, he planned to shuffle his holdings to provide each with greater visibility and boost the price of their paper, in preparation for the next leg of his acquisition campaign. "The financial posture in 1962 through 1964 was quite defensive," he remarked. "We had no surplus resources that would permit us to embark on an acquisitions program. Additionally we felt that our common stock was substantially undervalued for the long term."[7]

Ling's initial step was to establish three wholly owned subsidiaries: LTV Aerospace, LTV Ling Altec, and LTV Electrosystems. Each of these had virtually no assets except their articles of incorporation and common stock. Then Ling divided LTV into three unequal portions and exchanged the appropriate ones for all of the common shares of the three new entities. Thus, Aerospace received most of Chance Vought and a substantial part of Temco, Ling Altec obtained Altec and some miscellaneous properties, and whatever remained went into Electrosystems. In effect, LTV's only assets now were some furniture and office leases and three bundles of securities in a custodial account.

The next step was taken in April 1965, when LTV offered one-half share of each of these three companies, plus $9 in cash, for one share of LTV common tendered to the parent corporation. Ling hoped that as much as 800,000 shares would be offered, but the stockholders, by now aware that this maneuver would boost the earnings per share, which in turn would result in a higher stock price, held back. Moreover, some stockholders, and even analysts, had difficulty figuring out whether it would be a good deal. After all, there were no established market prices for the three subsidiaries. Could it be that 1 + 1 + 1 could equal more than 3? Ling suggested this was so—that the shares in three companies, each of which was in a single industry, would be worth more than that of a single corporation involved in three different enterprises.

This hardly was the way Little or Thornton had gone about transforming Textron and Litton into conglomerates. They proceeded from unity into diversity; Ling was reversing the process. Before LTV had become a true conglomerate, he was engaged in the process of deconglomerization, a practice that would fascinate Wall Streeters in the early 1980s. At the time, however, no one realized it, not even Ling himself. As ever, he operated from the seat of his pants.

In the end LTV received only 245,000 shares from the exchange offer. As a result (and the impact of a minor acquisition made with stock), LTV's capitalization was reduced to 1.8 million shares, and the three new entities had public stockholders, greater visibility, and eventually, the cachet of listings on the American Stock Exchange. Those who accepted the offer did quite well for themselves. The book value of the three companies at the time of divestiture was $7.9 million. The market value of the shares a year later came to $35 million. Thus, in a way, 1 + 1 + 1 worked out to around 14.

Ling went to great pains to explain that all three companies were autonomous. Their officers were supposed to behave independently from one another, although they shared a common parentage. Said Ling:

> Each is its own technological center. Each has its own profit centers. Each has its own separate markets. And, most importantly, each is its own management motivation center. Being publicly owned, each also is its own credit center, and has individual access to public and private financial markets. LTV does not guarantee, nor is responsible for the individual

indebtedness of each of its subsidiaries. The subsidiaries are
separate—literally and legally. No one subsidiary depends on
the purchasing power of another subsidiary—in the truest
sense, reciprocity does not exist.[8]

Was LTV a holding company, a conglomerate, or a closed end investment trust? It had elements of all three, and Ling did not care to quibble
over definitions so long as everything was working according to plan. Yet
there were inconsistencies. How could each of the three companies be
truly independent if LTV owned a majority of its stock, dictated its
choice of officers and members of the board, and had an effective veto
over long term plans? How could true independence exist when officers of
the three firms held posts at the parent and vice-versa? Finally, if independence did exist, why did Ling constantly refer to the companies as
"subsidiaries?" But such questions weren't asked in the afterglow of the
success of Project Redeployment. Once again the fans and critics were
heard from. The former considered Ling the most important creative
force in modern American business, while the latter observed that the
bull market then raging on Wall Street might have had more to do with
advancing prices than anything Ling had done.

It might be claimed in retrospect that LTV's definitive move into
widespread diversification came in October 1965, when it acquired
Okonite for $31.7 million in cash. This company was an old-line manu-
facturer of a wide variety of copper wire and cable, which had been
acquired several years earlier by Kennecott Copper, then attempting to
integrate forward into fabrication and marketing. Kennecott had up-
graded Okonite's facilities, and the firm was in excellent health, its
products in great demand at firm prices. Just then the Justice Department struck, claiming the takeover had been a violation of the antitrust
statutes. Thus, Kennecott was prepared to sell the holding, and Ling
rushed in to make his bid.

It seems Ling had used Okonite wire while a sailor in the Philippines.
He was favorably impressed with its quality and often referred to Okonite's product as "the Cadillac of the industry." Here was a chance to
take over a firm he had long admired, and to do so at an attractive price.
Ling grabbed for it, combining sentiment with business.

Now came the redeployment. LTV began by raising $20 million from a
consortium of banks, putting up as collatoral some $73 million worth of
its own securities, mostly those of the three subsidiaries. Then, as their
shares continued to advance, Ling sold additional stock in all three, using
the money to pay off some of the loans needed for the Okonite takeover.
Finally he turned around and sold 17 percent of Okonite. In this way, Ling
provided LTV with a fourth subsidiary, gave Okonite a market (the stock

responded by advancing), and secured for LTV more than sufficient funds to pay off whatever debts remained from the purchase. In effect, LTV had 83 percent of Okonite for virtually no cost save that of Ling's time. Okonite was able to contribute immediately to LTV's earnings, and the acquisition didn't result in an increase in total capitalization.

With this added fillip, LTV was able to report a modest increase in revenues and earnings. Net sales for 1965 came to $336.2 million against the prior year's $332.9 million, earnings were $6 million vs. $4.9 million, and per share earnings $2.82 against 1964's $2.32.

Project Redeployment had captured Wall Street's imagination, and the Okonite maneuver demonstrated that Ling truly was a magician when it came to securities. LTV common soared to 58 from a January low of 17; for Ling this was a crucial measure of success and acceptance. He was not alone in his thinking during this penultimate stage of the great bull market. Just as President Lyndon Johnson measured his accomplishments through popularity polls, so CEOs of that period looked to stock quotations as a sign of having done well or badly. By this measure, Ling was succeeding.

By then, too, Ling was on the prowl for other corporations that might be carved up and sold to the investing public. This meant he wanted large, complex companies; he generally was uninterested in the smaller and medium-sized operations that appealed to the likes of Thornton and Little. Ling would not nibble away at the fringes of corporate capitalism. Rather, he would strike at its core, and this made him more frightening to old-line businessmen and more a target for antitrusters than most other conglomerators.

In 1966 Ling fixed his gaze upon Wilson & Co., the nation's third largest meat packer, which had sales of close to a billion dollars, or more than twice as much as LTV's. Wilson had a good reputation and some modern facilities, but it was in an industry noted for slow growth, large capital requirements, and low profit margins. For these reasons its stock was out of favor with investors and was afforded a low price/earnings multiple. Management must have felt the same way, for the officers and board owned or controlled only a small fraction of the 2.4 million shares of common outstanding. Since the stock was selling for around 50 in late 1966, the securities market was valuing this large and famous company at less than $125 million.

Ling looked beyond the meat operation and saw a near-perfect candidate for a replay of Project Redeployment. While best known for packing operations, Wilson had four other interesting businesses, all of which developed out of the original concern. From the hides and skins came coverings for footballs, and out of this evolved Wilson Sporting Goods, which was the largest in its field and produced equipment for virtually every sport. Golfers who used Wilson clubs probably did not connect them with the meat company, but Ling (himself an excellent golfer) did. Then there was a pet foods division, which utilized parts of the slaughtered animals unfit for human consumption. From fats sliced from the carcasses came soaps, and some of these Wilson soap brands had national distribution. Finally, Wilson had a rapidly growing pharmaceutical business, which began when the company looked for uses for animal organs and wound up manufacturing steroids and hormones. Thus, out of the staid, undervalued Wilson & Co. might emerge three, four, or even five separate companies, and once again, the parts would be worth more than the whole.

Ling formulated his takeover strategy in late 1966, and referring to the pigskins, called this maneuver Operation Touchdown.

He began by setting his house in order—in effect, lining up his troops. As LTV common shares rose in price some of the debentures and warrants issued in previous takeovers had been converted into common shares. In what he called Project Retrieve, Ling exchanged more preferred stock and cash for the common, thus increasing the amount of senior paper outstanding in order to keep that of the common steady. As before, this tactic enhanced LTV's earnings per share.

As it happened 1966 was an excellent year for the corporation. Acceleration of military spending required by the Vietnam War was translated into higher profits at Electrosystems and Aerospace, and now Okonite's earnings were fully included in those of the parent. LTV earned $13.7 million, which was $6.47 per share, on revenues of $468.3 million. This leap in earnings came from higher profits and stable equity, resulting from Lyndon Johnson's policies in Southeast Asia and James Ling's Project Retrieve. But just as profits had more than doubled so did the amount of senior capital outstanding, which at the end of 1966 was $96.2 million, against the previous year's total of $42.9 million. As recently as 1960 LTV had only $5.7 million in senior capital. This didn't appear troublesome in 1966, though by then most Wall Streeters who cared about such matters knew that LTV was the most highly leveraged of the conglomerates. In time, however, this aspect of the corporation's structure would prove its undoing.

Ling was now prepared to go after Wilson. He began by raising the capital necessary for a tender offer; the approximately $14 million in LTV's treasury hardly would be enough. So Ling obtained a Eurodollar two-year loan at 7⅞ percent by pledging LTV securities, and Lehman Brothers brought in another $30 million by placing 6¾ percent three-year notes with warrants. Okonite "loaned" its parent $10 million, and more money came from a "loan" granted by the LTV pension fund.

In late December 1966, Clyde Skeen traveled to Chicago to break the news to Wilson's President Roscoe Haynie. Without much in the way of preliminaries he informed Haynie that Ling was prepared to offer $62.50 per share for 750,000 shares of Wilson common, which would give him 30 percent of the amount outstanding. Haynie was enraged, said the price was far too low, and vowed a fight. Skeen replied that Wilson had never traded for more than $58, observed that management owned few shares themselves, and predicted that the stockholders would disagree. Haynie did make some pro forma attempts to block the deal, but he must have known, even then, that there was no way for him to stop Ling.

Skeen was right; the offer was oversubscribed. Now Ling purchased additional shares on the open market, and within days had more than half of Wilson's stock, at a cost of slightly less than $82 million. Then he exchanged approximately $115 million worth of $5 preferred stock for the remainder. This deal transformed LTV into a $1.8 billion corporation, and had been completed with no dilution of equity, though the senior capital and short-term debt had been substantially enlarged. But not for long. Now Ling was in a position to exercise a redeployment that not only would boost LTV's earnings and earnings per share, but reduce that debt.

First Ling stripped Wilson & Co. of most of its cash, set aside four packing plants to be leased to the new meat company at fat fees, and transferred $50 million in European bank loans from LTV to Wilson. With all of this done, LTV's total cash investment was reduced to only $6 million.

The next step was a variant of Project Redeployment. Ling established three new "paper corporations," Wilson & Co., Wilson Sporting Goods, and Wilson Pharmaceutical & Chemical. Then, in exchange for their shares, LTV provided each with the relevant portions of the old Wilson & Co. It wasn't long before Wall Street had dubbed these three firms "Meatball," "Golfball," and "Goofball." The public now had the opportunity to invest and speculate in their shares. Ling sold 18 percent of Wilson & Co. to the public for $21.8 million, and a quarter of the shares of Sporting Goods brought in another $17 million, while 23 percent of Pharmaceutical & Chemical fetched almost $6 million. In all, Ling had more than $44 million from the sale, which came close to offsetting that $50 million in debt.

Almost immediately Sporting Goods and Pharmaceutical & Chemical became semiglamour issues, and their stocks took off. Even Wilson & Co. participated in the rally that followed the carving. Some of this was due to the bull market that resumed in 1967, but Ling's maneuvers rightfully received most of the credit. By autumn LTV's holdings in the three companies had a market value of approximately $250 million. The cost, as Ling calculated it, came to around $6 million in short-term debt and the $5.7 million annually to service the $5 preferred issue.[9]

Ling had become Wall Street's greatest hero during this phase of the most powerful bull market in American history, when "conglomeritus" was the rage. His sole rival in this regard was Harold Geneen of International Telephone & Telegraph, the only conglomerate larger than LTV. But ITT had been a mature corporation when Geneen took over, with almost $1 billion in revenues, while Ling had started fresh. Moreover, Geneen had a carefully calculated strategy, while Ling remained the supreme opportunist. Given the nature of the markets of this period, he was a more fitting symbol. As was LTV common, which soared to 169½ before splitting three for two in late 1967. That year the parent corporation reported a net income of $34 million, or $10.66 on the presplit shares.

Ling made passes at other corporations in this period, among them Rome Cable (which would have been added to Okonite) and Allis-Chalmers. He considered going after American Broadcasting and Sperry Rand, both of which would have been excellent candidates for redeployment. LTV did purchase Goldschmidt Chemical, which was promptly resold to Wilson Pharmaceutical. And the subsidiary companies entered the area; Ling Altec bought Allied Radio, and after the Rome Cable failure Okonite purchased Jefferson Wire & Cable and General Felt. But these were small potatoes, little more than exercises. Ling was a master at the *major* acquisition, made with borrowed assets paid back after restructuring. By 1967, he was interested only in the billion dollar giants.

Greatamerica Corporation was one of these, and it had the added virtues of being in his backyard and of being controlled by a close associate, Troy Post, who was willing to step down and exchange his holdings for LTV paper.

In his day Post had been one of the more spectacular wheeler-dealers in Southwestern insurance, and Greatamerica had been put together as an umbrella for his several holdings, among which were four insurance companies (Franklin Life, American-Amicable, Gulf Life, and Stonewall) and the First Western Bank & Trust Company. In 1964, when Post had ambitions of becoming a conglomerator, he acquired controlling interest in Braniff Airways, then a fast-growing regional operation, and he was in the process of taking over National Car Rental. It was after his attempt to acquire the Glidden Company aborted that he started thinking seriously about retirement. Greatamerica President E. Grant Fitts went to see Ling early in 1968 to explore the possibility of a buy-out. He arrived at the right time. Ling had just been frustrated in his quest for Allis-Chalmers and needed something like this to buoy his spirits and provide an arena for his talents. Not only was he interested, but he suggested the tender offer be made without delay.

Everything went smoothly. At the time Greatamerica common was selling in the low 20s. For every 100 shares, Ling would exchange $3,000 in LTV 5 percent debentures maturing in 1988, plus a warrant to buy ten shares of LTV common at 115. News of the tender caused LTV to jump to over 125, so the offer was most attractive. It was accepted, and now Ling was master of a financial empire, an airline, and a car rental operation, with Wall Street betting a new Project Redeployment was in the offing.

Once again Ling surprised his followers. Greatamerica wouldn't be deployed, but rather disassembled. Most of it would be sold in one of the most baroque dramas in American financial history, which coincided with Ling's grab for another giant prize, Jones & Laughlin Steel.

First of all, Ling got rid of most of Greatamerica's financial heart. Stonewall Insurance went for $15 million in early May, and a month later First Western Bank & Trust was sold for $62.5 million. Later, American-Amicable would bring in $18 million. In this way, Ling got back approximately one-fifth the face value of the bonds, and he still had Braniff, National Car Rental, and the two remaining insurance companies. And all of this while maneuvering for Jones & Laughlin.

Ling next tried to utilize these properties as vehicles by which to slash not only his debt but the equity as well. In October he established what his underwriters, Lehman Brothers and Goldman, Sachs, called a "unit," which was comprised of one share of Braniff Class A stock, 0.6 share of National Car Rental common, one share of National Car Rental Class A, 1.1 LTV warrants exercisable at 103.35 expiring in 1978, and one-third of a share of Computer Technology, a small entity Ling had recently put together in the service field (and for which there now would exist a market). Under his plan LTV would exchange these units in the following manner:

1.1 units for 1 share of LTV common
9.75 units for $1,000 of LTV 6.5 percent notes
10 units for $1,000 of LTV 6.75 percent debentures
6.7 units for $1,000 of LTV's new 5 percent debentures
9.5 units for $1,000 of LTV 5.75 percent debentures[10]

No one on Wall Street that day will ever forget the impact this offer had. What did it mean? Was it a good deal or not? Owners of LTV paper called their brokers for advice, only to find that the professionals were consulting with bankers, analysts, friends, and tipsters for help in figuring it all out. Was Ling a genius or a charlatan? No one quite knew, but all agreed that if he carried it off LTV would have a much lower total debt and/or far less equity, while retaining several important blocks of Braniff, National Car Rental, and other properties.

All of this had to be set against the backdrop of the Jones & Laughlin takeover, which was taking place at the same time and which, of course, complicated matters. These were simultaneous moves, designed to mesh with one another, while Ling also busied himself raising funds domestically and overseas—funds with which to absorb J & L. If everything fell into place, LTV would have almost $4 billion in total revenues, placing it on the edge of the dozen largest American industrial firms after little more than a decade of operation.

That Ling eventually would go after a large steel company should not have surprised anyone who appreciated the rationale behind the Wilson & Co. takeover. Like meat packing, steel was an aged, cyclical industry that combined large capital requirements with low returns on investment. The common shares of the major concerns hadn't participated in the great bull market, and in fact most were available at far below nominal book value, itself a greatly understated figure. But it was at this point that the resemblance to Wilson & Co. ended. None of the giant steel makers possessed the kinds of glamorous properties that Pharmaceutical & Chemical and Sporting Goods were proving to be. Rather, the American steel companies were laden with aging plants, obsolete technologies, and relatively unsophisticated work forces. But Ling thought a turnabout was possible and that J & L would lend itself to his familiar techniques. "There was (sic) more unknowns in the potential redeployment of a steel company than there are in other companies we had acquired," he conceded in 1969, adding, "And there were alternative methods of investing $425 million."[11]

Which was what it eventually took to bring J & L under the LTV umbrella. Would Ling have made the initial moves had he known at the time the ultimate cost, or the complications that would arise along the way? Or had he known more about the steel industry? Probably not, for the J & L acquisition would all but shatter his empire. Still, he did have some notion of the price in money, for LTV amassed a large war chest in preparation for the assault.

Rumors regarding the next big LTV acquisition echoed through Wall Street in the spring of 1968, the last, feverish year of the giant bull market. Among the more discussed candidates were Westinghouse, Bendix, North American, several medium-sized oil companies, and Youngstown Sheet & Tube. As it turned out Ling had made overtures to Youngstown, only to be rejected. Unwilling to make an unfriendly tender after being rebuffed by Allis-Chalmers and now intrigued by the steel industry, he sought another, similar firm, which is how he came upon Jones & Laughlin. Here was a billion dollar corporation whose common stock was mired around $50 per share. How much was J & L actually worth? The corporation's book value was $85 per share, but this surely was understated. J & L had recently completed a $400 million capital improvement program, which worked out to more than $50 per share, and the company seemed about to assume leadership in several key steel products. So Ling might have been justified in believing that this could be another Wilson & Co.

In April 1968, Ling met with J & L Chairman Charles Beeghly to discuss the possibilities of a takeover. Beeghly was not altogether surprised, since news of the Youngstown bid had spread through the industry. Close to retirement anyway and celebrating the capital improvement program as the climax of his career, Beeghly was prepared to step down. He would not fight the tender, assuming the price was right. After some dickering, they agreed upon $85 per share, the stated book value, and 70 percent above the current market quotation. Thus, J & L's shareholders were to receive a substantial premium. Ling said he would seek 63 percent of the stock in a cash offer, which would cost $425 million.[12]

That was where Greatamerica came in. The money from the sales of its assets went into the J & L war chest. In 1967 Ling had sold 600,000 shares of LTV at around $100, bringing in an additional $60 million. Another $200 million was raised by selling short-term notes in the United States and Europe. And of course the exchange offer involving those units was designed to sop up a great deal of the debt in preparation for the final absorption of J & L.

This was vital, for as a result of the acquisition LTV's total long-term debt had risen to $1.2 billion, up from $202 million in 1967. Something drastic had to be done to cut that debt substantially, which helps explain the unit exchange offer, and why Ling opted to sell off most of Greatamerica rather than deploy the corporation into several new entities.

That was sensible enough on its face, but had Ling moved too quickly? Wouldn't it have been more prudent to go after J & L *after* completing the sales at Greatamerica? Did Ling act so daringly because the J & L takeover wouldn't wait, or was this simply hubris? Timing was crucial. A slip could leave Ling, and LTV, financially embarrassed. On the other hand, it was an audacious plan, which if carried off successfully would have left LTV in fine shape, with Ling alert for his next giant acquisition.

Nothing worked out as expected. LTV was slammed by three separate blows that almost destroyed the corporation. A slow and painful recovery followed, but the J & L takeover marked both the peak and conclusion of LTV's spectacular acquisitions binge.

The first problem was the situation on Wall Street. Ling counted upon high stock prices to provide him with paper with which to purchase assets, and he always needed large sums of money at low interest rates to carry him along until he deployed sufficient assets to pay for the takeovers. Thus, he was in his element during the great bull market, when money was cheap and plentiful and stock prices often seemed to defy the financial laws of gravity.

All of this came to an end in late 1968. After advancing irregularly in late autumn and early winter, the Dow Industrials closed at 985.21 on December 3 and then started to decline. There would be intermittent rallies during the next year and a half, but by spring of 1969 Wall Street realized it was in a major bear market. The Dow slipped under 900 in June and crossed the 800 mark the following month before turning upward. Then it slumped again, closing the year under 800. It was even worse in 1970, when the Dow finally bottomed out at 631.16 on May 26th.

This topping out in 1968 coincided with Ling's complex exchange offer. Owing to confusion, but more to market conditions, not enough bondholders and owners of notes turned in their debt for units. To raise money to satisfy creditors, Ling had to dump other holdings in a bear market. At the time it seemed a replay of the 1961–62 experience with Chance Vought. Not only did Ling have to place the remaining Great-america holdings on the bargain table, but he also had to dump properties obtained through earlier acquisitions. All to pay for a steel maker whose immediate prospects, in the face of an economic decline, were somewhat in doubt.

The clearance sale began in February 1969, with the disposal of 2 million shares of Braniff, and continued for the rest of the year. LTV's remaining shares of Computer Technology went in April, and the following month LTV sold the rest of National Car Rental. These three fetched $84 million. Whitehall Electronics, disposed of in two stages, brought another $7.5 million. Then the subsidiaries entered the market. LTV Aerospace sold its shares of Computer Technology and sent the proceeds to headquarters. In December Wilson & Co. conducted its own version of Project Redeployment, establishing four subsidiaries: Wilson Beef & Lamb, Wilson Certified Foods, Wilson Laurel Farms, Wilson-Sinclair, and later, Wilson Agri-Business Enterprises. Portions of the first four were to be sold for cash, the idea being that the proceeds would be sent to the parent in the form of a special dividend.

The offering went poorly because of the bear market, and little was gained from this maneuver. Nor could Ling sell additional LTV shares in order to raise funds. The stock hit 136 in 1968 before starting to decline as a result of uncertainties surrounding J & L and the weight of the bear market on Wall Street. Ling would continue to wheel and deal, attempting to pull off yet another of his miraculous escapes from failure. Yet, the most dramatic chapter of his saga was still to be told when the conglomerate movement started grinding to a halt in the late summer of 1969.

5

Charles Bluhdorn: The Manipulator

They were making big splashes in their ponds. These, the new million-aires, all under the age of 40, were featured in *Time*'s cover story for December 3, 1965. The depicted faces were superimposed upon coins, apparently to symbolize their owners' uncanny ability to create fortunes for themselves and others.

Most were businessmen whose names were as unfamiliar as their faces to readers of general interest publications. Only one—the Broadway producer Harold Prince—was what might be called a celebrity, but *Time* thought others might soon become as well known. These men were the vanguard of a new breed, and in the next generation several could emerge as powerful, famous individuals in their fields.

None of this transpired. As it turned out, all but one of the group was close to or at his peak when the article appeared. Arthur Carlesburg's Rammco Investment Co. never became the force in California real estate the magazine thought it would be, and while Arthur Decio did better with prefabricated and mobile houses, his company, Skyline Homes, hasn't evolved into the giant its founder had envisaged. Nothing Harold Prince produced since has come up to his earlier successes such as *West Side Story* and *Fiddler on the Roof.* Of the cover-story subjects, only Charles Bluhdorn went on to become a more important person than he then was, and he did so in areas different from the one for which he had been singled out at the time.

In *Time*'s story Bluhdorn was identified as the "Manhattan-based chairman of Gulf & Western Industries, a widely diversified company specializing in auto parts." His purported objective was simple and well known within the industry, and could be summed up in the title of another article that had appeared earlier in the year in *Steel* magazine: "Gulf & Western's Goal: Become the GM of Partmakers."

It seemed an attainable and worthy ambition. There literally were thousands of manufacturers and suppliers in the field, most of them quite small, and G + W had gobbled up more than two dozen of them in the little more than six years of Bluhdorn's tenure as CEO. In 1958, the year after he took over, the firm (then known as Michigan Plating & Stamping) had revenues of $8.4 million and it posted a small loss. G + W's 1965 revenues amounted to $182 million, with earnings of $5.5 million. That year it entered the charmed *Fortune* 500 circle, and as number 341 on the roster was ahead of the likes of Fairchild Camera & Instrument, Outboard Marine, and Hewlett-Packard.

But the signs of strain were there. Talk was that Bluhdorn was having trouble integrating several of his units, and that G + W soon would lose several key managers. None of this was true, but still it was difficult to believe that the corporation could expand in the future at anything near the old rate. Yet, one might easily imagine Bluhdorn directing the activities of a coast-to-coast or international fabricator and distributor of parts, with G + W inching its way up the list, perhaps even entering the top 100 before its CEO retired. (Eaton Yale & Towne, with revenues of $701 million, was number 100 in 1965.) And had he managed this, the *Time* writer could have claimed that Bluhdorn had fulfilled the promise he had perceived in him in 1965.

Bluhdorn rejected this kind of destiny only a few months after the article appeared and at that time started transforming G + W into what for a while was the flashiest conglomerate of them all, one that grew even faster than LTV. In the process he performed some maneuvers that were almost as impressive as Ling's Project Redeployment. While Ling was demonstrating how to increase net worth and per-share earnings through successful takeovers and restructurings, Bluhdorn was showing others how to make millions of dollars by *failing* in attempted acquisitions. In 1969, while LTV was coming apart, G + W was prospering, earning $51 million from operations, and almost half again as much on the returns from foiled takeovers. All four years after Bluhdorn was labelled as a promising young auto parts executive.

As it turned out, G + W wouldn't have to wait until the 1990s to enter the ranks of America's 100 largest industrial firms. In 1968 the corporation was 69th on the list, and Bluhdorn, now 42 years old, was challenging Ling and Harold Geneen for the admiration of financial analysts and investors—and the attention of antitrusters in Washington.

To those who did not know him very well, Bluhdorn seemed an open and vivacious person, much given to animated and colorful talk, with a fiery temper he did not mind demonstrating. People could be put at ease by his informality, broad grin, and apparent warmth. But Bluhdorn was capable of swearing undying friendship one moment only to explode in a burst of pure fury the next, and then, soon after, to embrace the person against whom the wrath had been vented. Some of those who worked with him said this wasn't a simple expression of ego, that Bluhdorn was far from being the "Mad Austrian" he was dubbed in the late 1960s. Rather, this was an act designed to lead people to believe they were seeing the complete man, when in fact his emotional demonstrations served to disguise his ideas and intentions.

On the surface Bluhdorn seemed a showman, but underneath he was every bit as calculating and dispassionate as James Ling. At a time when Thornton, Geneen, and Ling were impressing securities analysts and business writers with the depth and breadth of their knowledge, Bluhdorn appeared to be leaping all over the business landscape, behaving in a flamboyant, almost playful manner and then suddenly becoming sinister and menacing. As a result, perceptive observers either dismissed him as a lightweight or categorized him as a disruptive corsair. Yet in several of his takeovers Bluhdorn demonstrated not only audacity but also serious thought and impressive skills. G + W was not guilty of the kind of press-agentry utilized by Litton or the razzle-dazzle financial operations featured at LTV. Alone of the great conglomerators of the late 1960s, Bluhdorn never stumbled badly, and he was usually well aware of limitations, knowing the mania could not last forever. When it was all over, G + W proved more durable than LTV or Litton, if not as sturdy as ITT and Textron. In large measure this was due to the corporation's depth of management. For all of his erratic behavior, Bluhdorn had a knack of retaining the loyalties and services of a talented team of executives. He was supposed to possess an oversized ego and terrible temper, but he also was capable of making room for the ambitions of others.

Little is known of Bluhdorn's early life. He was born in Vienna on September 20, 1926, to Paul and Rose Bluhdorn, and his father, a native Czechoslovakian, was in the import-export business. Sensing the coming of war in 1937, Paul Bluhdorn sent Charles to England, where he attended school for the next five years. Charles found his way to New York in 1942, got a job at a cotton brokerage, and took courses at the City College in the evenings. After a brief stint in the Army Air Force in 1945, Bluhdorn took a post at a small import-export house. Soon he was helping out in a wide variety of dealings. Bluhdorn had contacts in Europe, Latin America, and Asia, knew his way around the federal bureaucracy, was drawing a large salary, and had developed the cocky self-confidence for which he later became so well known.

In 1949, at the age of 23, Bluhdorn set up shop for himself as a coffee importer. Later, he handled other products and dabbled in the commodities markets. Things were going well, although on several occasions Bluhdorn lost substantial sums when commodities prices went the wrong way. Still breezy and arrogant at the job, he was becoming increasingly troubled by the unstable nature of his business and started looking for a more secure line of work, something to balance his broker-age operations. Bluhdorn found it in auto parts, a large, fragmented industry with plenty of room for growth. In the 1950s, was as close to being depression-proof as any. Casting about for a proper company in which to invest, Bluhdorn came across Michigan Plating & Stamping.[1]

It hardly could be considered an impressive property. Starting out in 1934 as Michigan Bumper, the firm had a single, decrepit 50,000 square-foot plant in Grand Rapids, an indifferent work force, and an aged management. In a period when most other parts manufacturers were thriving Michigan Bumper was on the skids, with revenues declining from $6 million in 1950 to half that amount three years later, and there were deficits in 1954, 1955, and 1956. Out of desperation management entered the plating and stamping business—and changed the company's name in 1955.

But Michigan Plating & Stamping was an interesting property. It had less than a quarter of a million shares of common stock outstanding, and a book value, clearly understated, of approximately $8.50 per share.

In 1956, when Bluhdorn became interested in it, the stock was selling for around $5 and was listed on the American Stock Exchange. What did he have to lose? Control could be purchased for a few hundred thousand dollars, and even if things turned out badly, Bluhdorn might liquidate the company for a profit. The trouble was that he did not have that kind of money. So Bluhdorn cast about for partners. One of these was John Duncan, an executive in his family's coffee business, whom Bluhdorn had run into as a trader. Duncan was interested, and contributed $112,000 to the coffer. David Judelson, who ran a small machine tool facility, put up another $50,000; Bluhdorn had met him on a vacation at Lake Champlain. Like Bluhdorn, Judelson knew next to nothing about auto parts.

The partners bought enough shares for Bluhdorn to ask for and get a board seat. Then he familiarized himself with the operation, explored the industry, and started stirring things up. In 1959 Bluhdorn eased out President and General Manager C. A. Woodhouse, named himself chair-man, and installed Duncan as president, with Judelson a member of the board. But even before then he had become the actual leader of the corporation.

Realizing little could be done with the Grand Rapids company, Bluhdorn set out to find other companies in related fields he might purchase at distress prices. The first of these was Beard & Stone Elec-tric, a Houston-based auto parts distributor probably uncovered by Dun-can, whose family lived in that city. This company was acquired in early 1958 for $1.1 million in notes and debentures. While in somewhat better shape than Michigan Plating & Stamping, it too was a rather lackluster operation. "Neither one amounted to a hill of beans," said Bluhdorn in 1969.[2] But they did provide him with geographic as well as product and services diversification, and the basis for a new name. In November 1958, to indicate the company's new aspirations and intended scope, Bluhdorn renamed it Gulf + Western Corp.

From the first Bluhdorn realized that the executives at Michigan Plating & Stamping lacked the backgrounds, ambitions, and perhaps even the talents to manage a large operation. Besides, an exotic cosmopolite such as he had little in common with the middle-aged, middle-class, middle Americans who were quite comfortable in Grand Rapids. As he became more involved in auto parts Bluhdorn would learn that these people were quite typical of the executives in that industry, and he knew he would never be at home with them. So he, Judelson, and Duncan recruited new talent for the home office, leaving the old managers in place so long as they followed directives and produced results.

This is not to say that Bluhdorn quickly became disillusioned with auto parts. The industry remained promising, and Bluhdorn had great ambitions for G + W. Still, it was a somewhat mundane business, and certainly lacked the glamour associated with electronics, pharmaceuticals, office machines, and even petroleum. Like Ling, Bluhdorn would get his satisfactions from front office maneuverings, not the actual operation of companies—at least not auto parts companies. He could do something about the place from which he operated, however—he could leave Grand Rapids. Bluhdorn and Judelson would have preferred to relocate to Manhattan, but Duncan wanted Houston. Besides, all three agreed that most of their expansion would be in the South and Midwest, and Houston was as good a place as any from which to function. So they went there.

The acquisitions program swung into action in 1959, when G + W purchased small firms with names like Car Parts Depot and Wood Time & Supply, paying for them with common stock. Others followed at the rate of one every two or three months. Auto Spring & Supply, Motor Supply, Spencer Auto Electric, Auto Precision Parts, Allbright Auto Parts, Jobber Service Warehouse, Marathon Automotive, Standard Auto Parts—all of these and others with less descriptive names were taken over during the next five years, and almost always for G + W common stock.

The corporation was exhibiting steady growth, the result of coordination of efforts, economies of scale, penetration of markets, and the development of new profit centers. By 1964 G + W was able to report net sales of $117.2 million. The common stock that Bluhdorn had purchased for around $5 was now selling for over $20 and was listed on the New York Stock Exchange. G + W was not yet the General Motors of automobile parts, but it had already become the largest and fastest growing company in the industry.

But was the company profitable? On the surface it seemed to be. In 1964, for example, G + W reported consolidated net earnings of $3.5 million, up from the $2.6 million of the previous year, while per share earnings rose from $1.71 to $1.81. Yet a good deal of this came from "special items," without which G + W would have had to report an earnings decline. Bluhdorn understood this—along with many new businessmen of the period he had become adept at "creative accounting." In early June he had learned just how bad things were from one of his vice presidents:

> The consolidated statement of earnings for the nine months ended April 30, shows that the automotive parts subsidiaries have made $1,123,000 before taxes. Of this amount more than a million dollars represented "special items" such as inventory bargain, taking Beard & Stone off LIFO [last in, first out], gain on sale of real estate at Reading, etc.; thus the true earnings of the parts companies are virtually nil for this year and I am extremely fearful of any detailed disclosures we might have to make in a registration statement.[3]

This was to be the first of Bluhdorn's experiments with funny money. He was learning how to mask stagnant or mediocre results with such special items. More spectacular ones would appear later.

Bluhdorn was more than happy to talk about the reasons for G + W's apparent success. It was able to provide the acquired companies with lines of credit, a chance to expand their markets and product lines, national advertising when appropriate, and coordination of efforts with others in the same industry. There was security to be had by becoming part of G + W instead of remaining one of the more than 17,000 manufacturers and jobbers trying to elbow their ways into new areas, where the failure rate in hard times could be quite high. Consequently, the owners of a parts distributing operation would exchange their business for G + W common shares. They would remain in command at decent salaries, and then take on new lines of products manufactured by other G + W companies. There would be cooperation with other distributors who had joined Bluhdorn, more visibility, and low-cost capital for expansion. Bluhdorn kept a tighter rein on his line managers than did Ling, for example, but in the end gave considerable leeway to those able to turn in good bottom-line figures.

But was it legal? Specifically, was G + W in violation of the antitrust strictures against reciprocity? That the company was aware of the problem was obvious, and in fact it was dealt with in a corporation manual.

> Reciprocity is that practice whereby one company seeks to obtain sales of its products by agreeing to buy from a supplier provided that the supplier in turn agrees to buy from it. Reciprocity embraces every form of agreement or arrangement to that end, whether expressed or implied, direct or indirect.
>
> It is the policy of this Company, that our purchases shall not be used as a means of effecting sales of our products. All products should be sold upon their own merits, using as inducement to the customer our own superiority in such items as price, quality, delivery, service, design, etc. In the same way, our purchases should be made with the same factors in mind, so that our needs are served by suppliers on the competitive merits of their own products and services.[4]

Yet newly acquired parts and distribution companies were fitted into the G + W system, and were likely to engage in practices which at the very least gave the appearance of reciprocity, and certainly violated the spirit of the law.

The parts manufacturers and jobbers knew this, which was one of the more important reasons they were willing to throw in with Bluhdorn rather than struggle along on their own. Eventually G + W developed what was known as the American Parts System, under which jobbers were guaranteed overnight delivery of orders. Whenever possible, these came from other firms in the G + W constellation. Seen in this light, the corporation seemed to resemble a cooperative as much as it did a unified corporation.

Increasingly Bluhdorn was willing to leave such matters as running the company to his management team. Duncan and Judelson were the de facto leaders when it came to coordinating and developing existing operations, and others soon arrived to augment the headquarters staff. One of the more important of these was Don Gaston, who left Ernst & Ernst to become an executive vice-president for financial affairs. The statistics he soon provided were the sort that Bluhdorn and Wall Street liked to see. Joel Dolkert, who had been there almost from the beginning, served as secretary and later took a vice-presidency as well. A New York-based attorney, Dolkert was considered an authority in the area Bluhdorn was coming to know best: mergers and acquisitions.

While there was a measure of collegiality in this inner circle, Bluhdorn clearly was in command. He did have a sense of his own limitations, however, and among the more important of these was his frequent impulse to act rashly. Bluhdorn counted upon the others, Duncan and Judelson in particular, to restrain him on such occasions. "The most important thing about this group is that they all know they can tell Charlie Bluhdorn to go to hell," wrote business analyst Chris Welles in 1967, "and they frequently have to, for in his gusto for making deals, Bluhdorn sometimes pushes beyond good sense."[5]

All the while he was learning how best to effect takeovers. Most of these were friendly enough; Bluhdorn could be charming when wooing a candidate. He would throw his arms around the prospect and whisper into his ear, "You and I are going to make a hell of a team." But he also was capable of throwing tantrums when encountering opposition from such individuals.[6] And Bluhdorn was also finding out how to maneuver in proxy battles when these became necessary. In 1964, for example, he outmaneuvered Spartan Corporation in a fight for control of Crampton Manufacturing, in a struggle marked by injunctions and a bidding war, the first in his experience. After it was all over Bluhdorn realized that he had paid too much for a company which at best was mediocre.

More important in terms of Bluhdorn's education was the attempted takeover of Muskegon Piston Ring. When its management tried to block his advances Bluhdorn retaliated by purchasing shares in the open market, thus bidding the price higher. Muskegon replied by seeking an injunction, claiming that G + W had violated the antitrust statutes in its acquisitions bid. Dolkert led the fight through an initial case and an appeal, and in the end Bluhdorn had to settle for representation on the Muskegon board and an agreement not to purchase additional shares. This arrangement hardly suited either party, and both looked for a way out. A few months later, by common agreement, G + W sold its Muskegon shares to AP Parts. The holding, which had cost an average of $17 per share, was sold at $32, yielding G + W a profit of around $2.7 million—which was reported as ordinary income, now a G + W practice. In this way, Bluhdorn learned that he might do even better by failing in a takeover than by succeeding.[7]

Struggles such as these interested Bluhdorn more than putting together a string of auto parts manufacturers and jobbers. Moreover, he was disturbed by the slow progress in earnings, and wanted firms with greater potentials for profit. His growing restlessness became evident in 1963, when G + W purchased Rocket Jet Engineering for $4 million in stock, its largest takeover to that date. Rocket Jet would put G + W into the more glamorous and promising defense industry at a time when Vietnam War orders were increasing, and it might lead to additional opportunities elsewhere. Bluhdorn also purchased Marson Musical Products, which hardly fit into the overall G + W picture.

By 1965 Bluhdorn had proven to himself and anyone else who cared that he could—with the help of his team—erect and operate a large auto parts corporation. Moreover, he was not a mere acquirer, lumping together a jumble of firms as others of the period seemed to be doing. Rather, where product lines were incomplete and no likely takeover candidate existed, he would order the creation of his own supplier. Bluhdorn claimed, with some justification, that fully half of G + W's growth was internally generated, and the American Parts System, for all its antitrust implications, was working. Yet profits, even when extraordinary income was added, grew at a slow rate. G + W was in an unglamorous industry not highly regarded on Wall Street in this period. The stock peaked at 44 in 1962 and then declined. Other advances followed, but in early 1965 the shares were going for between 32 and 34. Like Ling and Thornton, Bluhdorn wanted to do something to increase the price so as to use this paper for acquisitions. That he soon would take to the diversification path should have been evident.

But there were also other reasons for his choosing this direction. Despite all of his success Bluhdorn was getting bored—especially with auto parts and Houston. In effect he had climbed to the top of the mountain, only to discover it was the wrong peak. The parts business was fine in its own way, but that wasn't his way. Bluhdorn wanted to do something more interesting than anything that was happening at G + W. So together with several associates (and independent of his work at G + W) he purchased control of Ward Foods in 1963. A New York-based baking company with sales of $130 million, it was losing money and close to collapse; in this regard it resembled the old Michigan Plating & Stamping. Bluhdorn installed new management and within months they had turned the company around. Two years later he purchased control of another moribund operation, H. C. Bohack, a supermarket chain with more than $200 million in revenues but one of the lowest profit margins in the industry. Once again he reinvigorated management, and profits responded soon after.

Bluhdorn wasn't planning to abandon G + W for supermarkets and baked goods, however. For one thing, Ward and Bohack interested him more as vehicles for salvage and exercises in management than anything else. And for another, G + W was too important and powerful to turn one's back on. Bluhdorn had no intention of starting out again on his own. But he knew that if G + W continued along its present path it would become just another drab, capital-goods variety company going nowhere. In half a dozen years Bluhdorn had created his large auto parts supplier, but it was not as profitable as he imagined it would be. Still, he had learned some tricks along the way, and he was watching others developing new tricks he could adopt. Thus, he conceived the idea of utilizing G + W as a base upon which to erect a new, more exciting corporation.

As much as any other reason, this was how and why Bluhdorn turned to diversification.

As was the case with other budding conglomerates, G + W entered the zinc industry through happenstance as much as anything else. In mid-1965 one of his board members, Harold Zerbe, mentioned the growing dissension at New Jersey Zinc, the country's leading producer of the metal, and at Bush Terminal another firm of which he was a director. It seems that one faction at Bush, composed mostly of officers, wanted to invest Zinc's sizeable cash reserve in the business. Another group, most of whose members were outside directors and who were headed by Chairman Jacob Hein, thought the zinc business was ailing; they wanted to use the funds to enter new fields. A stalemate had been reached, which Zerbe thought could be resolved only by the entry of a third force. In the interests of both companies, then, he asked Bluhdorn to consider buying New Jersey Zinc.

Bluhdorn was sufficiently interested to send Judelson and others to look it over. They found a fully integrated though somewhat antiquated operation, with mines in six states and plants in four. The metal itself was used in a wide variety of industries, from paints to batteries to home construction. One of its more familiar applications was the galvanizing of iron and steel, so important in the manufacture of auto parts. Thus there was a link, though a trifle tenuous, between G + W and Zinc.

As Zerbe had indicated the firm had a clean balance sheet and a strong cash position, but it was in a stagnant, even declining business, and the price of zinc was subject to wild fluctuations. During strong years production and sales would rise sharply, only to collapse in slumps. The secular trend was downward, however, an indication that the Hein group was correct in opting for diversification. Still, Zinc was a large and profitable firm; revenues the previous year had come to $135.5 million and earnings to $7.5 million. Demand and price were rising in response to the needs of the Vietnam War. Hein would be tough when it came to negotiations.

Bluhdorn decided to make a play for Zinc, and to do so as an ally of the inside directors. That is to say, he was pledged to reinvest in operations, but he tacitly accepted Hein's rationale. Thus, he was an ideal mediator. Soon thereafter he initiated discussions, during which he captivated the officers. "The more you're around Bluhdorn," said President Lindsay Johnson, "the closer the moon is."[8]

Hein was not as easily charmed. In return for his group's 58 percent of Zinc stock he wanted $84 million in cash, at a time when G + W had only $5 million or so in its treasury. Bluhdorn knew he had to come up with the money quickly, for Hein indicated the offer would not remain open for more than a few weeks.

What happened next remained a source of contention between Bluhdorn and his critics, and it is one reason the latter often charged him with being the most devious and shady of all the conglomerators. Both sides agreed that the corporation would arrange for an $84 million uncollateralized loan from Chase Manhattan Bank, the proceeds of which were to be used to purchase Hein's shares. This amount was approximately twice that of G + W's total net worth. The transaction received little notice at the time, and soon was forgotten by all but those directly involved. It would be investigated throughly four years later, when G + W was called to testify before the House Antitrust Subcommittee of the Committee on the Judiciary investigating conglomerate corporations.

Bluhdorn and other G + W executives claimed that the loan was in accord with normal corporate practices. Moreover, since the funds were earmarked for the purchase of Zinc's shares, the security in fact was there. But under examination by the congressmen and their counsel, the witnesses were forced to admit that there was more to it than this—that, in fact, this was the beginning of an unwholesome nexus between the bank and the corporation.

The relationship between G + W and Chase went back to early 1964, when the corporation became one of the bank's customers. Chase was to handle only part of G + W's business, however, with the larger share remaining at the Bank of the Southwest in Houston, which remained Bluhdorn's base of operations. Roy Abbott, a Chase vice-president, was placed in charge of the G + W account. "This is a red letter day," he wrote after helping finance a takeover that year. "We are on the threshold of a breakthrough." He advised other officers to keep on the lookout for Bluhdorn, who might visit New York soon, "and roll out the red carpet when he arrives."[9]

Abbott looked upon G + W as one of his prime accounts, and he realized that Chase could earn large commissions and fees by becoming Bluhdorn's lead banker. From the first he established a warm relation with management, and tried to woo Bluhdorn away from his old lines of financing. "Charlie, I'm sure we can make this very attractive to you," he wrote regarding one such loan, adding he "would appreciate it if you could keep our friend in Newark [Prudential Life, which was one of G + W's sources of funds] out of the oil for the time being."[10] Given this kind of relationship and Abbott's known intentions, the quid pro quo for the $84 million loan—which he was in charge of arranging—wasn't difficult to figure out: Chase was to receive the bulk of G + W's financial business.

Bluhdorn understood this, and was perfectly willing to proceed along these lines, especially since he had every intention of moving to New York within the next few years, and Chase was a more prestigious bank than any in Houston. So the word went down to all the subsidiaries: in the future they were to direct as much of their business to Chase as was possible. "It is in our mutual interest for you to deposit your monthly withholding taxes with the Chase Manhattan Bank . . . rather than using local banks," was one such directive, and others followed. As expected, Chase replaced the Bank of the Southwest as G + W's prime financial source.[11]

None of this was either unusual or in violation of the letter of the law. When a Chase executive was asked in 1969 whether the bank expected additional business from G + W because of the loan he was quick to respond, "I think this is true of any banking relation. . . . When we make loans, this is improving our relationship and often with the improvement of relationship in the loan area there are also improvements in other parts of the relationship, too."[12]

Nor did Chase's practice of recommending takeover possibilities to G + W differ appreciably from the understanding between Lehman and LTV, and Lehman and Litton, or those of other investment bankers and their conglomerate clients. So it was that Abbott wrote Bluhdorn on August 10, 1965: "Having in mind your reciprocity with the automobile industry and, potentially the railroads and also some overlap into the trucking industry, I thought you might be interested in seeing some information on the Chicago Railroad Equipment Division of AMK. I am not sure whether or not Eli would have any interest in selling or on what basis he might be interested but, on the other hand, if it has any appeal to you, it might be an area for future discussion."[13] Other suggestions followed, and though G + W acted on few of them, the nexus had been created. And on February 21, 1966, Abbott left Chase Manhattan to become a senior vice-president at G + W.

It was then that the line between accepted practice and shady dealings seemed to some to have been crossed. Abbott maintained his contacts at the bank, a normal enough situation, and in fact became a prime go-between for Bluhdorn there. As such, he would inform his old colleagues about companies G + W intended to acquire—before the news broke, and the prices of their stocks advanced.

Two and a half months after taking up his duties at G + W Abbott dropped in at Chase for an informal talk with friends. "Roy also agreed to keep us better informed concerning proposed mergers and acquisitions and important investments," wrote Bruce Croccio, a Chase officer in a memo of the conversation, adding that Abbott would be "notifying us prior to announcements in the newspapers."[14]

Three years later Abbott testified about this arrangement before a congressional committee. On that occasion he claimed that none of this was in any way extraordinary, that exchange of information regarding takeovers was a common enough practice between banks and their corporate clients. But it was also clear that bankers provided with such knowledge might buy or sell shares in order to benefit themselves or their institution, and do so before the general public learned what was happening. Abbott claimed this was not the case insofar as Chase and G + W was concerned. Yet Wall Streeters of the period noted that there would be flurries in the volume and prices of certain stocks just prior to the announcements of tender offers, and that these were more pronounced with those involving G + W. That a pattern of leakage was being established was obvious to even the most casual observers. In the 1960s all parties involved protested their innocence, but many onlookers felt that the disavowals often strained credulity.*

While these Byzantine manipulations involved with the New Jersey Zinc takeover enabled Bluhdorn to hone old techniques and develop new ones, the company itself scarcely captured his imagination. This is not to suggest that Zinc wasn't a major acquisition and a valuable property. Rather, its potential simply did not intrigue Bluhdorn, who remained on the lookout for excitement and glamour. So he left its overall development to Judelson and others and sought out firms in industries that would provide the needed outlet for his creative energies.

That Bluhdorn was destined to become a conglomerator rather than an auto parts purveyor or the head of a mining and smelting concern had become obvious, if not to the investment community, at least to those around him. A man who delighted in the company of celebrities, Bluhdorn yearned to be one himself. He hardly could aspire to that status while G + W remained mired in mundane businesses.

That may have been the principal reason Bluhdorn went after Paramount Pictures in the spring of 1966. Of course there were other factors in the equation. Here was a well-known company with a depressed stock, selling far below its breakup value, as investors attributed more importance to losses on recent releases than to both the tangible and intangible assets in the form of its film library and its name, one of the most respected in the industry. Moreover, Paramount was in the midst of a power struggle somewhat similar to that which bedeviled New Jersey Zinc prior to G + W's entry. This suggested that Bluhdorn might come in with a reasonable bid acceptable to both sides and walk away with the company. Overnight he would become a show-business figure, and instead of having to glad-hand the avuncular, somewhat provincial auto

---

*As will be seen in chapter 7, similar investigations would establish a clear pattern of the use of inside information in such a way by those involved with the Penn Central collapse. Then, as in the G + W case, the bank claimed not to have utilized its privileged information. In the case of the Penn Central, as with G + W, the bank involved was Chase Manhattan.

parts and mining executives, he would wheel and deal with well-known jet-setters and motion picture tycoons and stars. As the head of Paramount Pictures Bluhdorn could combine his business talents with his growing fascination with the popular arts and media. It was an enticing prospect, which could hardly be resisted.

The Paramount takeover really began in the spring of 1965, when Broadway producer Ernest Martin joined with corporate raider Herbert Siegel to purchase almost 10 percent of the corporation's stock and then demanded and obtained board seats. Almost immediately these two clashed with the existing Paramount management, demanding to know why the company had been so slow to become involved with television, and why it had leased old movies to the networks at low prices. Others on the board pointed to rising earnings; Martin replied that this resulted from the sale of valuable assets and implied the program was a cover-up for inept administration.

Bluhdorn entered the picture a year later. After having sold some of Zinc's holdings he used the money to purchase 9 percent of Paramount's stock. Now he set out to woo Siegel. "Charlie flattered the hell out of him," said one of those involved with the matter. "He told Siegel his ideas for Paramount were marvelous but there was so much bitterness he never could get them across. But he, Bluhdorn, could carry Siegel's banner, vindicate his ideas—and also Siegel would be a big hero with his backers for selling out at a big profit."[15] Siegel and Martin agreed to go along with Bluhdorn's plan to make a tender offer for the rest of Paramount's stock. The deal was completed in October 1966. In all, G + W paid $165 million in its common and convertible preferred shares for Paramount, which at the time had admitted assets of more than $300 million, but whose actual worth was perhaps half again as much as that.

With other acquisitions Bluhdorn had been content to retain existing management—not so with Paramount. Shortly after the takeover was completed Bluhdorn named himself president and relocated to Hollywood, proclaiming his intention to shake up the company, make it an industry leader, and establish himself as a show-business personality. "I'm going to rebuild this whole goddamn town," he shouted, firing the old management and installing a new one, with former actor Robert Evans his studio head. Bluhdorn had a hand in producing new films, and on one occasion personally signed Jack Lemmon and Walter Matthau to appear in the Paramount version of *The Odd Couple*. He appeared on talk shows, made the rounds of the parties (often with a starlet on his arm), and was hailed as a tycoon of the new school. And he did show results. In 1967, Paramount's filming schedule reached its highest level since the end of World War II, and the studio started turning out hits. Losing ventures were closed down and new ones, especially those tied to television, were initiated. To speed up and augment Paramount's commitment to this fast-growing field, Bluhdorn purchased Desilu Productions, named after its founders, Desi Arnaz and Lucille Ball, for $16 million in preferred stock. Then Desilu and the existing television operations were consolidated into Paramount Television Enterprises, with an ebullient Bluhdorn confidently predicting it soon would become an industry leader.

Later, critics would charge—with some justification—that Bluhdorn juggled the books in order to show even better profits than were actually obtained. Even though he reorganized the company, some said Paramount was little more than an ego trip for Bluhdorn. "He's acting like the rubber-stamp cliche of the show biz novice who's after glory and excitement," said one Wall Streeter. "The man simply has no taste, no sense of the artistic."[16]

Yet, there was no arguing with the published results, verified by audit and accepted by the Securities and Exchange Commission. In 1966, largely as a result of the New Jersey Zinc and Paramount acquisitions, G + W reported revenues of $519 million against the previous year's $277 million, while earnings rose to $22.8 million from $11.4 million. G + W common advanced by over 50 percent in the first half of the year, only to slump badly in the third quarter. But this was due more to the general decline of the period than to any lack of results in the areas of revenues, earnings, prospects, and most importantly, image. Hardly known to any but the more sophisticated investors two years earlier, G + W now was considered one of the faster-growing and more interesting conglomerates, and if Bluhdorn was not yet in the same league as Ling, Thornton, and Geneen, he seemed to be closing rapidly.

Early in 1966, even before he made the initial commitment to Paramount, Bluhdorn purchased 75,000 shares of South Puerto Rico Sugar for G + W, and soon thereafter took a seat on that corporation's board. Little was made of this move at the time. Bluhdorn's interest in foodstuffs was well known, and it was assumed that this was yet another way for him to play out fantasies, not unlike what was happening with Paramount. While refusing to deny plans for an eventual takeover, Bluhdorn had said that "the food industry would be pretty far fetched for G + W," and most analysts were content to let it go at that. But several noticed that for all of their disparities there was one feature both companies had in common, namely that the market was valuing their shares at substantially less than net asset values. In its own way, South Puerto Rico Sugar might be as much a bargain as Paramount.

Nothing happened for nearly a year and rumors regarding a takeover faded, as Bluhdorn acquired Desilu and a handful of small firms involved in the manufacture of capital goods. Then, in February 1967, G + W announced plans to purchase South Puerto Rico Sugar for slightly more than $62.7 million in debentures, with many of the details to be handled by Chase Manhattan. Judelson now spoke of his "great belief in agriculture," and of G + W's new commitments to help feed the world in the face of the population explosion. On Wall Street, analysts noted that the takeover would help boost G + W's earnings and earnings per share.

In fiscal 1966 South Puerto Rico had earned $3.5 million on revenues of more than $61 million. Despite its name, most of the corporation's operations and assets were in the Dominican Republic, and included prime shoreline acreage that might be converted from sugar to tourist and vacation home uses. South Puerto Rico's assets were carried at $68 million, but they clearly were worth more. Given large-scale financing, it might easily be transformed from a sugar firm tied to the cyclical peradventures of that crop to a lucrative resort-based operation. This apparently was on Bluhdorn's mind in approving the takeover, and within a year plans for such a switch were being discussed.

And the planning was accompanied by the customary transfer of a newly acquired company's banking business to Chase Manhattan. Ronald Sherwood, an officer at the bank's San Juan office, reported on a discussion with Roy Abbott less than a month after the tender offer was announced. "Roy stated that as soon as the merger is finalized he will have the accounts moved to our Puerto Rican branch. In the meantime, he does not 'want to make any waves until they are in the fold.'"[17]

Now G + W became a feature at the New York Stock Exchange, its shares helping to lead the way in the recovery of 1967. There was much talk of the "synergy" between Paramount and South Puerto Rico Sugar, with the two firms becoming the base for a new entertainment-leisure time-vacation enterprise. As for the auto parts and zinc businesses, these would remain, providing the needed earnings which would be plowed back into the more glamorous parts of the enterprise.

Bluhdorn was being hailed as one of the most dynamic businessmen of the time. G + W now was number 135 on the Fortune 500 list, and as the third-fastest-growing corporation on the roster, seemed destined to enter the top 100 circle before the decade ended. As though to signal this coming status, Bluhdorn announced that the firm would soon move its headquarters from Houston to Manhattan, where it would be housed in a new skyscraper located at Columbus Circle. With typical verve, he told reporters, "It will make the General Motors Building look like peanuts!"[18]

Whether or not the forty-four story G + W Building was an architectural triumph is a matter of taste—though most critics thought it flashy and derivative, with one saying that in this regard it was a proper reflection of its sponsor. More spectacular were Bluhdorn's merger activities the following year. Not even James Ling, busily acquiring Greatamerica and Jones & Laughlin by means of financial legerdemain, could match him in this regard. Moreover, Bluhdorn demonstrated an uncanny knack of earning more money when one of his attempted takeovers failed to materialize than when one succeeded.

Early in 1967 Bluhdorn had drawn up a short list of potential acquisitions. Most of these were large, old, asset-rich firms, that, due to erosion of markets or management failures, had lackluster records and so might be purchased for a low prices. Bluhdorn thought along the same lines as other conglomerates in this regard, but at least some of his acquisitions bore more than a passing relationship to existing operations.

E. W. Bliss was one of these. A company with roots going back to 1857, Bliss turned out a wide variety of industrial machinery and equipment, and perhaps was best known for its dies, a large number of which were sold to automobile manufacturers. Well entrenched in highly cyclical fields, it turned in an undistinguished performance. On revenues of $157 million the previous year Bliss had reported net earnings of $6.1 million. But the company did have net assets of $58.2 million and a clean balance sheet, and could be had relatively inexpensively.

Universal American was another old-line capital-goods manufacturer; its top lines included special machinery and bearings, and, like Bliss, it numbered the automobile companies among its major customers. Universal's 1966 sales totaled $181 million, on which it had earned $9.3 million before deductions for a one-time loss. With net worth of more than $44.5 million, it too was underpriced by the market.

That both Bliss and Universal American had a place in G + W should have been obvious. There would be a neat fit with the existing automotive-related operations, and their acquisition could contribute to Bluhdorn's continuing pledge to turn his corporation into the General Motors of auto parts.

Consolidated Cigar was another matter entirely. Here was a company whose sole products were low- and medium-priced cigars. Consolidated grew some of its own leaf on farms in Connecticut, and it owned several warehouses. What did any of this have to do with auto parts and entertainment? A case might have been made for a "fit" with South Puerto Rico Sugar, in that some cigar tobacco might have been grown in the Dominican Republic. But the G + W people didn't think much of this possibility. Instead, Roy Abbott spoke of the company "as a base on which to build a diverse retail trade for cigar, candy-store type of products," and added that Consolidated had perfected a new kind of synthetic wrapper for use on cheaper cigars that might prove highly profitable. Still, cigars hardly were a growth item. Consolidated quite simply was another fine old company, mired in a stagnant industry with dead-end products, whose stock might be picked up cheaply. On revenues of $159 million in 1966 it had earned $9.9 million, and its net worth came to slightly less than $78 million. As with other firms acquired by G + W this last figure was understated: Abbott noted that the Connecticut farmland was worth far more than its carrying price. An acquisition of Consolidated might boost G + W's per share earnings and increase its book value the first year, but little more could be expected thereafter. The purchase of this kind of property would signal the acceptance of the philosophy of size for its own sake and little else.

Bluhdorn announced these three takeovers within days of each other, and all became parts of G + W on January 11–12, 1968. In 48 hours he had almost doubled the size of his corporation. Taken together, Bliss, Universal American, and Consolidated Cigar had revenues of more than $500 million; in 1967 G + W had reported sales of $649 million.

This was the beginning of a whirlwind acquisitions campaign. While not as far reaching as those overseen by Geneen or as spectacular as Ling's, the campaign came close in both regards. During the rest of that year Bluhdorn took in 19 other companies. Most of these could be justified as augmenting existing operations. For example, East Publishing, which owned Stax and Volt Records, clearly had a place beside Paramount, as did North Brevard Cable Television and Orange CATV, all of which came together with several others to form the Leisure Time Division. Atlas Metal Products, WCM Machine Tools, General Steel Products, and Gardner Clark Spring Co. fit in well with Bliss and Universal American in the Manufacturing Division. Wheels Inc. and Detroit Supply augmented the large Distribution Division, which still concentrated on auto parts. Consolidated Cigar was to become the base for a Consumer Products Division, while South Puerto Rico did the same for Agricultural Products. An obscure entity, Chicago Thoroughbred Enterprises, which apparently had something to do with horse breeding, was intended as an initial foray into that field; later on Bluhdorn would purchase the Arlington Park Racetrack, take an interest in Hollywood Park, and make a play for Resorts International.

The "big three" takeovers of January and the others that followed provided two legs of an acquisitions triad that occupied Bluhdorn in 1968. Owing to the triad, revenues would rise to $1.3 billion that year, which placed G + W in the 69th slot on the Fortune 500 roster. Earnings from operations came to $67.7 million, up from the previous year's figure of $59.5 million, while book value per share shot up to $19.93 from $9.55.

As impressive as all of this might have been it had no important impact upon the prices of G + W common and convertible preferred shares, which actually declined during much of the year. The reason was no secret: Wall Street believed Bluhdorn simply was gathering up cats and dogs to dress up his year-end figures. There was no glamour in companies like Consolidated Cigar and E. W. Bliss, and not much more even in Paramount. Because of this, G + W common fetched the lowest price/earnings multiple of the more familiar conglomerates. This—and the convertible debentures based upon the common—was the paper Bluhdorn had to use in his takeovers.

The low price meant he had to exchange more shares and their equivalents for properties than would have been required if the multiple had been as high, say, as that afforded a company like Litton. Thus, while Thornton acquired, in exchange for his high-priced paper, firms whose share prices were low in relation to earnings and so boosted Litton's per-share results—the opposite often was the case with G + W. In vain Bluhdorn tried to point this out, claiming with some justification that G + W wasn't involved in this particular "funny money game" that was the talk of the financial district in 1968. In fact, several of his takeovers actually resulted in lower per-share earnings than might have been reported had they not taken place. But this would soon change, as Bluhdorn engaged in a ploy quite different from that employed by Thornton, but equally effective, to advance his earnings.

This was the third leg of the triad, one that was so simple and obvious as to lead one to wonder why others hadn't attempted it earlier in the movement. Specifically, G + W would establish an equity position in a company, doing so as quietly as possible in order to obtain the shares at a low price. Then Bluhdorn would make a tender offer for the rest of the shares, always much higher than the going quotes. Thus, the initial position would appear as a beachhead from which G + W intended to mount the main assault. This was the way Bluhdorn had gone about acquiring New Jersey Zinc, Paramount, Desilu, South Puerto Rico Sugar, and several smaller firms. If he succeeded, G + W would have a new unit, but failure also might be profitable. Should Bluhdorn have to abandon the quest he might dispose of those original shares, almost always at a price closer to that of the tender offer than that he had paid for them.

Bluhdorn had some experience with this technique prior to 1968, but he always employed it as a sideline to his more pressing and central objectives, namely to enlarge upon his holdings and expand into new areas. Conditions that year, however, enabled him to use it in such a way as to produce a huge one-time capital gain—close to $52 million—from abandoned acquisitions. Bluhdorn received more credit for this than had been accorded him for most of the takeovers and turnarounds he had engineered, and there are Wall Streeters who to this day consider the abandonments his most clever and original ploy. While clearly enjoying the praise, Bluhdorn vigorously, and with some justification in several cases, denied having sought such profits. With a straight face he told reporters that he wished things had worked out otherwise. This was necessary. For to have sought profits in such a way would have constituted a serious violation of federal laws.

Bluhdorn's initial move in this sphere didn't work out as expected. It was familiar enough to those who had followed Ling's acquisition of Wilson & Co. There was Armour & Co., a $2.2 billion a year company which in addition to its meat-packing operations turned out household products, chemicals, and a variety of industrial goods. In late 1967, while completing work on the Bliss, Universal American, and Consolidated Cigar takeovers, Bluhdorn started accumulating Armour shares, so that by January 1968 G + W had a fraction below the 10 percent holdings that would have required reporting the position to the Securities & Exchange Commission. But Armour's management knew of his activities, and was willing to cooperate in a takeover, assuming the price was right. And so it was. On January 16th the two companies announced their intention to merge, with G + W issuing convertible preferred stock and warrants for all outstanding Armour shares. The value of the tender came to around $374 million, which worked out to slightly less than $50 per Armour share.

At a press conference following the announcement Bluhdorn spoke of Armour's undervalued assets and alluded to plans to make better use of them. He pointedly compared the company to "a girl pregnant with a lot of babies that are more valuable than the mother."[19] Was Bluhdorn planning a Ling-like deployment of assets? It was a possibility. Moreover, some of Armour's component firms would fit in well with others in G + W's Manufacturing and Distribution divisions. Wall Street thought well of the takeover. Armour's stock, which was selling for a fraction below 45 at the time, soon went over the 50 mark; that was approximately 10 points above the price Bluhdorn had paid for his initial stake, on which he now had a paper profit of approximately $7 million.

At this point the Justice Department entered the picture. Antitrusters there had studied the conglomerate movement for more than a decade, attempting to determine whether the takeovers violated existing statutes. No important cases had been initiated, but this wasn't considered the equivalent of giving the conglomerators a clean bill of health. Rather, there seemed no way to prosecute a company for making acquisitions that didn't increase market share significantly in a specific industry. And since the Lings, Bluhdorns, and Thorntons were diversifying away from existing bases they seemed safe so long as no new legislation was framed and passed. As a matter of course they consulted the Justice Department prior to making sizeable takeovers; G + W had done so with South Puerto Rico Sugar, New Jersey Zinc, and Desilu, for example, and had received the go-ahead. Still, the antitrusters felt in their bones there was something unhealthy about conglomerate diversification. If only they could come up with some kind of formula under which to prosecute the big companies. But none existed in late 1967 and early 1968.

Nevertheless, the antitrusters managed to find a roundabout way to challenge the Armour takeover. Under the terms of a half-century-old consent decree meat packers were limited in the businesses they might enter. The Justice Department claimed that the merger would transform G + W into a meat packer—with interests in a wide variety of other businesses. There was talk of requiring spin-offs of South Puerto Rico Sugar and Consolidated Cigar in return for permission to acquire Armour, something Bluhdorn was unwilling to do.* Nor was he prepared to contest the Justice Department's position, for in 1968 this seemed just the kind of test case the antitrusters had been seeking to establish an opening wedge in the fight against the conglomerates. Finally, news of the government's position had resulted in major sell-offs of conglomerate stocks at the exchanges, with G + W leading them on the way down, falling 13 points before leveling off. The paper Bluhdorn had offered for the meat packer was now considerably shrunken in value, and Armour Chairman William Wood Price was having second thoughts about the deal. He bridled at Bluhdorn's suggestion that Armour purchase G + W's block—at $60 per share, which translated into an $18 million profit on the deal. In a clever countermove, Price announced that Armour would repurchase 20 percent of its own shares at 50, which was a few points higher than the current quote. If the shares were tendered and retired this would have increased G + W's holdings of Armour to 12½ percent of the outstanding stock, transforming it into an "insider," and according to SEC rules insiders were prohibited from realizing short-term profits from the sale of a company's shares. In order to avoid this unhappy circumstance Bluhdorn would have been obliged to tender a quantity of his shares to Armour at the $50 price. This would have resulted in a nice profit to G + W, but hardly the bonanza Bluhdorn had anticipated.

Bluhdorn struck back by seeking and then finding another company interested in Armour. This was General Host, a smallish (less than $150 million in revenues) food company that formerly had been known as General Baking, and now was attempting to diversify and perhaps eventually transform itself into a conglomerate. Bluhdorn arranged to sell 150,000 of his Armour shares to General Host at 56, and he gave that company an option to purchase the rest at 60. The option was exercised, and in early 1969 General Host acquired Armour. Later, Bluhdorn would

---

*This was the initial attempt to work out a deal with the conglomerates, a deal which eventually was accepted by LTV and ITT.

claim to have made $16.2 million on the deal, or $11.7 million after taxes.[20]

Bluhdorn next went after Allis-Chalmers, a major manufacturer of farm and construction equipment; it also turned out products for the electric power industry. Here was yet another old, somnolent operation, the kind Bluhdorn often found attractive. The corporation had earned only $5 million on revenues of $822 million the previous year, but most industry observers believed this was due to management lapses and an ill-considered venture into steam generation equipment then being abandoned. Allis-Chalmers had done better in the past; as recently as 1965 it had posted earnings of $22.1 million while grossing $714 million. Estimates of potential earnings once the company was repositioned ran from $20 million to as high as $30 million. That was why A-C had so many suitors, all of whom thought they could turn it around. General Dynamics was interested, as was James Ling, who perhaps recognized a splendid opportunity for redeployment. But these and others had been repelled by a management eager to remain independent.

Knowing all of this, on May 7th Bluhdorn went ahead with a tender offer. He bid for and obtained 3 million shares of A-C in exchange for cash and G + W securities, the total of which came to $117 million, or approximately $39 per share, at a time when A-C common was being quoted at a fraction above 33. As expected, A-C's management promptly announced it would fight the takeover and, recognizing it had an ally in Washington, spoke of violations of the antitrust statutes. The Federal Trade Commission agreed to look into the matter, and a month and a half later notified Bluhdorn that "formal proceedings" would be instituted. Specifically, the FTC charged that the acquisition would have an adverse affect on competition in a wide number of subindustries, including paper-making machinery, metal-forming presses and punches, and engine pistons. The case was weak, since the merged companies wouldn't have been the prime factor in any of these product areas, and even the more ardent antitrusters agreed that the commission had made its stand on an almost indefensible front. But it did cause Bluhdorn to have second thoughts about the takeover, while A-C cast about for a friendly acquirer that might rescue it from G + W with a merger offer of its own.

The parties came to an agreement in early autumn. White Consolidated Industries, a large capital goods manufacturer then involved in an aggressive acquisitions campaign of its own, agreed to purchase the A-C shares but not seek a direct takeover of that company. Rather, White would be allowed to name some new members to the board and then try to use its leverage there to improve conditions, thus enhancing the value of the investment. Bluhdorn was agreeable to this arrangement, since he stood to get another hefty capital gain from the transaction while avoiding bothersome litigation. Besides, he already had started out on his next campaign and was eager to put the messy A-C situation behind him. On October 31st White agreed to purchase the A-C shares owned by G + W for $122 million, thereby providing Bluhdorn with a $5 million profit.[21]

Bluhdorn had investigated the airline industry in the spring of 1967, and later that year concentrated his attention on Pan American World Airways, one of the largest in the field. But it wasn't until the following January, when LTV acquired Greatamerica and along with it control of Braniff, that he made his move. Open market purchases began in January and continued through the summer. By September G + W had accumulated some 1.6 million shares, or slightly less than 5 percent of the total, and Bluhdorn made his interest known to Pan Am's officers.

Bluhdorn always contended that he never expected to acquire Pan Am, that this was an investment, pure and simple. And in fact G + W never did put forth a tender offer. Perhaps the most important reason for this was opposition from his own board members, some of whom had negative opinions of the airline industry. In time Bluhdorn came to agree with them, and he sought a proper purchaser. In January 1969, he sold the Pan Am holding to Resorts International, which at the time was seeking to develop a string of vacation and gambling-based hotels in the Caribbean. The price was $17.2 million, of which $16 million was paid in cash and the rest in Resorts International shares and warrants. G + W's profit on this transaction came to $6.5 million. Meanwhile, G + W held a stake in Resorts, which at the time seemed intent on taking over Pan Am; at some future date should G + W make a takeover bid for Resorts, it would thereby gain the entire bundle. This firm would make a nice fit with G + W's racetrack interests and its undeveloped property in the Dominican Republic. Or so it appeared in 1969.[22]

Bluhdorn astonished even those who thought his ambitions were virtually unbounded by the audacity of a move he took just before the final Allis-Chalmers settlement. More than any other of his deals, this one provided evidence that he was more concerned with wheeling and dealing and capital gains from failed takeovers than in actually acquiring new properties.

The previous summer Roy Abbott had targeted Sinclair Oil for a tender offer. Here was a company with revenues of $1.5 billion, which meant that it was more than twice the size of G + W. The tenth largest factor in the petroleum industry, Sinclair had assets of nearly $1.6 billion and earnings in 1967 of $95.4 million. Abbott observed that Sinclair common was selling in the low 80s, while having an understated book value of $96 per share. With only 12.5 million shares outstanding it was one of the most thinly capitalized of all the major oil concerns. Moreover, it was a bargain that couldn't possibly involve G + W in an antitrust suit.

But there was one major obstacle—besides the anticipated opposition of Sinclair's management. The corporation had close relationships with Atlantic Richfield, and in fact even then was considering a merger with that petroleum company. Any attempt on Bluhdorn's part to acquire Sinclair was bound to result in a fight, one which G + W had little chance of winning. But he knew that even a defeat in such a contest could result in a major profit.

Bluhdorn began in a familiar fashion, by purchasing approximately 7 percent of Sinclair's stock on the open market. He got that stake for approximately $89 million, a price that averaged slightly in excess of $77 per share. Then he announced a tender offer, just a week before the final sale of the Allis-Chalmers shares to White Consolidated. Bluhdorn was proposing to exchange paper then valued at $114 for each share of Sinclair, then selling for a fraction above 95. The total value of the offer, then, was more than $1.4 billion—this from a corporation whose assets then were under $400 million.

As expected, Sinclair contested the bid, while the Justice Department asked the usual questions, thereby complicating matters. In a series of newspaper advertisements Sinclair urged its stockholders to reject Bluhdorn. G + W had no experience in the petroleum business, possessed inadequate resources to run so large an enterprise, and in any case hardly was a fitting partner for a respectable corporation. Sinclair also noted its growing relationship with Atlantic Richfield, which now entered the picture as a direct competitor. Bluhdorn responded by upping his offer, while Sinclair's shares shot over the 110 mark.

In the end G + W came to terms with both Sinclair and Atlantic Richfield. On January 8, 1969 Bluhdorn agreed to sell his 618,360 shares of Sinclair to Atlantic Richfield for $130 per share plus warrants to purchase a like number of Atlantic Richfield shares. Thus, G + W took in $80.4 million in cash, while the warrants were valued at around $32.5 million. The total worth of the package came to $112.9 million. G + W's profit from this particular exercise was $24.2 million.[23]

Two other acquisitions—both of which were partial—merit mention. Bluhdorn went after Brown Co. while wooing Armour. After taking in 23 percent of the shares by means of an exchange of debentures and warrants for Brown stock he increased the G + W stake to 69 percent. Brown was a $200 million a year forest products company whose major product was paper; one Wall Street joke of the period was that Bluhdorn wanted it because he would need paper in which to wrap Armour's meat. In fact Brown was just another undervalued sleeper, fascinating to Bluhdorn, who hoped to turn it around to show a large profit.

More important was the acquisition of Associates Investment Company, a large lending institution with assets of over $1.7 billion; it cost

Bluhdorn over $346 million in convertible debentures. This was a period during which many conglomerates were seeking finance and insurance companies, largely because their assets were underpriced, but also in the expectation of milking them to provide cash for takeovers of more interesting firms. Prior to this acquisition Bluhdorn had gone after Security Insurance of Hartford and Security Life as well as several others, but nothing came of those bids. Associates turned out to be a well-managed firm that made a contribution to G + W, but as far as Bluhdorn was concerned, it was only a consolation prize.

It also was the last of G + W's important takeovers. From 1969 onward Bluhdorn had to content himself with developing those properties already in hand. This wasn't because his penchant for takeovers had waned. Rather, it was due to the same combination of corporate, political, and economic problems that affected Litton, LTV, and the other conglomerates: an economic slump, a stock market crash, government investigations, and declining earnings. The G + W statistics told a story of both mediocre management of mature, cyclical companies, and profits from the failed takeovers that by then had become Bluhdorn's hallmark.

Gulf + Western Operating and Financial Results, 1966–1969 (figures in millions of dollars)

	1966	1967	1968	1969
Net Sales and Revenues	317.5	649.5	1,320.5	1,563.6
Net Earnings	20.1	46.2	69.8	72.1
Net Earnings Excluding Gains on Securities Sales	19.3	45.4	67.2	51.0
Net Earnings Per Share	$1.98	$2.85	$3.13	$3.15
Net Earnings Per Share Excluding Gains on Securities Sales	$1.90	$2.80	$3.00	$2.15

Source: *Gulf + Western Annual Report, 1969*, pp. 30–31.

The glow was gone, revealing the tinsel. At its peak in 1968 G + W common sold at a fraction above 64, or around 20 times earnings, far below the multiple afforded LTV and Litton and not nearly as high as those of Textron and ITT. At its low the following year G + W was 17½, so that its fall from grace was deeper than that of any of the others except the wallowing LTV. This occurred in the face of apparently stable earnings. Part of the reason was the general malaise, but Bluhdorn himself was a factor in the decline. More than the others, he was mistrusted. One might admire Thornton's vision, be impressed with Ling's daring and ingenuity, find Royal Little a refreshing original, and be awed by Harold Geneen's power and thrust. But Bluhdorn had none of these qualities. He had not turned G + W into "the General Motors of auto parts" as once had been promised. The machine-tool companies and South Puerto Rico Sugar were in pretty much the same shape as they would have been on their own. Nothing significant had been altered at New Jersey Zinc and Consolidated Cigar. The unwelcomed raids that gained large profits had captured the attention of Washington's antitrusters and helped spark one of the few reformist movements of the Nixon administration. The one area in which Bluhdorn did show flair was show business. Paramount was recovering nicely, and G + W was committing more of its attention and capital to leisure time activities. But this did not redeem him in the eyes of Wall Streeters or the business community at large. To most observers Bluhdorn was one of the lesser beasts in the corporate jungle, a jackal capable only of imitation and scavenging.

6

Harold Geneen: The Master

At the peak of his career, during the second half of the 1960s, Harold Geneen was generally conceded to be the greatest businessman of his time, and the only conglomerator whose impact upon management transcended the conglomerate movement. Students of the subject studied his techniques and philosophy as they had that of Alfred Sloan of General Motors in the previous decade and the strategy and structure utilized and created by the likes of John D. Rockefeller and Andrew Carnegie even earlier. In both popular magazines and specialized journals Geneen was hailed as an extraordinarily astute leader, the man who finally rationalized the conglomerate movement and made it respectable. Not for him were the feints and jabs of a Charles Bluhdorn or the convoluted manipulations practiced by James Ling.

Geneen had a nose for bargains every bit as keen as that of Royal Little, but he was no piker and was prepared to pay full value for properties. International Telephone & Telegraph, his great creation (or recreation, in both senses of the word) had solid underpinnings, which was more than could be said of Litton; its earnings advances were based upon achievements, not bookkeeping tricks. In these respects Geneen indeed was outstanding, and even now those who despise the man and consider him a malevolent influence concede as much.

Hatred arose from perceptions of Geneen as a man willing to bend the law so as to benefit his corporation, prepared to corrupt officials and even to participate in the overthrow of a government for the sake of ITT. Much of this can be shown to be quite exaggerated or simply false, yet the image persists, in part due to Geneen's personality, but also because there was more than a bit of truth in several of the allegations, and the problems were compounded by blunders at the highest corporate level. For all of his supposed shrewdness, Geneen possessed an uncanny knack (matched in this regard by Richard Nixon, to whom he often was compared) of shooting himself in the foot. So it was that to many reformers

ITT became the symbol of the evils and excesses of American corporations. Ralph Nader attacked ITT, not Litton or Textron, in his critique of conglomerates. The Justice Department paid as much if not more attention to Geneen's takeovers than to those of Ling or Bluhdorn, though for the most part his were "cleaner," and in only one case was a true contest mounted. When the time came for journalist Anthony Sampson to single out the one firm to serve as a scapegoat for business excesses he turned to the biggest target, and wrote *The Sovereign State of ITT,* published in 1973, when the corporation was under siege. Rarely had an author been so favored by events with so ripe a publication date. Today many of Geneen's real accomplishments have been forgotten. But the image of an amoral entrepreneur using ITT's considerable muscle to exercise his will remains, annealed in the public perception.

Only the sketchiest of information is available regarding Harold Sydney Geneen's early years, and he doesn't welcome inquiries on the subject. There seems to be nothing of consequence to hide, but rather the outlines of a life that was more bleak than those of most of the other conglomerators, and of a person who later compensated mightily for what appears to have been a deeply ingrained feeling of inferiority and inadequacy.[1]

Geneen was born on January 22, 1910, in the seaside resort town of Bournemouth, not far from London. His father, S. Alexander Geneen, was a small-time impresario who booked vaudeville acts and the like, and who made no discernible impact on the show business world of his time. In any case he abandoned the family before Harold was five years old, and could not have made much of an impression on the boy. In common with all of the other great conglomerators of the post-World War II period, Geneen was an outsider from a broken home, and like Little, Thornton, and Ling, was raised by his mother.

Aida DeCruciani Geneen, who emigrated with her husband and children to the United States when Harold was a year old, was an independent and strong-willed woman, who made a fairly comfortable living as a singer. Due to her need to be on the road much of the time she placed Harold and his younger sister Eva in boarding schools. Aida saw little of her children while they were growing up, yet Harold always thought warmly of her, and he was closer to her than to anyone else he ever would know.

In 1917, at which time he was seven years old, Harold was enrolled at the Suffield Academy in Connecticut, where he would remain for the next nine years. A small, shy, unathletic boy, he had few friends there, and became even more withdrawn. Rarely could he turn to his mother for help, for she was busiest during the holidays, and when the other boys went home, more often than not Harold remained in the dormitory or was sent to summer camp.

Graduating from Suffield in 1926, Geneen took a job as a runner at the New York Stock Exchange, while taking business courses at New York University at night. This was somewhat unusual for graduates of private academies, who generally aimed for the Ivy League. Perhaps Aida Geneen suffered a financial reversal in the mid-1920s, or Harold lacked the interest to attend college full time. Later Geneen would imply that the former was true. He once told a reporter of having subsisted on meals of taffy and bread. "They had one cent sales on taffy, two pounds for 9 cents, and bread filled me up."

That he was ambitious was obvious. This was the heyday of the bull market on Wall Street, and Geneen was delivering messages to some of its stars. The way upward was clear: experience at the Exchange combined with a degree from N.Y.U. would enable him to step forth when opportunities beckoned. Already his foot was on the first rung of the ladder of success—soon he would start climbing and by dint of hard work, pluck, and luck might get to the top. Not by means of a dazzling intellect, for in this period Geneen doubted his own abilities; instead, he would succeed by working twice as hard as anyone else.

If James Ling bore some resemblance to Jay Gatsby, Harold Geneen was an amalgam of all the heroes ever created by Horatio Alger.

The crash of 1929 shattered this dream, as along with thousands of others on Wall Street Geneen lost his job. For a while he worked as a salesman for the *New York World Telegram* and then as a junior accountant for Mayflower Associates. There were other low-paying, usually temporary jobs for him in the 1930s. Meanwhile Geneen plugged away at his business courses at night school. He also married, though when and to whom is one of Geneen's guarded secrets. But the marriage failed, and the Geneens were divorced in 1946.

Geneen received his degree in accounting in 1935, a year when the economic picture was brightening but the unemployment rate remained over 20 percent. He applied for junior jobs at several firms, willing to accept almost any salary just to get a start. Fortunately, there was an opening at Lybrand, Ross Brothers, one of America's top accounting firms. When asked how much money he expected Geneen asked for a salary of $20 per week and later said he would have taken less. As it happened Lybrand Ross's minimum was $30, which was what he received.

This was a turning point of sorts for Geneen, not so much in terms of career, but in the way his personality started to change. He would spend seven years with Lybrand, Ross, during which his shyness and lack of self-confidence was replaced first by feelings of self-esteem, and then by cockiness. As an auditor he would analyze the books of many corporations, learning how they operated and seeing the result of both well-considered and foolish programs—and in the late 1930s there were more of the latter than of the former. Geneen learned to recognize errors in judgment, at first in retrospect, but later in prospect as well, and he wondered how supposedly adept executives—with salaries many times that of his—could err so badly. By observing the mistakes of others Geneen not only was obtaining an invaluable postgraduate course in management, but in addition was becoming more secure in his sense of his own worth. He became aware that in many respects he was more astute than the people whose books he was auditing.

One of his accounts was American Can, which on the eve of America's entry into World War II had received a contract to manufacture naval torpedoes, but had no idea of how to structure its operations for the task. Geneen came into the discussions, primarily to provide cost estimates, and he created an organizational blueprint which was quickly adopted. This led to an offer of a top accounting post at American Can, which Geneen accepted.

Now Geneen obtained his initial exposure to management in practice. Participating in negotiations with government and union officials as well as with counterparts elsewhere in industry he honed his talents and after a while offered suggestions for long-term objectives as well as financial operations. He could see American Can evolving into a multi-industry concern, drawing away from what to him seemed the stodgy business of turning out a line of tin cans and other containers.

All of his suggestions were ignored by top management. These were men who had devoted their lives to a single company, or at most several firms in the same field. They were uncomfortable with defense work and yearned to settle down into the old groove after the war. By then Geneen knew there was no future for him at such a concern. This was also during the time that his marriage was breaking up, and he might have wanted a change for personal reasons.

Geneen left American Can in 1946 to become controller at Bell & Howell, which then was a minor factor in the camera business. The firm was controlled by Joseph McNab, an elderly and ailing man. Geneen clearly wanted to succeed McNab, but won few allies with his hard-driving personality and growing intolerance of inept performance. Now in his late 30s, he was ready for the top post somewhere, but he couldn't convince the Bell & Howell people to give him the job there. McNab died in 1949 and was succeeded by Charles Percy. Knowing he could not hope for power in that company, Geneen left, but not before marrying his secretary, June Elizabeth Hjelm.

Now Geneen became controller at Jones & Laughlin, the company that a generation later would become the centerpiece for Ling-Temco-Vought, and which at that time was the nation's fourth largest steel company. J & L's physical plant was run-down and operations were generally flabby. Geneen was there to tighten controls, eliminate inefficiencies, and help refinance the long-term debt. All of this was done and, aided by the economic boost provided by the Korean War, the company went on to post high profits. Geneen received some of the credit for this, and as a reward was given a vice-presidency and enlarged responsibilities.

He wasn't to remain long at J & L, however. Geneen was an oddity in an industry noted for its clubbiness and suspicion of outsiders. He argued for diversification, and that was an unwelcome prospect to men who were dedicated to steel, who had no experience in other industries, and who had no desire to change. Geneen encountered more opposition there than he had known at either American Can or Bell & Howell. Utterly frustrated, he looked for another post.

In 1956, while attending a management seminar at Harvard, Geneen learned of an opening for a financial vice president at Raytheon, then a medium-sized electronics company that specialized in military products. He applied for the position, made a favorable impression on President Charles Francis Adams, Jr., and was hired. Not only would he be responsible for financial matters, but Geneen also took on direct managerial responsibilities as executive vice-president.

Geneen entered into the kind of love-hate relationship with Charles Francis Adams one sometimes encounters at large American corporations, in which one person defends the status quo and his own position while the other wants rapid change and added power. Both have positions of authority, yet they have to work with one another. The situation bore a resemblance of sorts to that at Hughes Aircraft, where Howard Hughes and Tex Thornton respected one another's abilities, but neither could accept the other's ideas for the company's future.

Adams was quite different from Hughes, but no less determined to have his way with Raytheon, which he meant to continue as a supplier of military ordnance. There was a great deal of American history in his name. A descendent of two American presidents as well as scholars and diplomats, he had excellent contacts in Washington and on Wall Street. Adams hoped to use these to bring new business to Raytheon, and he looked to Geneen as an ideal plant manager who would see that the products were turned out at the proper price and delivered on time.

For a while it seemed that the idea might work. Geneen shook up the company, nudging deadwood elsewhere and bringing in sharp new talents. Productivity and efficiency improved, but at a price. The atmosphere at Raytheon became superheated; few could stand the fast pace

Geneen set, and there were defections as he created antagonisms and made enemies. Adams saw what was happening, but didn't interfere. Geneen was bringing about necessary changes, he thought, and he was willing to let it go at that for the time being. Far too self-assured to be cowed by his executive vice-president, Adams nonetheless was not one of his ardent admirers.

At the heart of Geneen's reorganization was the establishment of a divisional structure somewhat similar to that created for General Motors by Alfred Sloan in the 1920s. Geneen established twelve semi-autonomous units, each with its own manager, and all reporting directly to him. There would be formal monthly meetings, at which each manager reported and "performed." These occasionally degenerated into brutal affairs, with Geneen entirely capable of humiliating those who weren't well prepared or who turned in bad results. Several of the survivors later claimed that this could be an edifying experience, goading them to higher levels of excellence. Geneen rewarded them with promotions, salary increases, and added responsibilities. Others who failed or who could not stand the pace might resign, ask for reassignment, or be fired. (But not by Geneen. Despite his apparent ruthlessness, he had difficulty telling a man to his face that he had to go.) And Geneen himself was rewarded. In late 1957 the corporation created an "office of the president," comprised of Adams, senior vice-president Percy Spencer, and Geneen, who in addition obtained a seat on the board.

Raytheon was about to undergo a period of rapid growth. Led by Adams, the corporation's Washington staff obtained several major missile contracts, while Geneen made certain that they could be delivered upon. In the immediate post-Korean War period revenues had fluctuated between $175 million and $182 million, with a profit peak of $4.5 million in 1954. Now they rose sharply. Revenues were a record $259 million in 1957 and earnings, $4.8 million. For 1958 the figures were $375 million and $9.4 million, and the following year—when Raytheon was listed 90th on the Fortune 500 list—they would be $494 million and $10.5 million.

Geneen was perfectly content to receive most of the credit for this showing, as newspapers ran stories about this new production genius, several of which appear to have been planted. While this rankled some at headquarters, Adams let it pass. After all, Geneen was performing superbly at his tasks, and was of no threat to Adams, who in addition to being president also was chief operating and executive officer and in firm control of the board. Geneen appreciated this, and started casting about for another position.

Occasionally he spoke of his ambitions with his few close associates, and almost always these involved leadership of a major enterprise. Unlike Thornton, Bluhdorn, and Ling, he had no intention of starting small and creating a giant corporation from a single seed. There was virtually nothing of the entrepreneur about Geneen, then or later on, and he seemed to know his limitations. Rather, he had become an expert in dissecting ailing large firms, presenting a diagnosis, and then acting upon it to transform a stale operation into a vital one. This was what he had hoped to do at J & L and Bell & Howell, and what he had succeeded in accomplishing at Raytheon. His job there had been completed by 1958, and Geneen was eager for a new challenge, one in which he would have complete authority.[2]

It was in this period that International Telephone & Telegraph was searching for a new leader. During the mid-1950s the corporation had been rent by a struggle between two factions, one supporting Chairman Sosthenes Behn, who had founded ITT in 1920, and the other an insurgent group behind President William Henry Harrison, who had been brought in to help revive the ailing domestic business. Harrison died suddenly in 1956, and after Behn's attempt to regain power failed the board selected an interim leader, Edmund Leavey, and then searched for someone to take over permanently. Geneen was a natural for the job, and the announcement of his selection came on May 20, 1959. Wall Street's reaction was prompt. Raytheon common lost 6½ points, shaving some $19 million from the total value of the shares, while ITT rose by only half a point. This might be interpreted as meaning the market believed the former company would suffer from Geneen's departure but wasn't at all certain what he would do for ITT.

Of course Geneen didn't doubt his abilities, and later took credit for having saved a collapsing firm from utter extinction. "There's a question how long it would have gone on before it cracked wide open," he said less than two years after taking over. "If this had gone on for three or five more years, maybe no one could have brought it back."[3]

That simply wasn't the case. Although ITT was a loose, poorly coordinated corporation in need of overhaul, it hardly was at the point of dissolution. In fact it possessed elements of genuine strength that were recognized within the industry and on Wall Street. ITT never was in danger of collapsing. Rather, it was a declining corporation that could have gone on that way for a decade or more, growing sluggishly, increasing its assets but not earnings in any significant way. This is a picture of a prime takeover candidate, a firm that might be acquired and then deployed by Ling, ensnared by Bluhdorn, or gobbled up by Thornton to become the heart of some new Litton division. Geneen's contribution was to halt this decay and reshape ITT, to turn it into a pursuer rather than one of the pursued.

The numbers tell part of the story. In 1959 ITT would report revenues of $765 million, placing the corporation in the 52nd slot on the Fortune

500, just below Jones & Laughlin and B. F. Goodrich but above Caterpillar Tractor and National Steel. Revenues had tripled over the past decade, but earnings had not kept pace. Profits that year were $29 million, which worked out to a 3.8 percent return on sales and 7 percent on invested capital, one of the worst showings in the industry. But the balance sheet was in good shape; by year's end total current assets were $471 million and current liabilities, $249 million, hardly a dangerous ratio and certainly not that of a corporation on the verge of collapse. In 1950 ITT's working capital had been $120 million; in 1959, the figure was $222 million.

Nor were ITT's prospects unrecognized on Wall Street. The corporation's stock had doubled in 1958—the year before Geneen's arrival—far outdistancing the Dow Jones Industrials, which rose by slightly more than 20 percent in the same period. That December, Leavey had announced a two-for-one split, and the dividend was boosted the following March. At one point in 1950 ITT common sold for less than ten; the stock peaked at 65 in late 1958, prior to the announcement of Geneen's impending arrival. Contrary to the impression he so assiduously tried to give the press and the business community, the board had not turned to Geneen out of desperation.

ITT's major problems in late 1958 were a lack of focus and direction, an inability to come to terms with what it was, and an unclear idea of what it might become. Originally intended as a global equivalent of American Telephone & Telegraph, by the late 1920s ITT had operating telephone companies in Europe and Latin America, a worldwide cable operation, and a holding company (International Standard Electric) that owned factories that turned out telephonic and telegraphic equipment. The corporation came close to bankruptcy several times during the 1930s, and some of its plants and telephone companies suffered confiscation during World War II. It was then that Behn and his associates decided to concentrate upon the American market, first by producing for the military and then, after the war, specializing in consumer durables. Almost from scratch Behn created Federal Electric, which by 1945 had become one of the nation's most important manufacturers of military telecommunications gear. Using the profits from this business together with the proceeds from the sale of foreign holdings he purchased such well-known firms as Farnsworth Television & Radio, Capehart Radio, and the Coolerator Co., hoping that when combined with Federal and several other properties they would establish ITT as a major domestic concern.

It didn't work out according to plan. ITT had no experience in competitive markets such as those for television sets, radios, refrigerators, and air conditioners; the firm stumbled badly. Federal was unable to maintain its wartime momentum. Harrison, who had been brought in from Western Electric to run the domestic businesses, failed to turn them around. This, then, was ITT's major weakness in 1959.

The overseas operations of International Standard Electric presented a far brighter picture. Its British company, Standard Telephones & Cables, received important contracts for the manufacture and installation of telephonic equipment in that country. France's Compagnie Général de Constructions Téléphoniques and Le Materiel Téléphonique developed new switching equipment technically advanced beyond anything yet known. In Germany, Standard Elektrik Lorenz literally rose from the ashes to become one of the fastest growing concerns in all of Europe, while the Belgian operation, Bell Telephone Manufacturing, did almost as well. In early 1959 ISE was a $500 million a year corporation, accounting for almost three-quarters of ITT's revenues and the bulk of its profits. By then ITT had assets of close to $400 million, of which only $84 million was in the United States.

This was the problem. Having been so badly scarred by confiscations during World War II Behn had struggled to create a domestic corporation. Meanwhile the European components flourished. The ITT board hoped that Geneen might succeed where both Behn and Harrison had failed, and while he agreed that this would be one of his primary tasks, he had an agenda of his own to pursue.

He also had a clear idea of who could best help him achieve it. That Geneen had a low regard for many old-time ITT managers became obvious even before he arrived at headquarters, when he announced that several of his Raytheon associates would be joining him. One of these was William Marx, who was to be senior vice-president. Geneen said that Marx would have the "important assignment of integrating our widespread global staff activities with our area line managements, as well as responsibility for our personnel, planning, and organization functions." That was a roundabout, bureaucratic way of saying that Marx was supposed to rid ITT of those executives who either could not or would not accept Geneen's plans and discipline, or who were unable to maintain the kind of pace he insisted upon. Moreover, Marx was to search out promising, aggressive men within the organization and at other corporations and place them in positions where they would be both responsible and visible. Promotions for those who passed muster would be rapid; the others would be demoted or dismissed.[4]

Marx helped engineer one of the most rapid management shifts at a large corporation in recent history. By early 1964, after less than five years in command, Geneen was able to boast of a "dynamic management team" of 728 executives, and of this number 118 had arrived during his tenure, and an additional 131 were promoted from within the system.

Approximately one out of every three top executives had replaced men appointed by Behn, Harrison, and Leavey, or they held newly created positions.[5]

Just as Thornton had his Lidos, so ITT developed a roster of graduates from what some reporters called "Geneen University." With Marx as admissions officer and Geneen the professor, ITT became a school for executives who, after surviving the course, would be hired to head some other corporation in the hope that they would infuse it with some of the "Geneen magic." Such was his reputation by the mid-1960s.

During his first three or four years in office Geneen concentrated on tightening controls, pruning some hopeless subsidiaries, and infusing ITT with a new aggressive spirit. He talked about doubling ITT's revenues and profits within five years, with most of the growth expected to come from a thorough revamping of the domestic units. There was little thought of acquisitions in this period, and not a hint of plans for widespread diversification in Geneen's public statements or interviews with reporters.

Instead, what one reporter later dubbed "The Geneen Machine" shook up ITT's somnolent American companies. Led by Louis Rader, formerly a General Electric executive and now group vice-president with special responsibilities for domestic commercial markets, a team of newcomers worked its way through Federal, discovering duplication of effort and inefficiencies. A recent arrival from Temco, Nevin Palley, was sent to Federal with a broad mandate to reduce costs and restructure procedures. Known as a hard-bitten engineer who kept a bullwhip on his office wall, Palley reduced employment from 7,300 to 6,300, eliminated several hopeless projects, reduced inventories, and within a year turned the company around.[6]

Shortly after taking office Geneen embarked on the first of several European inspection tours. Usually with Marx at his side, he would rush through factories and laboratories, asking questions, absorbing information, and trying to locate flaws in operations. Geneen immediately realized that the companies there were in far better shape than the domestic operations, but were laboring under what to him seemed an outmoded and crippling heritage from the old regime—intense nationalism that mitigated against cooperation and coordination of efforts.

Each of the ISE companies concentrated upon a single customer, the post office of its host country, which was responsible for operating its national telephone system. Thus, Standard Elektrik Lorenz wooed the Bundespost, and as part of a consortium headed by Siemens was virtually assured of a segment of the German business; similar situations existed in the United Kingdom, France, and elsewhere. Bell Telephone Manufacturing was somewhat different in that it had developed into an aggressive merchandiser beyond Europe, but this was due more to the small size of the Belgian market than to anything else. Each ISE firm stayed out of the others' backyards, and there was little contact, much less cooperation, between them. Thus, SEL was on more intimate terms with Siemens than with Standard Telephones & Cables.

Geneen hoped to break down this isolation and make at least a start toward integration of effort. He appreciated that each unit would have to remain bound to its one major customer, but he saw no compelling reason why there shouldn't be a greater sharing of information and cross-licensing of patents. In effect, he was trying to create an ITT—or at least an ISE—spirit and sentiment in Europe where none really existed. For the first time managing directors of the national companies came together to present reports and to discuss projects and plans. One of those who attended an early session recalled the atmosphere at the time. "You could sense the gasp spreading around the table. The French couldn't conceive of giving the Germans information, the Germans giving the British information, etc. This was a whole new ball game."

It didn't work. When forced to do so the national managers would meet with one another and listen to reports. Geneen's requests for information couldn't be ignored, but they were complied with reluctantly and with a minimal effort. His hopes for integration never really faded, but after a while Geneen turned to other matters that had higher priority. This did not mean Europe would be ignored; on the contrary, ISE's share of development funds actually increased in the early 1960s.

In the 1962 annual report Geneen noted the completion of 15 new facilities, all but two of which were in Europe, and each initiated by his predecessors. Then he announced his own construction program. There would be six projects in Germany, five in the United Kingdom, and two each in Spain and Belgium, with others in France, the Netherlands, Portugal, Austria, and Sweden. "The major portion of our initial expansion is taking place in Europe," he explained, "to provide needed production increases in the fast-growing Common Market." ITT was also committed to a Puerto Rican facility for the manufacture of telephone equipment. Finally, there would be a single new domestic installation, one intended to expand the capabilities of Jennings Radio Manufacturing, which was one of Geneen's initial acquisitions.

Thus, Geneen expanded upon ITT's European legacy, but he did so with some reluctance. Ironically, this most famous of America's international executives did not feel comfortable dealing with foreigners. Geneen never developed the enthusiasm for the overseas businesses that he had for the domestic. For all of his scope, Geneen was surprisingly provincial. Bold and adventuresome on the American scene, he was cautious when it came to Europe and crudely jingoistic in regard to Latin

America. This narrowness intensified when Fidel Castro seized an ITT subsidiary, Cuban Telephone, and soon after Geneen had to fight the nationalization of several Brazilian properties. He feared a Communist takeover in France and Italy, with subsequent expropriations of ISE units there as well. He would approve the purchase of small companies on the continent, especially in the early years, when business was expanding at a rapid rate, but he rejected the notion of acquiring large firms that would dramatically alter ITT's situation there. Significantly, his one major European takeover was of Alfred Teves, a German-based manufacturer of original parts for automobiles. Geneen often expressed the belief that alone of the West European countries, Germany would stand strong against both communism and socialism.

There were few takeovers of any kind during those early years, and none of these represented a change of direction for ITT. Rather, Geneen started out like the other conglomerators by purchasing companies that manufactured products that fit in with those already being turned out. For example, there was L. C. Miller, a minor factor in the electromagnetic vibration equipment business, and a telephone company based in the Virgin Islands. In 1961 ITT purchased Jennings, Suprenant Manufacturing (a producer of wire and cable), and Alpina Buromachinen (a German manufacturer of telephonic equipment). Six small European firms were added in 1962, all of which augmented existing operations. In addition Geneen purchased one domestic company, National Computer Products, which despite its name specialized in electronic components.

That year ITT's revenues passed the $1 billion mark for the first time, placing the corporation in the 41st slot on the Fortune 500. Yet the growth rate during these first three Geneen years hadn't been appreciably greater than it had been from 1956 to 1958, when first Harrison and then Leavey had been in command. Nor was there any dramatic change in profit margins. The price of ITT common advanced, going from 32 (adjusted for a two-for-one stock split in early 1959) to 58 in early 1962, before it plunged to 33 later that year—but in so behaving it followed the general trend of the market. Yet Geneen still was credited with having transformed the company into an emerging giant. Newspapers and magazines carried stories of his idiosyncracies and brilliance, usually stressing his insistence upon results that would show up on the bottom line. In this period, however, ITT did not live up to its billing.

In late 1962 Geneen organized a task force charged with identifying likely takeover candidates. Rumors regarding forthcoming acquisitions—always in fields related to ITT's existing businesses—started appearing in the press and were heard on Wall Street. There still was no hint of a drive toward diversification. Yet the prospect was very much on Geneen's mind. He wanted growth and was ever aware of his promise to double revenues in his first five years: this would be the best way to do it. But there was more to it than that. Geneen was confident to the point of arrogance about his abilities to manage an enterprise—any one, in virtually any industry. Transforming ITT into a conglomerate would enable him to demonstrate this belief and justify his reputation. Moreover, diversification was a logical outgrowth of his ambition to strengthen the domestic business and lessen ITT's dependence upon the ISE companies. Finally, and perhaps most importantly, Geneen considered implementation of this strategy a way to shield his and other corporations from the vagaries of the business cycle. While Ling, Bluhdorn, and Thornton spoke of the excitement of entering new areas, in many of his public statements Geneen stressed the defensive elements of the strategy. In an internal document drawn up in early 1963, he summarized his purposes for diversification in a logical, almost geometrical, and essentially conservative fashion:

1. To diversify into industries and markets which have good prospects for above average long-term growth and profitability;

2. To achieve a sound balance between foreign earnings and domestic earnings;

3. To achieve a sound balance between high risk capital-intensive manufacturing operations and less risky service operations;

4. To achieve a sound balance between high risk engineering-labor-intensive electronics manufacturing and less risky commercial and industrial manufacturing;

5. To achieve a sound ratio between commercial/industrial products and services, and consumer products and services;

6. To achieve a sound ratio between government/defense/space operations and commercial/industrial/consumer products and services in both foreign and domestic markets; and

7. To achieve a sound balance between cyclical products and services.[7]

At first glance this appears the kind of program that might have been conceived by some detached philosopher of business rather than by a leading practitioner. On closer examination, however, it may be interpreted as a rationalization for the same kind of large scale diversification utilized by other managers attempting to enter new industries. Virtually any company Geneen might have acquired could be justified under one or more of the seven points. But he would not have budged without first carefully setting down his thoughts. This was as much part of his style as financial pyrotechnics were to Ling, airy talk of synergy was to Thornton, and raiding was to Bluhdorn.

In reality Geneen did not set about creating his new ITT from a collection of blueprints or a vast design. The seven points were objectives and desiderata, not a strategy or set of tactics. Like the others, Geneen would enter the movement gradually, over a period of several years, and even now it is difficult to identify the specific steps by which ITT became a conglomerate. He was as opportunistic as any of the others, usually trying to select the most promising candidates from among those companies that came his way or were singled out by his acquisitions people. But there was one significant complication: early in the game Geneen and ITT became a special target for reformers both in and out of government.

The pace of acquisitions picked up in 1963, with most of the newcomers involved directly or peripherally with telecommunications. There wasn't anything unusual in this; Geneen seemed intent on obtaining technologies, plants, and work forces to augment existing operations at a time when business was booming. ITT was issuing more common and preferred shares in exchange for assets, an already quite familiar practice. Geneen was impressive, but hardly spectacular.

Three of the takeovers did break the mold, and although it didn't create much of a stir at the time, their acquisition might be interpreted as Geneen's entry into the conglomerate camp. First came General Controls, a manufacturer of a wide variety of automatic control devices, most of which were used in household appliances. Then there was Bell & Gossett, the country's largest producer of industrial and commercial pumps. Finally, ITT purchased Nesbitt, which specialized in turning out heating, ventilating, and air conditioning equipment for schools.

In explaining these acquisitions Geneen observed that they were part of his plan for balancing military sales from the domestic companies with revenues and earnings from the civilian sector. In addition, all three companies were involved in the production of climatizing equipment, and so there appeared a certain logic to taking them in together. But there was more to it than that. Geneen's fears of confiscation of ITT properties overseas had increased. In private meetings at headquarters he alluded to French plans to license the export of capital and to the growing anti-Americanism exhibited by President Charles de Gaulle. Italy was rent by a wave of strikes and was headed leftward. In the United Kingdom the Labour Party was considering an ambitious program of nationalizing several large companies, including Standard Telephones & Cables. Geneen also feared the consequences for the ISE companies of a greater economic integration of the Common Market. ITT would have to expand its domestic operations rapidly if the corporation was not to be crushed by one or more of these blows. The seizure of ITT's overseas properties during World War II had almost destroyed Behn. Geneen was intent on making certain that it didn't happen to him.

In 1964 Geneen made a more dramatic move toward transforming ITT into a conglomerate. In exchange for nearly $40 million in common and preferred shares he obtained Aetna Finance, a consumer-based organization with activities in half the nation's states; its assets were more than $90 million. Then he purchased a half interest in Great International Life Insurance, which was based in the United Kingdom. To these he added several credit operations at the domestic companies, and out of this came ITT Financial Services, a new subsidiary. There wasn't much glamour in finance and insurance companies during the early 1960s, however, and the Aetna takeover was interpreted by Wall Streeters as little more than a prudent purchase at a reasonable price.

In early 1965 Geneen announced that revenues for the previous year had been $1.5 billion, against $766 million in 1959; he had delivered on the pledge to double the size of ITT in five years. Several analysts suggested that this was the real reason for the acquisitions—vanity, not sound business. Net income rose from $29 million to $63.1 million in this period, but earnings per share had gone from $1.90 to $3.11, a lower percentage increase owing to the issuance of additional shares to pay for the acquisitions. The 15.5 million shares of 1959 had grown to 19.3 million five years later—a disturbing degree of equity dilution without a dramatic alteration of the corporation's fortunes and image.

The investment community still did not perceive ITT common as a glamour stock. While earnings and dividends were boosted and the price/earnings ratio rose, ITT's shares weren't in the same class as those of Xerox, Polaroid, Texas Instruments, or Litton, where Geneen thought they belonged. The stock seemed conventional, rising and falling in harmony with the Dow Jones Industrials. Geneen yearned for a strong rally in the shares, not only as a vote of confidence in his leadership but in order to use them for major purchases without undue dilution. He vowed to alter the stock's image over the next decade, during which he anticipated another doubling of revenues and earnings. This could be accomplished only by means of takeovers, and of the kind that would excite Wall Street's imagination.

Geneen needn't have taken the path of large scale diversification. With its solid base in telecommunications ITT could have sought only firms in the same or related fields. But widespread diversification was in tune with Geneen's developing concept of the corporation and his own personality. For a while he would try to pursue both goals and it was only after disappointment in the first that he turned to the second. In 1965 he found the right person to lead him down that path.

Early in the year Geneen's attention was drawn to Avis, Inc., which was less than a quarter the size of Hertz, but was the fastest growing company in the auto leasing business. Avis was in need of continual refinancing, and so would fit in well with the Financial Services unit. Out of auto leasing could come other acquisitions, the most obvious being parking lots, hotels and motels, and credit cards. Geneen was intrigued, and ordered his staff to go ahead with the deal.

Although Avis was a publicly owned company, nearly a third of its shares were held by the investment banking firm of Lazard Frères & Co., which was brought into the discussions at an early stage. Representing the Lazard interests was Felix Rohatyn, then 37 years old and a partner since 1961. Considered one of the shrewdest acquisitions men in the field and a special protégé of senior partner André Meyer, Rohatyn impressed Geneen with his astuteness, bargaining ability, and polish. Some later said that Rohatyn absolutely mesmerized Geneen, and from then on he was a major factor in ITT's development, bringing in most of the big acquisitions for Geneen's approval, in effect deciding the direction he would take. This story is rather exaggerated—Geneen was too strong and intelligent a person to play Trilby to anyone's Svengali—but Rohatyn's influence did grow. He joined the ITT board soon after; from there he was ideally suited to play the role of acquisitions consultant.

Avis was acquired for $55.7 million in ITT common and preferred shares, making it Geneen's most expensive takeover to then (Lazard's fee for this operation was $135,000). Rohatyn then presided over the purchase of Airport Parking, and a number of related companies followed—National Auto Rental, National Truck Rental, Mears Motor Livery, and Yellow Cab of Kansas City among others. In 1967 ITT made an initial foray into motels by purchasing Cleveland Motor Inns; the beachhead was fortified, and ITT had entered a new industry.

While acquiring additional finance-related firms and adding to the core provided by Avis, Geneen also sought new areas. One of these was publishing, wholly unrelated to any previous ITT business. In 1966 he purchased Howard S. Sams, a midwestern complex best known for its trade and text subsidiary, Bobbs-Merrill. Sams was expanding rapidly and it needed the kind of cash infusion Geneen was prepared to offer. Other conglomerates and some old-line companies were buying publishing houses in this period; there was much talk then of a "knowledge explosion" and publishing companies were in vogue. Litton had acquired American Book, which Thornton characteristically promised would be in the vanguard of high technology publishing. Geneen was also in character by viewing Sams as a base from which to expand vertically.

Books were sold in stores and used in schools. Concluding that the latter was a more reliable (and captive) market, he set about acquiring secretarial and vocational schools. Scarcely a month went by during the next three years in which ITT wasn't investigating, negotiating for, or purchasing one or more schools. Most were small, local affairs, and ITT's commitment to publishing and education was never very important. More than anything else, it was an indication of the vast reach Geneen was developing, and where he intended to lead the corporation.

More important than any of this—finance, auto rentals, publishing— was the merger that failed. Had ITT acquired the American Broadcasting Companies, a firm that Geneen fairly ached to possess, the corporation's history would have been radically different from what it became, as would the reputation of its CEO.

ITT and ABC had dallied with one another before, when in 1951 Behn and ABC's President Edward Noble came close to uniting to create a major telecommunications-entertainment enterprise. The match of ITT's Capehart, Farnsworth, and Federal units with the nation's third largest television network was close to being ideal. Had it come about ITT-ABC would have resembled RCA, which also was in electronics and broadcasting. One company would have fed into the other, with more magical synergy than would be shown in diversification. Negotiations broke down, however, and two years later ABC merged with United Paramount Pictures.

Whether or not Geneen knew of Behn's aborted merger attempt is unknown, but in 1963 he ordered a survey of the broadcasting industry. There was much talk of a takeover of Gross, Corinthian, Storer, or some other small network, but nothing came of it. Then Geneen concentrated on bigger game—none other than Columbia Broadcasting. But before he could make a move in that direction he learned that ABC might be had for a reasonable price.

In that period, prior to his association with Rohatyn, Geneen utilized the services of several "finders" or "marriage brokers" in locating, negotiating for, and finally acquiring companies for ITT. One of these was Gerald Tsai, who was a well-known mutual fund manager for the Fidelity Group. In 1964 Tsai's Fidelity Capital Fund had a large block of ITT in its portfolio as well as shares of ABC. He knew that the network had been approached about the possibility of a takeover by West Coast industrialist Norton Simon, who had developed Hunt Foods & Industries into a wide ranging conglomerate and who now hoped to enter broadcasting. ABC's President Leonard Goldenson had developed a marked dislike for Simon, who had already started purchasing shares in the open market and who was demanding representation on the Board. Needing a savior desperately, Goldenson had approached General Electric, and

General Telephone & Electronics, but neither was receptive. Litton was interested, but lacked the muscle to make the move. In December 1964, Tsai suggested that Goldenson consider a merger with ITT. The ABC president reacted favorably; he asked Tsai to act as go-between, and soon after met with Geneen to explore the possibilities.

This would be no small move on Geneen's part. The asking price for ABC was in the neighborhood of $250 million, which would require a considerable dilution of equity and a probable decline in ITT's per-share earnings. And it appeared that Geneen would have to slug it out with Norton Simon. Most important, such a merger would require approval by the Federal Communications Commission, which would entangle Geneen with Washington's bureaucrats, a breed for which he had often expressed contempt.

Nonetheless, he went ahead. The announcement of the ITT-ABC merger was finally made on December 7, 1965. The terms called for an exchange of stock, and although the actual dollar figure could not be determined until later, it worked out to around $200 million in ITT paper. Geneen had gotten the price down, but ABC was no bargain, nor was it so perceived on Wall Street. When rumors of the takeover appeared ABC common was selling in the high 50s. By early December, after the announcement, it shot up to 74, and added a dozen more points within the next three months, while ITT traded in a narrow range.

It doesn't require much imagination to see why Goldenson and ABC's shareholders wanted such a merger. More interesting is what Geneen expected from it.

As had Behn, Geneen considered television a major growth industry and an important outlet for ITT's technological and managerial capabilities. In conversations and interviews he spoke of the possibility of using ABC's facilities to transmit business correspondence during the off-hours, and of a world-wide network bouncing signals off space satellites. Even before consummating the merger he committed $7 million to construct six cable television systems, which were then used to bring existing programs into fringe areas where reception was poor. An additional $10 million was budgeted for this purpose in early 1966, by which time Geneen was considering the purchase of more than 20 other cable operations at a cost of more than $100 million. ITT was also exploring the possibilities of pay television and television in theaters.

Geneen's thinking was years ahead of most executives already in the industry. Doubtless he had given the matter much study and effort, concentrating upon it to the exclusion of some of his other enterprises. Had the merger taken place Geneen would have transformed himself into a show business figure. And he liked the idea of becoming something of a celebrity, shuttling back and forth between New York and Hollywood, mixing with directors and artists, deciding what the public should view on television. Only a few months earlier he had been deeply concerned with rental cars and the future for submersible pumps. Now he was expounding on the virtues of "Batman," one of ABC's most successful programs, and wondering how to build upon it.[9]

The ITT-ABC combination would have had revenues of $2.2 billion, making it larger than RCA-NBC, and shaking up the industry as never before. CBS would have become the smallest of the three, and within weeks of the ITT-ABC announcement came rumors of a marriage between CBS and General Electric, which might have set off sparks between RCA and some other giant. As analysts wondered where it all might end ITT became an interesting holding, and the price of its shares inched up. That was reason enough for Geneen to want the acquisition to succeed. ITT was now becoming a well-known corporation, basking in instant recognition, which helped give its stock a higher multiple.

Geneen believed visibility to be one of the key ingredients in a firm's success, and now because of ABC, ITT was receiving its proper share. "You can stop 15 people in the street and not one will know what ITT is," he once told a *Time* reporter. "That bothers me. We have to get identification through products or companies." He was irritated that people who knew about Avis hadn't heard of its parent; ABC would alter this situation and enable the company to raise its prices. On one occasion Geneen was shown a new electronic device turned out by an ISE subsidiary. When told it would sell for $30, he shot back that if the letters on it were IBM instead of ITT it could have fetched twice as much. If true, this alone would have justified the ABC price tag.

If it were only up to the Justice Department and the Federal Trade Commission the merger might have sailed through with little difficulty. But the Federal Communications Commission had jurisdiction in the matter, and its mandate was far broader than those of the other two agencies. Not only might the FCC reject a takeover if the merger tended to lessen competition, but it might do so simply if a majority of the commissioners decided that the takeover was not in the public interest— which could be interpreted to mean just about anything. The FCC had this power because the airwaves belonged to the entire nation, with broadcasters using them on sufferance only so long as they hewed to the FCC's well-monitored standards of conduct. The line between the acceptable and unacceptable was fuzzy in the mid-1960s, as it had been since the agency was chartered.

Representatives of both corporations appeared before the FCC in September to present their cases. Goldenson inferred that ABC was on the edge of bankruptcy, and in addition needed at least $140 million in new funds to convert to full-time telecasting, erect new studios, and in general keep up with its two major rivals. ITT was willing to provide this much and more, said Geneen. To allay fears of undue influence on the network, he testified that ITT would enter into an arms-length relationship with ABC. Although he didn't say as much, the model for all this would be the situation already existing between RCA and NBC, which the commission had never challenged. The corporations made a strong case and for a while appeared to have favorably impressed enough commission members to make the merger possible.

The situation changed dramatically in late September and early October. Senator Gaylord Nelson (D-Wis.), who was chairman of the subcommittee on antitrust and monopoly, came out against the takeover alleging that it would lessen competition within the industry. Donald Turner, who headed the Justice Department's Antitrust Division, disagreed, and asked for new legislation before any action be taken. He was supported by Senate Majority Whip Russell Long (D-La.), while Attorney General Nicholas Katzenbach, the key figure in the decision, remained mute. But then Katzenbach resigned to take a post at IBM, and he was replaced by Ramsey Clark, a judicial activist with strong ties to prominent reformist organizations, who promptly supported Nelson's position. This brought him into conflict with Turner, and the two men jockeyed for position within the Justice Department in November and early December.[10]

It was against this murky background that the FCC handed down its decision on December 21st. The merger was approved by a vote of four to three. Ordinarily, the decision would have been considered final. ITT and ABC would have proceeded as planned, and Geneen would have wound up being a television executive.

The minority fought back, however. Led by Nicholas Johnson, the three challenged the decision, and sought a rationale with which to block it. A close ally of Ralph Nader and like him a critic of conglomerates and multinationals, Johnson called the action "a mockery of public responsibility." He took note of ITT's extensive overseas operations, and argued that Geneen could attempt to manage the news so as to benefit his interests. "Of all the large American corporations there are few whose particular business interests are so clearly of the type which should not be joined with major broadcasting facilities as are those of ITT." But Johnson could offer no evidence to support this generalization, while the majority noted that such hadn't been the case with other corporations—RCA and Westinghouse among others—engaged in both broadcasting and foreign business. Pressed hard on this point, Johnson observed that one ITT executive was a member of the French National Assembly while two more sat in the British House of Lords. As it turned out both were directors of ISE companies in their own countries, and had nothing directly to do with the parent. It was grasping at straws, as even the minority must have realized.[11]

Ramsey Clark now entered the picture, asking for a delay while he considered an action of his own to block the merger. Did the ITT-ABC merger violate any antitrust statute? Clark thought so, offering novel arguments in support of his contention. He noted that if ITT acquired ABC it would have to divest itself of all cable operations so as to hew to existing FCC regulations, and that if not this merger would lessen competition in that segment of the industry. He criticized the FCC for accepting at face value Goldenson's contention that ABC needed funding. On the contrary, said Clark, "rather than planning to invest large amounts in the capital improvements of ABC, ITT appears to have expected ABC to produce a large cash flow which would be available to use outside of the broadcasting industry." Such a charge was impossible to prove, but it was picked up by several reporters, and probably was instrumental in causing the FCC to reopen the hearings. In reporting the story, the *Wall Street Journal* observed that "the FCC's handling of the case has been attacked by the Justice Department's Antitrust Division, the American Civil Liberties Union, congressmen, journalists, and even auto safety critic Ralph Nader," all of which was true.[12] Not since the late 1930s had a corporation been singled out for so much criticism as ITT was during the ABC merger period.

The hearings began on April 10th and continued for two weeks. Both sides presented the same arguments as before, but there was a peripheral development that had an important bearing on the case. Several reporters testified to having been approached by ITT officials who complained that their coverage had been slanted. They told of threats, and of having been subjected to "nasty and accusatory language." One ITT employee had told *New York Times* business writer Eileen Shanahan that her reporting had been "unfair from the beginning."[13] Such testimony cast doubts on Geneen's claims that ITT wouldn't interfere with ABC news, but more important, it provided the press with additional ammunition to use against the corporation. From then on, in the eyes of a significant number of reporters and columnists ITT became the symbol of much that was wrong with American business.

The second round of hearings ended as the first—the FCC once again approved the merger by a four to three vote. As expected the minority returned to the attack and, together with Attorney General Clark, put pressure on Donald Turner at the Antitrust Division. Somewhat reluctantly, Turner announced on July 20 that proceedings would be instituted, and the stage was set for what promised to be a lengthy legal battle.

Neither Geneen nor Goldenson relished the idea of a fight; both were thoroughly disgusted and weary. They agreed to call off their merger and announced their decision on New Year's Day, 1968. The Antitrust Division then dropped its action, and the parties went their respective ways. ITT was not to be an electronics-entertainment company after all. Geneen set about dismantling his cable and other television operations, selling them off as rapidly as possible as if to rid ITT of everything that reminded him of this deep disappointment. And as though to compensate for this loss, he set about conglomeratizing as never before, gobbling up companies with verve at a pace that surpassed even that of Ling and Bluhdorn.

Mergermania had been accelerating through the early and mid-1960s; it peaked in 1968. That year ITT acquired 20 domestic concerns with combined assets approximating $1 billion at a cost of slightly more than that in securities and cash. In addition it purchased a handful of foreign companies while accelerating the development of properties already under the ITT banner. It was as though Geneen had elbowed his way into some giant smorgasbord (dished up by Rohatyn for the most part) and was piling his plate high with all sorts of interesting items. Under the circumstances it was little wonder that ITT later suffered from corporate indigestion.

The process actually began while Geneen was occupied with ABC. Through Rohatyn's good offices ITT learned that Levitt & Sons, the nation's premier home-building operation, whose 1965 revenues came to $60 million, was on the block. There were several obstacles to be overcome, however. William Levitt, the company's flamboyant and often erratic president, was willing to come to terms but insisted upon a high price, semi-autonomous authority within the ITT constellation, and a large amount of development capital to transform his company into a worldwide operation. Geneen wooed Levitt assiduously, but the builder realized that ITT was concentrating on ABC, and complained bitterly about delays in completing the deal. It was only after Levitt threatened to seek another partner or even transform his own firm into a conglomerate, that Geneen gave the signal to proceed. A merger was announced on July 22, 1967, with the completion date to be determined later.

Levitt & Sons would not become part of ITT until February 11, 1968, more than a month after the ABC merger was abandoned. The price came to slightly less than $92 million in ITT common, which was twice the amount that the stock market had valued Levitt & Sons before negotiations. Some on Wall Street assumed that Geneen had rushed into the takeover to slake his hunger after the ABC disappointment, and that Levitt had taken advantage of the man's demoralization by upping the price, but this really wasn't so. Geneen seemed truly convinced that home-building could be as glamorous as television, and he spoke expansively of Levitt's possibilities. The company was "the ideal vehicle for ITT to participate in the United States and abroad in the revolution in housing which will take place in the next decade and of which we intend to be a part." He spoke of projects on four continents and predicted that the company would have annual revenues of more than $1 billion by 1980. This would be made possible by infusing Levitt with the money previously earmarked for ABC. In that respect, perhaps, Levitt became a surrogate for ABC.

Geneen now engaged in the kind of expansion from a one subsidiary base he had earlier demonstrated in telecommunications, finance, and publishing, and that he was continuing in rental cars and parking lots. Sheraton Corporation of America, one of the world's largest hotel chains, provided a good fit for Avis on the one hand and Levitt on the other. But unlike the home-building firm, it was a stagnant, poorly operated concern, many of whose properties were run-down, outdated, and located in declining areas. While Levitt commanded a premium, Sheraton might be had for a knockdown price. In late 1966, when ITT first raised the idea of a takeover, Sheraton's revenues and assets each exceeded a quarter of a billion dollars, but the value of its common stock was less than $60 million. When the transaction was finally completed on February 28—slightly more than two weeks after the Levitt deal—the price in ITT paper came to $193 million, which was more than Wall Street had ever valued Sheraton.

Now ITT executives and consultants swarmed all over Sheraton, trying to uncover the reasons for its shabby performance, identify and ease out incompetent managers, develop alternate strategies and tactics, all in the hopes of boosting its image and earnings. From the start it appeared certain that large amounts of money would be needed for these tasks, and as was the case with Levitt, Geneen stood prepared to spend. But, no one had any clear idea of how much it would take, and it is doubtful that Geneen appreciated the magnitude of the problems he had acquired with Sheraton.

The following year Geneen announced a five-year plan to expand operations, update facilities, and triple the number of rooms in the system. The cost was to be $865 million, plus another $81 million for hotel properties constructed for Sheraton to manage.[14] Financial analysts began to suspect that the hotel chain was a white elephant that Geneen would gladly dispose of if given a chance to do so with a modicum of grace. Indeed, one analyst dubbed Sheraton "ITT's Vietnam." If Geneen really wanted to get into the lodging business he might have done better by starting fresh rather than trying to revive this antiquated corporation. In the end Sheraton would be turned around and prove a money maker, but the costs were enormous, and whether it was worth it remains a matter of debate.

The next major acquisition came out of Rohatyn's stable. Rayonier was a medium-sized forest products company that had fallen on bad times. It was one of the world's largest producers of wood cellulose, used primarily in the manufacture of acetate and rayon. Each fabric was losing ground in its major markets to nylon and other synthetics. Moreover, Rayonier had a weak balance sheet and had suffered from indifferent management. On the other hand, it had several recently completed modern facilities and nearly a million acres of land in Georgia, Florida, and Washington, as well as a new leadership team, headed by Russell Erickson, eager to expand into new areas and regain old markets.

One might easily imagine Geneen's assessment of this situation. There was an obvious fit with Levitt. The home-builder needed land upon which to construct its units, and Rayonier not only had that in abundance—close to settled areas—but it also had the lumber with which to build them. More important for the short run, however, was the fact that cotton prices were rising, and some experts thought there soon would be a similar increase for petroleum and natural gas feedstocks used to create synthetic fibers. If this occurred, rayon and acetate might undergo a rebirth, making Rayonier a prime company, assuming it was prepared to exploit its advantages.

Geneen couldn't resist such a prospect, and Rohatyn proved most convincing. Rayonier was acquired in April, at a cost of $293 million in ITT common and preferred. This worked out to more than $47 per share of Rayonier common, which was twice what the stock had been selling for prior to the announcement.

Shortly after the takeover, Erickson and his staff travelled to New York to meet with and report to ITT management. Erickson had decided to make a big splash, and ask for $85 million for a new cellulose facility, to be on stream in late 1969 or early 1970, when he expected the price for that material to be substantially higher than it was then. This was a complex program that would occupy much of the corporation's attention, especially since the mill and related facilities would be rushed to completion. To his surprise Geneen approved the plan readily, and then asked, "What else have you got?" The ITT chairman either didn't appreciate the difficulties involved with lumber and other forest products or was a higher roller than had been thought. Whatever the reason for Erickson's actions he decided to plunge ahead and present a bold and expensive project that had been in the back of his mind; prior to his meeting with Geneen it had seemed destined to remain there. Rayonier might acquire a huge tract in Canada, roughly the size of the state of Tennessee, upon which it would erect the largest and most modern milling and processing facility in the world. Such grandiose projects always interested Geneen, who after some study gave the signal to proceed.

Thus was born the Port Cartier operation, which sustained ever-increasing losses that bled Rayonier white, and which a decade later had to be written off at a loss of $320 million.[15] The analyst who had described Sheraton as ITT's Vietnam sensed Geneen's vulnerability but had the wrong subsidiary in mind. Eventually Sheraton would turn a profit, but Rayonier never worked out as planned.

To complement this initial commitment to natural resources, Geneen acquired Pennsylvania Glass Sand, an important manufacturer of silica, the basic raw material used in the manufacture of glass, as well as other products and raw materials used in the chemical industry. The company was in good shape, requiring neither capital nor management changes. It therefore commanded a premium price, $112 million in ITT common and preferred, for assets valued at $46 million. The takeover was completed on June 27th, and while little more was heard from the company over the years, its revenues and profits continued to grow.

Continental Baking, the last of 1968's major acquisitions, was the most puzzling. This was not because it was run-down or troubled. On the contrary, it was a well-managed concern, with bakeries in all parts of the nation, and it was a growing factor in snack foods and frozen foods as well. Among Continental's better known products were Wonder Bread and Morton pot pies. Twinkies and Hostess cupcakes could be found in the lunchboxes of many of the nation's children, while Profile was the leading diet bread. Continental's facilities were the most modern and efficient in their industries, and its marketing practices were widely imitated. With $620 million in sales it was the largest baking concern in the land.

But what did Geneen hope for in this particular industry? Continental could hardly expand at a rapid rate; revenues had doubled over the past decade but as a result of acquisitions rather than enlargement of the market. Profit margins were low at under 4 percent and not likely to rise. Unlike Sheraton there were no inefficient units that might be sold to raise capital and increase margins. Continental was the classic case of a corporation that had gone about as far as it could in its markets. Nor was the stock on the bargain counter. Due to persistent takeover rumors it rose to 40 at midyear, its highest price in history and twice what it had been in 1966.

Later, ITT would claim Geneen visualized Continental as a logical extension of the hotel business, but this was rather farfetched. Some believed that he had been lured into the merger by Rohatyn, who had observed that in this way ITT would enter an important consumer goods area while at the same time expanding the base of the domestic business. Then too, this was a period when it appeared that the conglomerators could work magic. It might have been that Geneen—like Ling, Bluhdorn, and Thornton—had started to believe his own press notices, and thought he could perform his tricks even at Continental.

The price worked out to $280 million in common and preferred shares, or about the same as had been paid for Rayonier, which had $100 million more in assets and at the time was considered a more likely growth candidate. This came to $68 per share, or around 19 times earnings for a stock that traditionally sold for a multiple of about ten. In retrospect it appears that Geneen had overpaid for Continental, but at the time several rather cynical observers commented that he had merely exchanged his bloated paper for the inflated shares of the baking company.

Prudence might have dictated a pause, a period of consolidation after the Continental acquisition, but that was not Geneen's style. Moreover, he was swept along with the other conglomerators in the frantic current of the times. In the superheated atmosphere of early 1969 Geneen accumulated companies at a record pace. Six were added in March alone, ranging in size from the Paterson School of Business (for less than a quarter of a million dollars in cash) to United Homes of Seattle, a sizeable regional construction outfit (which took $13.6 million in stock). Five more were added the following month. Electronics Institute of Technology, a minuscule entity, cost ITT only $50,000, indicating that Geneen's eye indeed was on the sparrow. On the other hand, Canteen Corporation, a dominant factor in vending machines and one of the largest suppliers of on-site feeding services, took close to a quarter of a billion dollars in stock, and by most standards was a major acquisition. Five more companies were added in May and eight during the next four months, as Geneen prepared for another big move, the takeover of Grinnell Corporation.

Grinnell was a large old plumbing and foundry products concern as well as the nation's leading manufacturer of fire protection systems; the company's annual sales of $340 million would make it Geneen's largest takeover in the capital goods area. Grinnell's systems might be installed in Sheraton's hotels and motels, Levitt's homes, Continental's bakeries, and ITT factories around the world, so the "fit" was quite satisfactory. Moreover, Grinnell's management was eager for the merger. The company had recently lost an antitrust case and had been obliged to divest itself of several properties and to abandon attempts to acquire additional companies in its industry. Short of capital and wanting another means of expansion, Grinnell welcomed Geneen's overtures, and there was little difficulty coming to terms. But completion of the acquisition, as was the case with Canteen, would have to await final Justice Department approval, and that was delayed until 1969.

The Justice Department's Antitrust Division questioned both the Canteen and Grinnell takeovers, but at the time their doubts were overshadowed by their more important concern with the LTV-Jones & Laughlin merger. ITT's legal team travelled to Washington to meet with the antitrusters and work out a compromise. After several rounds of bargaining both sides agreed the takeovers could proceed, but that Canteen and Grinnell would be maintained as separate entities until the courts decided on the legality of the acquisitions.

But there was no possibility of compromise when it came to Geneen's next important acquisition, the largest of his career and even more contentious than ABC.

Hartford Fire Insurance was one of the nation's oldest and largest property, casualty, and fire insurers. In 1968 it reported assets of nearly $2 billion with a premium income of $969 million. A well-funded, conservative operation, Hartford had a capital excess of some $400 million, which theoretically might be remitted in the form of dividends. Critics charged Geneen with seeking that plum. In the process of its acquisition and expansion programs ITT had enlarged its long-term debt from $310 million in 1964 to $932 million at the end of 1968. Hartford's surplus could be used to shrink that figure considerably.

Geneen repeatedly protested that he had no such intention, but he wasn't convincing. As it turned out he was quite sincere. ITT internal documents that later were turned over to the government bore out his contention and revealed that he had another, more complex and interesting plan for Hartford, one which suggested violations of reciprocity codes to the antitrusters. ITT planned to use Hartford to fund the Sheraton expansion program. The fit with Levitt was obvious. "Levitt has sold homes to 80,000 homeowners and is building new homes at the rate of 6,500 per year," wrote one ITT executive. "Within five years this figure will exceed 11,000. These purchasers require homeowners' and mortgage insurance, which may be offered through special marketing programs."[16] In addition, ITT companies might be nudged into taking out policies from the insurer, and employees and even stockholders might be approached—more than 200,000 in each category. The possibilities were almost endless. One can imagine ITT executives spinning out a picture of a corporation tied together by hotels, insurance, rental cars, and other products and services coming from within the corporation. Similar thoughts were entertained by attorneys at the Antitrust Division. Later one of them would conjure the image of a Sheraton hotel, financed and insured by Hartford, using Grinnell fire protection devices, with Canteen providing food services (including Wonder Bread and Twinkies from Continental?), while Avis enjoyed a preferential position at a lobby location. None of this need be mandated in any specific way; each unit would know what was expected of it. "Where the large diversified company makes substantial purchases from many suppliers, these suppliers are going to feel a 'reciprocity effect' even without affirmative use of reciprocity by the purchaser," was the Justice Department's view. "The creation of such power, regardless of whether it is overtly exercised, may have a serious anticompetitive effect."[17]

Whether ITT believed that it would have troubles with the Justice Department is unknown. Settlements of the Canteen and Grinnell difficulties appeared possible in late 1968, which might have caused a mood of optimism to prevail. The Johnson Administration was winding down, and Ramsey Clark soon would leave the Justice Department. Better treatment for corporations would likely have been expected from Richard Nixon and his attorney general, especially since the incoming President had singled out Clark for special condemnation. On the other hand, Hartford's Board hadn't welcomed ITT's overtures, and there were already indications of a fight in the making. Ralph Nader and other reformers were preparing for the attack. This was to be Geneen's first experience with an unfriendly takeover, and he didn't relish the idea. There was also the Connecticut Insurance Commission to consider; even if all went well, this body would have to approve the merger. Still angry and bitter over his experience with the FCC, Geneen was worried about the possibility of yet another rejection.

Nonetheless, he pressed on. In early 1969 Geneen and his circle devoted much time to the Hartford takeover, while other candidates were in the wings, awaiting consideration. At the same time, across town at Columbus Circle, Bluhdorn, Judelson, and their associates were making plans for a new resorts-entertainment-land development project in the Caribbean, while in Dallas James Ling poured over Jones & Laughlin's organization charts, preparing for another deployment of assets. Textron may have become quiescent while Litton was suffering from a loss of credibility, but the conglomerate movement appeared strong and viable. In retrospect we know that this was the high noon of this most vital and significant managerial development of the postwar period. At the time, however, Geneen, Ling, Bluhdorn, and the others seemed about to shift into a higher gear, with larger acquisitions in the works.

7

Antitrust and the Penn Central Fiasco

The conglomerate phenomenon was carefully tracked by analysts, journalists, and Justice Department antitrusters. Men like Ling, Geneen, Bluhdorn, and Thornton made good copy, and rumors and anecdotes about them overflowed from the financial pages to the gossip columns to the front pages. There was talk that Geneen had purchased a handful of restaurants to please the CEO of the newly acquired Canteen Corp., a man who long had yearned to expand into this field. "What the hell, they'll cost only a few million," he was purported to have remarked. "Let him have them if that's what he wants." Or the yarn that Ling was disappointed to learn that the Bank of England was a public institution, since he had thought to acquire it, split the bank into quarters, and then sell off the parts to financial interests in France, Germany, Switzerland, and Belgium. One of the more persistent Wall Street tales was the so-called "inside story" on why Bluhdorn had gone after Paramount. "Charlie likes girls," opined one analyst, "and owning studios eliminated the middle man." Financial journalist George Goodman, who wrote under the pen name of "Adam Smith," offered a scenario in which a new conglomerate planned and successfully executed a takeover of AT&T through an unfriendly tender offer. Wall Street chuckled—but afterward wondered just which conglomerate Goodman had in mind.

Most telling, perhaps, was the joke about the conglomerator whose son found a mongrel in the streets and brought him home. The businessman asked, "How much do you think he's worth?" to which the boy replied, "At least $30,000." Trying to let his son down as gently as possible, the father explained that such a dog hardly could fetch even one dollar. But the following afternoon the boy returned, and proudly informed the conglomerator that he had sold the dog for $50,000. The man was dumbfounded. "Do you mean to say some fool was willing to give you so much cash for that mangy mutt?" he asked. Well, not quite," was the reply. "I traded him for two $25,000 cats." The family business would be in good hands.

The pace and numbers of large mergers increased substantially in the late 1960s, with more of these involving conglomerates than ever before. In 1964 there had been 91 mergers of firms with assets of more than $10 million, and of these 62 were of the conglomerate variety. There would be 192 such mergers in 1969, with conglomerates accounting for 161 of them. The total assets of merged firms that year came to $12.6 billion, and all but $1.4 billion of the amount went into the conglomerates.[1]

There were those in the Justice Department who fairly ached to institute antitrust actions to prevent some of the larger and more spectacular takeovers. In the marrow of their bones they felt that the likes of Geneen, Ling, and Bluhdorn were violating custom and tradition—and so they were, unabashedly so. Traditionally the department had been staffed by attorneys of two disparate persuasions—graduates of prestigious law schools who were devoted to established norms, and reformers itching for crusades; the conglomerators offended the sensibilities of both. But the more sober and judicious of them (all of whom were of the former category) knew that there was no basis for prosecution either in statute or common law. That is to say that they wanted to haul the conglomerators to court, and sought a way to do so, either through the use of existing legislation or the framing of a new antitrust law. The search for such a rationale was one of the more fascinating legal developments of the conglomerate era.

The most recent legislation bearing upon mergers and industry position was the Celler-Kefauver Act of 1950, which placed prior restraints upon companies seeking takeovers that might appreciably lessen competition. The framers had in mind vertical and horizontal mergers, and the legislation may have encouraged takeover-minded executives to seek acquisitions of firms in nonrelated industries. To the extent that it did, the Celler-Kefauver Act may be considered the Magna Charta of the conglomerate movement.

Donald Turner, a sober, reflective, and scholarly man, became head of the Antitrust Division in 1965; he would serve in that post until the end of the Johnson administration. The holder of both a Ph.D. in Economics and an LL.B. from Yale, Turner had clerked at the Supreme Court and during the preceding eleven years had taught at Harvard Law School, to which he would return in 1969. Only 44 years old when he came to the Antitrust Division, Turner was one of the most respected legal minds of his generation, an acknowledged expert in the area over which he would preside. He was convinced there was nothing yet in the law to prevent conglomerate takeovers. "I do not believe Congress has given the courts and the FTC a mandate to campaign against 'superconcentration' in the absence of any evidence of harm to competition," he wrote in a stinging rebuke of critics of conglomerates who refused to attempt to draw up legislation to prevent such mergers. "In the light of the bitterly disputed issues involved, I believe that the courts should demand of Congress that it translate any further directive into something more formidable than sonorous phrases in the page of the Congressional Record."[2]

Such a person was an improbable candidate to lead a crusade against the likes of Geneen, Ling, and Bluhdorn.

Still, the drive to develop a workable doctrine for use against the conglomerates continued. During the second half of the 1960s the Federal Trade Commission probed the movement from almost every angle, seeking a handle upon which to hang cases, while Senate and House committees sought, largely in vain, to frame legislation to restrict if not actually cripple the growing mergermania.

Meanwhile, the Supreme Court groped toward an anticonglomerate stance. Its big opportunity came in 1967, when it heard arguments in an FTC complaint seeking to prevent Procter & Gamble from acquiring Clorox. The commission argued that the nation's largest soap manufacturer was trying to dominate the liquid bleach industry. The FTC conceded that Procter & Gamble turned out superior products at low prices, thus benefiting consumers, and that it hadn't engaged in unfair practices against competitors. Still it said that such a merger was of the type that "hurts, not helps, a competitive economy." In its defense, P & G denied competition had been adversely affected by the merger, and went so far as to deny there was any such thing as a "liquid bleach industry," since that product competed with solid bleaches. Finally, the company observed that it hadn't been charged with violating any statute, the Celler-Kevauver Act in particular. Notwithstanding, the high court found for the government. The merger was dissolved amid cries that the FTC had embarked upon an antitrust campaign without proper legislative support, and that it was being encouraged by a Supreme Court that seemed more interested in framing social and economic policy than interpreting the statutes.

As it turned out, the P & G case did not signal the start of an all-out crusade against large-scale takeovers. Both the FTC and the Antitrust Division urged Congress to pass a statute to guide them, and wouldn't take further action until one was in hand. "The law respecting the anti-competitive impact of conglomerate mergers has not been established," said FTC Commissioner Mary Gardiner Jones. "It is the duty of the Department of Justice not to bring a case simply on the basis that it thinks it *can* win, but to bring only those cases it thinks it *should* win," added Donald Turner, who ruled out harassment tactics urged by reformers. "I think this is far too important an element in our national economic policy to be handled that way."[3]

When Ramsey Clark replaced Nicholas Katzenbach as Attorney General in late 1966 he almost immediately clashed with Turner over antitrust policy. Clark played a role in preventing ITT from merging with ABC, a clear signal that he intended to take a more vigorous stance against takeovers. Toward this end he asked Chicago Law School Dean Philip Neal to head a commission to study the matter, hoping Neal would bring in recommendations that would lead to actions in both the executive and legislative branches. Turner approved of the Neal Commission and reluctantly went along with his chief in the ITT-ABC matter while indicating that he did not view this as setting a precedent. For the next two years these men would quarrel repeatedly, with Clark arguing for an all-out crusade and Turner fighting a rear-guard action while awaiting the commission report and new legislation.

The Neal Report, published toward the end of the Johnson administration, sustained the positions of both men, but in the end came down in favor of the Turner stance. While critical of conglomerate mergers it concluded there was nothing in existing law to prevent them. The commission recommended legislation to prevent large firms (with revenues of more than $500 million or assets in excess of $250 million) from acquiring "leading firms" in other industries, which were defined as those with more than 10 percent of the market. Clark could do little but accept the Neal Report, and slaked his antitrust thirst by pushing ahead in other areas, most notably an action designed to break up IBM. That was the situation as Richard Nixon prepared to assume the presidency.

Few expected judicial activism from Nixon, especially in antitrust matters. After all, he had spent the preceding five years on Wall Street, as a lawyer specializing in corporate affairs. One of his partners, John Mitchell, had served as his campaign manager and was attorney general designate. "This country is going so far right you won't recognize it," said Mitchell shortly after the announcement. His deputy was to be Richard Kleindienst, one of Senator Barry Goldwater's closest allies and if anything more conservative than Mitchell. Richard McLaren was to replace Turner at the Antitrust Division. A senior partner at a leading Chicago law firm, McLaren had devoted a good deal of his time over the preceding 20 years to defending corporate clients against the Justice Department and recently had served as chairman of the Antitrust Section of the American Bar Association. This led liberals to expect the new administration to support and be supported by the "business community."

This might have happened, had such a thing existed. But "business community" was a vast oversimplification of the situation in American industry. There was seldom unity on important matters, but instead frequently conflicting special interest groups. Outsiders, especially reformers, perceived real unity where none existed, or where "unity" was at most a number of loose, temporary alliances. That helps explain crusades such as those against "the trusts" and "malefactors of great wealth," usually led and supported by people with little actual knowledge of the complex business landscape. To them the conglomerate movement seemed quite similar to the trust creation activities at the turn of the century. Large concentrations of economic power were being fashioned with the help of Wall Street banks and powerful allies in Washington. These had to be opposed in the name of freedom and democracy. Or so it appeared to the kinds of individuals who bemoaned the passing from the scene of Ramsey Clark and who expected few if any antitrust prosecutions from the likes of Nixon, Mitchell, and McLaren.

In fact, Nixon would preside over one of the most vigorous antitrust crusades in history, one directed against the conglomerates, which dumbfounded those who assumed that anyone who attacked business must do so from the political left. Actually, the conglomerators had more enemies and critics among conservative businessmen than any other group. They might not be as eloquent and well advertised as the liberals, but they had more at stake—their very existence as independent operators. Any CEO of a large, relatively stagnant company whose stock price didn't reflect its underlying worth had reason to fear a raid from Bluhdorn, Ling, or some other conglomerator. Critics like Ralph Nader and Ramsey Clark who considered Nixon to be the defender of a mythological business community against "the people" couldn't have been further off the mark. In reality, the incoming president favored the old business elites against the rambunctious newcomers.

McLaren gave the warning during a conference with Mitchell and Kleindienst, at which he predicated acceptance of his new post upon a set of conditions. There was to be "a vigorous antitrust program," and the Justice Department was to "decide all matters on the merits" leaving politics aside. The new attorney general agreed that "we would follow my beliefs with regard to what the Supreme Court cases said on conglomerate mergers, and the restructuring of the industry that I thought was coming about in an almost idiotic way." Which was what might have been expected from a person who had spent the preceding few years defending his corporate clients against the onslaught of various conglomerators. Mitchell became quite outspoken on the matter. In June 1969, he decried "super-concentration" in American business, and so that no one could mistake his meaning, added that it "discourages competition among large firms and establishes a tone in the marketplace for more and more mergers."[4] All of this pleased his former associates at the Wall Street law firm of Nixon, Mudge, Rose, Guthrie, Alexander, and Mitchell, noted for its roster of old-line corporate clients.

Still, McLaren lacked adequate ammunition for his campaign. The courts had enunciated no clear principle in regard to conglomerates. Congress still had not enacted the legislation Turner had wanted, and without which he claimed there could be no important prosecutions. Little consolation might be derived from the Neal Report, and the newcomers at Justice hadn't any fresh ideas to bring to bear on the issue. So, as Clark had before them, they went outside government for another report, one from a group headed by George Stigler, a conservative University of Chicago economist noted for his antipathy to business practices that tended to restrict entry into markets.

In light of his record and publications, Stigler was expected to develop a rationale for the attack, one that had eluded McLaren. To the surprise of top leaders at Justice (but not to his fellow academicians who knew him better) Stigler did no such thing. Recognizing the nature of the conflict between the old and new business establishments, the professor appreciated the nature of the challenge conglomerators posed to established corporations, and knew they were acting to stir up rather than consolidate the industries in which they were entering. Moreover, he seemed to know that Mitchell, Kleindienst, and McLaren were trying to use him, and the always independent and irascible Stigler had no intention of being treated in that fashion. In his final report, Stigler stated that conglomerates "pose a minor threat to competition." In a sharp reproach to the new administration, Stigler urged it "to resist the natural temptation to utilize the antitrust laws to combat social problems not relating to the competitive functioning of markets."[5]

Clearly McLaren could expect nothing from such an individual. But he had one more hope. Shortly after the election, the House Antitrust Committee of the Committee on the Judiciary scheduled an investigation of conglomerates. The Chairman, Emanuel Celler (D.-N.Y.) was a veteran reformer who had served in the House since 1923, and who on previous occasions had sharply criticized "corporate raiders." If McLaren could obtain little from the New Right, perhaps something could be gained from the Old Left.

The subcommittee began its work in February 1969, announcing the selection of five conglomerates whose representatives were to be called to testify. There were LTV, Litton, G + W, ITT, and National General, the last being a fairly new entry into the conglomerate world. (Later, Leasco Data Processing, which really wasn't a true conglomerate, was added to the list.) From the start it was evident that Celler and his fellow congressmen intended to concentrate on the first four. The chairman said that the purpose of the hearing was to answer the question: "If a multi-industry company merger does not substantially lessen competition or tend to create a monopoly, and thus does not violate the antitrust laws, is there any effect that nonetheless needs to be corrected by legislation?"[6]

The hearings took place that summer. Into the committee room came Bluhdorn, Ling, Thornton, Geneen, their staffs, attorneys, accountants, and assorted experts. The congressmen learned of how Bluhdorn had used his connections at Chase to bring about acquisitions, and about Litton's explorations into synergy, and they tried to understand how Ling used imaginative financings to take over huge corporations. Geneen dazzled them with a recitation of conglomerate philosophy and with his encyclopedic grasp of facts. Thousands of documents pertaining to takeovers were produced and perused. The congressmen criticized some practices and questioned others, but in the end they did nothing of consequence. In 1970, after nearly a year of study, the subcommittee recommended that Congress pass legislation prohibiting the use of taxable funds to finance takeovers. And that was it. There was nothing in the final report useful to McLaren in developing his anticonglomerate crusade.

By then, however, the Antitrust Division had come up with two rather weak weapons to use in the attack.

The first was the familiar stricture against reciprocity, which as already indicated, means that a corporation musn't oblige one of its divisions to sell to or buy from another without offering equal access to potential and existing competitors. Thus, Bluhdorn had to demonstrate that his auto parts manufacturers hadn't been obliged to purchase raw materials and finished goods from each other, Geneen stood prepared to answer allegations that Avis had a preferential position in Sheraton hotels, and Thornton that Ingalls was not favoring other Litton companies when it came to the award of subcontracts on its ships. Yet it was quite clear that opportunities for such favoritism not only existed, but would be difficult if not impossible to resist. As Columbia Law School Professor Harlan Blake put it, "Reciprocity is as inevitable a result of widespread conglomerate structure as price rigidity is a consequence of oligopoly structure."

The other weapon McLaren intended to use was the assertion that size alone could provide the rationale for an antitrust case. This notion had been bandied about for decades, usually by liberal activists critical of large corporations. It had been heard in 1901, when United States Steel was put together by J. P. Morgan. Woodrow Wilson and Louis Brandeis believed this philosophy, and the idea can be found in their speeches of the pre-World War I period and in sections of the Clayton Antitrust Act. Could it be used against the conglomerates, however, none of which dominated any particular industry? Turner hadn't thought so, but McLaren believed otherwise. Referring to what he termed "aggregate concentration," he would say that "what we were shooting for, from the beginning of 1969, was to stop this merger trend that was leading more and more toward economic concentration." As far as he was concerned, the conglomerate phenomenon was "a merger movement where concentration of control of manufacturing assets will be substantially increased and the trend to further concentration will be encouraged."[7]

Weak reeds upon which to build a major assault against the conglomerates. McLaren was too experienced in antitrust statutes and decisions not to have realized this. Nonetheless, barely two months after taking office, he had his campaign planned and shot off the first barrage.

On Saturday morning, March 22, 1969 McLaren placed a call to a member of the law firm that represented LTV to inform him that an antitrust brief would be filed to prevent the Jones & Laughlin takeover. Ling recorded his own reaction to the news, which was "absolute, utter disbelief." While lacking a legal background he knew that the takeover would not increase concentration in the steel industry, and had been led to believe that this was the view of the Justice Department as well. "The antitrust laws are part of the rules of the game" said Ling. "You consult your attorneys before you make any move that might involve those laws, and unless they think you're in the clear, you don't make the move."[8]

Ling had done this and had been assured that all would proceed without a hitch once J & L's management accepted the idea of joining LTV. Donald Turner hadn't protested when the announcement of the acquisition was made in December. Nor had there been the slightest hint that Ramsey Clark, the Justice Department's most vocal critic of takeovers, would attempt to block this one. The new administration was in place by February 5th, the day LTV registered its tender offer, and there had been no reaction from Mitchell, Kleindienst, and McLaren. Ling's surprise—and indignation—was understandable as he considered the possibilities of a drawn-out court battle.[9]

The filing took place on April 14th. McLaren charged that the LTV-J & L merger would lessen competition in the steel industry, involve reciprocity violations, and result in an increase in aggregate concentration. The first two allegations would be difficult to demonstrate, since LTV had no other steel interests and the possibilities for reciprocity between J & L and existing LTV units were slim. As for the matter of aggregate concentration, this was a vague, imprecise, and untested doctrine. Nonetheless a beginning had been made.[10]

The same day on which McLaren struck against LTV he met with the ITT legal team, newly arrived in Washington to discuss the Canteen takeover. ITT offered to maintain the company as a completely separate and independent entity if allowed to proceed with the acquisition. Thus, Canteen might be divested of with a minimum of pain if the courts so ordered. After some skirmishing McLaren accepted these terms. Canteen became part of ITT on April 25th, and three days later the Justice Department initiated its antitrust suit; the charges were almost identical to those in the LTV-J & L brief.[11]

McLaren fired his third salvo in May, this time supporting B. F. Goodrich in its attempts to ward off unwelcome overtures from Northwest Industries, a company Ben Heineman had transformed from an ailing railroad into a conglomerate. As in the LTV case, McLaren utilized arguments based upon reciprocity and aggregate concentration, claiming that for these reasons the merger would be against the public interest. It didn't work this time. The Justice Department's request for a preliminary injunction was denied on the grounds that McLaren hadn't sufficiently demonstrated a basis for suspicion of reciprocity; the count also cast doubt on the claim of aggregate concentration as a justification for blocking takeovers.

Now the outlook at LTV and ITT brightened. Ling proceeded with plans to purchase additional J & L shares, while Geneen added five companies to his collection in May and eight more during the following four months, all of which were small and none challenged by the Justice Department. But McLaren was neither particularly dismayed nor about to pull back on the antitrust front. He had no trouble discerning the possibilities for reciprocity between Grinnell and ITT, and he monitored Geneen's struggles with the Hartford's board with increasing interest. Sensing that Justice was preparing a new attack, Geneen asked Donald Turner, now back at Harvard Law School, for an opinion on the Hartford acquisition. Not surprisingly, Turner responded that the combination unquestionably was within the law as then written.

McLaren disagreed. On June 24th he announced his intention to file a suit, and on August 1st the Justice Department issued its briefs challenging both the Grinnell and Hartford acquisitions.

Thus, the stage was set for McLaren's great confrontation with the conglomerators, most notably Ling and Geneen. In this contest he would lose every battle, but in the end win the war. The victory might not have been possible, however, without the assistance of developments at the securities market. The conglomerate movement wasn't slain by the Justice Department's antitrust suits so much as by the most important stock market decline since 1929-33.

Neither the ITT nor LTV acquisitions campaign of the late 1960s would have been possible were it not for the buoyant stock market of the period, which boosted the value of the paper Geneen and Ling hoped to use to obtain the very real assets of Hartford and Jones & Laughlin.

Others were doing the same. This was about the time Bluhdorn was making his bid for Sinclair, and for a while he seemed capable of pulling it off.[12] The targeted company fought back in a series of newspaper advertisements aimed at its shareholders. "Would you willingly exchange your stock in Sinclair and turn its management over to a company that is not in the oil business and could end up with $4 billion in debt?" it asked. Apparently many would; Bluhdorn told reporters he had "every reason to be confident of success." Nor was he the only minnow trying to gobble up a whale. As we've seen, Bluhdorn sold his block of Armour stock to General Host after being foiled in his attempt to purchase that meat packer. Only a smallish conglomerate (1968 revenues: $201 million), General Host was now taking off after Armour (1968 revenues: $2.4 billion). Meanwhile, the freshly minted conglomerate, Data Processing Financial & General (1968 revenues: $17 million), was exploring the possibilities of obtaining a major interest in another of Bluhdorn's holdings, the Great Atlantic & Pacific Tea Co., the nation's second-largest supermarket chain (1968 revenues: $5.4 billion). About to enter the conglomerate ranks, Continental Can acquired printing-press manufacturer Miehle-Goss-Dexter and was eyeing Nekoosa Edwards Paper. Walter Kidde, which had been turned back by Continental in the Miehle-Goss-Dexter bidding, consoled itself by going after United States Lines, the nation's biggest ocean shipping operation. And so it went, but only as long as the shares of the acquiring company remained high.

In late 1968 the Dow Industrials seemed poised to shoot past the 1000 mark. This was familiar territory; the Dow had gone as far as 943 the previous year before topping out, and in 1966 it actually went beyond the three digit figure, to 1001.1, but then declined, not reaching bottom until later that year, by which time it had shrunk by more than 25 percent. But in 1968 the situation seemed different. For one thing, Nixon had defeated Hubert Humphrey for the presidency, and he was considered far more favorably disposed toward business. Also, Nixon had spoken of a "secret plan" to end the Vietnam War, which by then had become one of the most bearish elements in the market. Then too, there were persistent rumors that President Charles de Gaulle was about to devalue the franc, which caused disruptions in the European money markets and led to a flow of funds to New York. The bulls believed that these factors alone would suffice to push the Dow over 1000, and they continued to buy, pushing the Dow to 985 on Friday, November 29th, up 9 points for the session and 18 for the week.

Yet all was not well, and cracks were starting to show. Those investors and speculators who had sold their shares to the bulls had reason to suspect a decline was in the making, though few suspected how deep and prolonged it would be. Nixon had vowed to bring down the inflation rate (which was over 5 percent at the time), and to do so he would have to adopt deflationary measures. Nothing good could come out of Vietnam. A continuation of the fighting would be economically harmful and morally depressing, while any settlement would result in decreased military spending, and this could upset the economy. The same people who had cheered the Nixon victory were now troubled by the uncertainties ahead.

Wall Street was the scene of hyped-up speculation in late 1968. Not only was there a wave of takeovers—a new one every day, or so it seemed—but the stocks of young companies were coming to market where they shot up to twice the offering price in a matter of minutes. Fundamentalists were troubled by the lack of strong leadership and by the higher stock prices in the face of economic uncertainty. Money was getting tighter too, an indication that interest rates would be boosted, and this surely would be interpreted as a bearish omen. Market technicians observed that some indicators had started to turn downward, and that in making its third attempt to break through the 1000 level the Dow was tracing a classic "head and shoulders formation," which could mean that prices would decline substantially. Newton Zinder of E. F. Hutton, a respected market observer who took into account both fundamental and technical data, was troubled by these signals, even as the Dow shot ahead that November 29th. "From a technical point of view the market continues to be in overbought territory, suggesting that a period of some consolidation many not be far away." Zinder didn't anticipate a serious decline, however; the correction "should be followed by further upside progress," with the Dow ending 1968 on a firm note.

Zinder was correct about the downturn in stock prices but overly sanguine about the possibilities of a recovery. On Monday, December 2nd, the Chase Manhattan Bank boosted its prime rate to 6½ percent and others soon followed. The news reached the exchanges at a time when the Dow was over 994, up by more than 9 points over Friday's close. Caught by surprise, the bulls hesitated and then, in one of the most rapid conversions in recent market history, went over to the bear camp. The Dow plunged more than 20 points in two hours before recovering toward the close of trading, ending the session at 983, down by two points from the previous close.

It was the beginning of the end. While there would be feeble rallies over the next year and a half, the general direction was downward. Not until late May 1971, when the Dow stood at 631, would the bottom finally be reached. It was a sharper correction than those of 1966 and 1967-68, and with a far more significant and lasting psychological impact. The conglomerate movement slowed down and seemed to be over. The market would recover in time, and there would be flurries of activity on the takeover front. But neither the conglomerates or Wall Street possessed the vitality and drive they had demonstrated in the 1960s.

In retrospect this appears to have brought an end to the movement's major, innovative phase—what followed was qualitatively and quantitatively different. At the time, observers couldn't have known this, of course, and as far as they were concerned this was merely a pause in the action, which would be resumed once the market straightened itself out. Not until mid-1970, when one of the giant conglomerates actually failed, was it clear that the party was truly over.[13]

It was the Penn Central, organized in 1967 through a merger of two of the nation's oldest and most prestigious railroads, the Pennsylvania and the New York Central. Although no giant, with revenues of over $2 billion the Penn Central was in the same league as Armour or Firestone, while its assets of $6.2 billion were close to those of Sears Roebuck or U. S. Steel. Penn Central was by far the nation's largest transportation system, owning one out of every eleven American locomotives and freight cars and operating 20,000 miles of main track of the nation's 340,000. By industry standards it was a behemoth or, more appropriately, a leviathan, for like the ship of that name, it was doomed to failure.

The merger had been made out of desperation and approved by the Interstate Commerce Commission in that spirit. Railroading was an ailing industry that defied all conventional means of resuscitation. For decades shippers had been turning to trucking and passengers to automobiles and airplanes. While the western long-line carriers were able to make a go of it, even they had become involved in more promising areas, such as land development and the exploitation of mineral reserves. Most eastern lines lacked such resources, and with the exception of the coal carriers their markets hardly were promising, so merger seemed the best solution to their problems. Thus, the Erie had united with the Delaware, Lackwanna, and Western; the Chesapeake & Ohio with the Baltimore & Ohio; and the Norfolk & Western with the Virginian. Both the Pennsylvania and the New York Central had cast about for other merger partners before coming together in 1967, with the vigor and interest largely on the part of the former. Although they had been century-long rivals it appeared an ideal match—for just that reason. Since the two companies serviced many of the same areas, in time they might eliminate thousands of redundant miles of track and as many workers, transforming two invalids into a strong regional competitor. This was the hope and the prospect offered by analysts who understood the numbers better than did the managements involved.

These two lines were quite different. The Pennsylvania was a major coal carrier, accustomed to dealing with an undifferentiated product whose time of delivery wasn't as important as price, and which had tended to neglect passengers in order to concentrate upon freight. The Central hauled a wide variety of industrial and consumer products, and its customers had completely opposite priorities from those of utilities that burned coal. Moreover, its top management clung to the idea that somehow the railroads could maintain their grip upon passenger traffic.

Alfred Perlman, the Central's CEO, was an industry maverick, a graduate of M.I.T. and the first Jew ever to head a major railroad. He had a record of success, having taken the Denver and Rio Grande Western from bankruptcy to solvency in the 1930s and 1940s by upgrading equipment, revamping operations, and providing excellent service. Arriving at the Central in 1954, Perlman soon attempted to do the same there, but progress was slow, due in large part to competition from trucks, barges, and airplanes. Within a few years he came to believe that salvation lay in mergers and economies, and not so much in increased revenues. Some lines would have to be abandoned, but others could be cultivated and made to grow. Perlman envisaged a lean company, operating fewer but more modern and efficient trains, servicing both freight and passenger customers better than ever before. By the mid-1960s he had inculcated this idea and vision in his managers and workers, often by comparing what he was doing to the stagnation at the Pennsylvania. Rivals for more than a century, the two lines had developed differing corporate cultures, and the New Yorkers relished the idea of another round in their ongoing contest with the Philadelphians.

The Pennsylvania had been headed since 1963 by a CEO whose background, personality, and temperament differed sharply from Perlman's. In his heart Stuart Saunders really wasn't a railroader, though he had been in the industry for nearly a quarter of a century when elevated to the Pennsylvania's chairmanship. A medium-sized, stocky man with a bald head and a bulldog expression, he could be quite impressive when talking to outsiders, but those within the industry had a low opinion of his abilities. His selection troubled many veteran Pennsylvania executives who wondered why a more qualified and dedicated person hadn't been chosen. Moreover, Saunders had joined the Pennsylvania from another line, and this rankled those in the organization who had been passed over.

Saunders was a West Virginian who had graduated from Roanoke College and then took a law degree from Harvard. He struggled along on his own during the Great Depression and in 1939 gave up his practice to join the Norfolk & Western as an assistant general solicitor. During the next two decades Saunders inched his way up the ladder, going from assistant general counsel to general counsel in 1951. Then came the executive vice-presidency, and in 1958, the presidency itself.

Controlled by the Pennsylvania, the N & W was a solvent, healthy line, a major coal carrier most of whose customers had long-term contracts. It operated in a strong territory with few rivals, and Saunders took over when business was expanding. By accepted standards the most viable of the eastern lines, the N & W almost ran itself. That was fine with Saunders, who always had been more comfortable in board rooms and country clubs than in roundhouses and along the tracks. Leaving the actual operation of the company to others, Saunders embarked upon an acquisitions campaign, hoping to grab smaller lines to consolidate the N & W grip on the region and expand it further into the coal fields. In 1959 he merged with the Virginian, and then started to explore the possibilities of taking over the New York, Chicago, and St. Louis (more familiarly known as the Nickel Plate) and the Wabash. Were this done, the N & W would emerge as the third largest northeastern line, behind the Pennsylvania and the Central.

James Symes, CEO of the Pennsylvania, applauded this ambition, in part perhaps because at the time his line controlled the N & W, but also because he believed such consolidations were necessary if railroading were to have a future in that part of the country. For a while there was talk that there might be a union of the Pennsylvania and the N & W, with Saunders becoming Symes' heir apparent.

Nothing came of this, largely because Symes was more interested in uniting with the Central, at the time headed by Perlman but controlled by Robert Young. Symes and Young put together a merger plan in 1957, whereby the interests of both managements would be preserved, but the Pennsylvania would be the senior partner on a 60-40 basis. Symes persisted even after Young's death in 1958 and despite Perlman's continued reluctance which was based on the hope of finding a more junior merger partner. As part of his plan, Symes expected to divest himself of the N & W and several other interests. He informed Saunders of this in 1961, at the same time indicating a willingness to assist in the Wabash acquisition. Saunders was delighted to be on his own, especially since Symes was showing such an interest in him. As for Perlman, he saw most of his merger candidates disappear into new combinations, and with no little reluctance and trepidation, he approached Symes and indicated a willingness to see the Central and Pennsylvania come together.

All that was needed now was approval by the Interstate Commerce Commission, the unions, and the stockholders. Symes didn't foresee too much trouble on these fronts, and with everything falling into place he decided it was time to retire. Why he plucked Saunders from the N & W to become his successor is something of a mystery. Perhaps Symes thought Perlman could run the combined lines while Saunders took care of problems in the executive suite and Washington. He certainly couldn't have gauged the dislike both men would develop for one another and their inability to work in harness. Nor could he have appreciated the bitterness felt by those who were passed over in favor of Saunders. But Symes stepped down in 1963, and Saunders assumed command, his first order of business being to unite with Perlman in bringing their two lines together.

Matters of personality and ambition aside, Saunders and Perlman had differing views about where the new Penn Central should head. Perlman, who was to become president and chief operating officer, still wanted a modern and efficient railroad. Saunders, the chairman and chief executive officer designate, believed railroading in the East incapable of significant revival and hardly worth the effort. While prepared to make major financial commitments to the line, he tended to look upon it as a potential money pump for more promising ventures.

The Pennsylvania had a tradition of diversification; in the 1920s it had taken major positions in companies that were the predecessors of Greyhound and Trans World Airways, and like many other railroads it had extensive real estate holdings. Now Saunders meant to build upon it. His takeover activities at the N & W had whetted his appetite. Chance had placed him there and in railroading, but his ambitions were elsewhere.

Milton Shapp, a businessman who later would become Governor of Pennsylvania and an opponent of the merger, testified about Saunders' aspirations and model. "I've been at several parties with him where he had a few drinks and he was always talking about Litton Industries and how Litton and those other conglomerates had cash coming in and were putting it to good use, getting good returns. He said he wanted to keep the money for real estate investments instead of putting it in the fucking railroad. That's what he said, the fucking railroad." Shapp wasn't alone in realizing the nature of Saunders' intentions. "There's no doubt Saunders wanted to get out of the railroad business even during the merger controversy."[14]

His vehicle in this would be the wholly owned Pennsylvania Company, which had been organized in 1870 to take control of trackage west of Pittsburgh and which in 1918 became the repository for all the corporation's miscellaneous properties, including its shares of the N & W. Saunders was prepared to take the plunge and had the vehicle with which to perform the task. All he lacked was a person who could perform the actual mechanics of takeovers, isolate likely properties, and above all, provide him with a plausible rationale and strategy.

Saunders found all four in David Bevan, the Pennsylvania's chief financial officer since 1951. The trouble was that the two men did not like one another. Bevan had recognized Saunders' apparent shallowness early, when the latter was still at the N & W, and had spoken openly of it. Furthermore, Bevan was one of those passed over by Symes for the chairmanship, and so had a natural resentment of the new CEO.

Nonetheless, Saunders and Bevan cooperated in transforming the Pennsylvania Company into a conglomerate. In 1963 they purchased a one-third interest in the Buckeye Pipeline for $28 million in cash and preferred stock, and the rest of its shares were acquired in the next two years. The eighth-largest processor of crude oil in the nation and one of the most important suppliers of jet fuel to the airlines, Buckeye was a sound company in a growing industry. It could be counted upon to provide a boost to the Pennsylvania's earnings, which in turn would lead to a higher price for the railroad's stock, making it the currency to be used in future takeovers. Such had been the path taken by Litton. Apparently Saunders hoped the same magic would strike the Pennsylvania.

The following year Saunders purchased a 60 percent interest in the Great Southwest Corporation, a land development operation with several properties, the most important of which was an amusement park in Dallas known as Six Flags Over Texas. In 1965 he purchased another 20 percent of the firm, which by then was being perceived as possessing "another Disneyland," riding the crest of a growing industry. Saunders seemed to be wagering that the future—amusement parks—would help salvage the past—railroads. More important, however, was his growing conviction that the Pennsylvania should expand rapidly into real estate. Thus he purchased a controlling interest in the Arvida Corporation, which owned approximately 100,000 acres of Florida land. Macco Realty, a California-based company, came next. Then, in a flurry of activity, Saunders acquired Strick Holding Company (a manufacturer of aluminum trailers and containers with an interest in mobile homes), made loans to Executive Jet Aviation (which hoped to develop a large charter business), and increased the Pennsylvania's equity in Madison Square Garden (Symes had obtained shares in exchange for Manhattan real estate). All were initial steps in his plan to transform a large, respected, but declining railroad into a glamorous conglomerate. Ben Heineman was doing as much at the Chicago and North Western, a road that operated even more miles of track than did the Pennsylvania. By 1967 he would transform this ailing line into Northwest Industries, and then divest himself of all railroad operations. Thus, the caterpillar became a butterfly. Saunders' ambitions were not identical, but he obviously wanted to do something along similar lines at the Pennsylvania.

Such was the situation on February 1, 1968, when the Penn Central came into being. Perlman was intent on creating a viable railroad, while Saunders hoped to make it a base for a conglomerate. As for Bevan, he seemingly despised Perlman and rejected his vision, while sharing Saunders' aspirations but apparently considering him second-rate at best.

All of this would become public knowledge later on. At the time, however, the outlook seemed bright. The press dwelled on Perlman's superb record. Saunders appeared on the cover of *Time* and was designated by the *Saturday Review* as "businessman of the year." Bevan was generally acknowledged to be one of the industry's most intelligent, imaginative, and respected financial officers. Who could doubt that such a team would raise the Penn Central to heights that neither of its component lines might have realized on its own? Or that once things were sorted out at the railroad Saunders would use some of its increased profits to diversify, making the Penn Central a true conglomerate, one whose stock would soar in the vigorous bull market on Wall Street?

The answer was that it was doubted by just about everyone who really understood the situation. The dubious included Bevan and Perlman and others at the Penn Central—but not Saunders, who remained confident that all would turn out well, despite growing evidence to the contrary.

The Penn Central's board was dominated by members from the Pennsylvania, and the corporation's organizational structure dispelled any doubts that the merger wasn't really a takeover by the Philadelphians. At the apex was Penn Central Transportation, a holding company with two major and separate properties: the railroad and its various interests and the old Pennsylvania Company. Saunders intended to have primary responsibility for the latter, while a united Pennsylvania and Central staff, directed by Perlman but under Saunders' supervision and control, would manage the railroad's activities. As for Bevan, he would make certain that capital flowed smoothly into both segments. In time the railroad and the investment company might be completely separated, and if this transpired Saunders would go with the Pennsylvania Company, which by then would be a full-fledged conglomerate. But there was no time. In less than three years the Penn Central would crash, in the greatest and most traumatic corporate failure in American history.[15]

When it was all over some of the Penn Central's apologists argued that it had been done in by a faltering economy, that were it not for the recession that began shortly after the merger the company would have remained afloat. The evidence doesn't bear this out. From the first there were inefficiencies, personality clashes, mismanagement, and even incompetence. Prior to the merger both Perlman and Bevan had testified about the difficulties involved, but even they hadn't imagined it would be as bad as it turned out. Some of the blame could be assigned to the core economic problems of eastern railroading, which had affected the performance of both railroads while they had been independent. Had it not been for the merger, however, each would have survived independently longer than they did as a single entity. They might have lasted to this day, declining slowly, suffering from financial arthritis, their equipment falling apart—but still operating.

The two lines simply couldn't and wouldn't mesh, and rather than realizing efficiencies and economies, costs actually rose. Attempts to harmonize operations backfired as freight piled up and was misrouted at the unified marshalling yards. To complicate matters the two railroads had different computer systems so they couldn't exchange information. Customer dissatisfaction intensified throughout 1968 and 1969, leading to losses of business to other lines and to truckers. Moreover things weren't improving. The Central's staff in New York had little contact with the Pennsylvania's in Philadelphia, and when they came together there were arguments, recriminations, and shouting matches. Things got so bad that Bevan and Perlman refused to talk with one another, while the animosity between Perlman and Saunders intensified.

The public got a hint of the troubles early, during the annual stockholders' meeting on April 1, 1968, two months after the merger. Saunders reported operating revenues had fallen from $1.7 billion to $1.6 billion (on a consolidated basis) while return on investment from railroad properties had been 0.8 percent compared with 2.7 percent the previous year. He blamed this poor showing on the recession. When national prosperity returned, said Saunders, the Penn Central would prove profitable. Bevan was less optimistic; he conceded the railroad's income was "alarmingly low in relation to our investment in transportation facilities," and hinted that unless conditions improved the corporation would be in a financial bind. Perlman said little, looked morose, and left for New York as soon as he could.

The situation didn't improve. Transportation revenues for 1969 came to $1.9 billion. Saunders claimed that the Penn Central had earned $0.18 per share, but this had been made possible by the remittance of large dividends from subsidiaries to the parent. Then too, there was an "extraordinary loss" of $5.22 per share, so the corporation really had a deficit of $5.04 per share. Even so, Saunders paid a dividend, though it was decreased from $2.40 to $1.80 per share. He apologized for this, pledging to restore the old rate when conditions improved.

Things still weren't getting better. Feeling that his warnings were going unheeded, Bevan submitted his resignation in June, and agreed to remain only after impassioned pleas from Saunders, who knew that Bevan's departure would be frowned upon by the bankers. But Perlman went, "promoted" to the meaningless post of vice-chairman after another argument with Saunders. He was to be replaced by Paul Gorman, then president of Western Electric, who had a fine record, especially in the area of cost controls, but no real knowledge of railroading. Gorman said he wouldn't be able to take over until early December, but Bevan—who knew the situation was critical—urged him to advance the date. "Paul, if you are coming, the quicker, the sooner, the better." Gorman wanted to know if things were really as bad as all that, to which Bevan replied, "No, they are worse." But Gorman couldn't leave Western Electric due to provisions of his contract there, so for more than three months the Penn Central drifted.[16]

Wall Street had only a vague inkling of the seriousness of the problems in 1968. Later that year Standard & Poor's thought "the capital stock is an interesting long term speculation," by which time shares were going for 61, down from the postmerger peak of 86 but hardly the subject of panic selling. The price drifted lower with each poor quarterly report, falling below 50 in mid-1969, 40 in the autumn, and ending the year under 30.

Later it would be learned that several directors and officers, among them Bevan, were selling their Penn Central holdings in this period. Moreover, Bevan had a serious conflict-of-interest problem, in that in 1962 he had organized a private investment group known as the Penphil Corporation, which had dealt in some of the more important stocks in the Pennsylvania's portfolio. Bevan continued on at Penphil after the Penn Central was organized, and the later revelation of his investment practices would place him under a cloud.

This can of worms, together with the incredible mismanagement of the railroad and the overarching problems of the eastern rails, would dominate analysis of the collapse.

Saunders believed that he had a budding conglomerate in the Pennsylvania Company, but as it turned out there was no time for germination. The railroad, which was supposed to provide profits for reinvestment in other companies, hemorrhaged so badly that rather than providing transfusions, it needed them, even before its birth.

While at the Pennsylvania Saunders and Bevan had sold off railroad properties accumulated by their predecessors, realizing over $163 million from the Norfolk & Western and another $65 million from the sale of the Long Island Railroad. Most of this money was used to purchase such properties as Macco Realty and Great Southwest, but some was plowed back into the Pennsylvania, then in the midst of an expensive modernization program. Far more railroading capital was needed during the fewer than three years of the Penn Central's precrash history—more than $460 million, in fact.[17] Bevan spent most of his waking hours scurrying from bank to bank, trying to raise needed capital, while additional funds were raised through the sale of properties. The situation recalled the railroad epics of early silent movies, when firemen ripped coaches apart and used the lumber to feed the engine in order to keep the locomotive going. Throughout its history, the Penn Central would be obliged to dispose of assets in order to obtain funds to operate the railroad.

It was a desperate and futile exercise. In 1968 Bevan arranged the sales of the Bryant Ranch and Six Flags Over Georgia, both parts of Great Southwest; Six Flags Over Texas, the most successful of the amusement parks, went soon after. Saunders didn't dare seek buyers for Buckeye, the most successful of his acquisitions, for to do so would signal Penn Central's desperate condition and probably frighten off the bankers. Rather, in a move meant to indicate confidence, he organized the Penn Central Company, which acquired the common stock of Penn Central Transportation on a share-for-share basis. He said he would use this new company as an umbrella for both the Transportation and Pennsylvania companies and "future acquisitions." Of course there would be none of the latter. Rather, Saunders was attempting to create a structure in which the Transportation Company might be distanced from the Pennsylvania Company. He was setting the stage for possible bankruptcy, in which event he might be able to salvage the investment company while the rest of the Penn Central went down the drain. While this ploy was hardly as subtle as Ling's machinations, it was the best that could be done under the circumstances.

Meanwhile Bevan stripped the subsidiaries of their assets to feed the railroad. Merchant's Despatch Transportation, a moderately successful trucking operation owned by the Penn Central, reported a 1969 profit of $2.8 million, and was required to remit $4.7 million to the parent that year. Another trucking subsidiary, New York Central Transport, had profits of $4.2 million, and yet paid the Penn Central a $14.5 million dividend. These and other wholly owned companies were being bled white and would never recover from their financial emaciation. It was as though a cancerous vampire were devouring some of its offspring and sucking the blood from others, without improving its own health.

The conglomerate movement often resembled a corporate explosion, with aggressive new or reinvigorated corporations expanding all over the business map. Engaging in the fallacy of extrapolation, some critics warned that before the end of the century all of American business would be controlled by a score or so of giant conglomerates. The dismantling of the diversified company, as practiced by the Penn Central, was akin to implosion, the shrinkage of the tentacles until nothing remained but the chronically ill core. Were it not for Interstate Commerce Commission strictures and simple pride Saunders and Bevan might have separated the Transportation Company from the still-solvent Pennsylvania Company, taken steps to place the former in bankruptcy, and gone on to develop the latter. (In fact, this was pretty much what happened later, under different leadership.) But this wasn't possible in 1969 and early 1970. Instead, the corporation moved quickly toward failure. The ironic result of this was that railroading resembled the critics' worst-case scenario, when after the collapse the eastern railroads came to be dominated by Conrail, a government-sponsored monopoly.

Penn Central suffered through major problems in early 1970. It was a brutal winter with heavy snows, requiring more than $8 million for snow removal alone, and far more was lost due to stoppages. In March, when the outside auditors came they found a railroad in disarray. Bevan met with them while Saunders went to Washington to seek assistance. Conceding there might be losses on the order of $100 million for that quarter, Bevan said they would be made up. He proposed to do that by transfers from the Pennsylvania Company, updating the sale of some N & W shares, and the use of financial ploys, one of which would be an attempt to sell $100 million of Pennsylvania Company bonds, the proceeds of which were to be used to purchase three Transportation Company properties worth less than half that amount. The underwriters recognized that this was a chancy and perhaps even shady operation, while Bevan all but pleaded with them to go along with him, the alternative being bankruptcy. By then the chief financial officer had become Penn Central's key figure, upon whose persuasive abilities the railroad's fate rested. (Whenever such a person achieves such status it is an almost inevitable sign that the enterprise is close to its destruction.)

Railroad revenues would come to a record $485 million in the second quarter of 1970. This performance was made possible by an economic upturn, rate increases, and rising efficiencies. Nevertheless, in what even Saunders might have conceded were the best of circumstances, the Transportation Company reported a deficit of $12 million. These figures provided an epitaph for the Penn Central. The railroad was doomed. The only questions that remained were how the corpse should be treated and whether the nascent conglomerate might be salvaged.

The general public knew that the Penn Central was in trouble, but there was as yet no strong hint that it might collapse. The corporation's banks knew the worst, and started dumping their holdings in late April. A month and a half later the underwriters rejected Bevan's pleas for assistance, and on May 28 he announced the withdrawal of the $100 million bond flotation. The end was close at hand.

Saunders, Perlman, and Bevan were fired at a special board meeting on June 8; that was the price extracted by the banks for continuing to assist the railroad. Gorman moved into the chairmanship of both the Penn

Central and the Transportation Company; his major task now was to obtain support from the bankers and perhaps the government as well.

Help wasn't forthcoming. The Penn Central Transportation Company declared bankruptcy on June 21, 1970. There was shock on Wall Street (but not at the banks, which by then had virtually emptied their portfolios of Penn Central paper). Rumors abounded regarding other railroads, and even industrial firms, which might follow it down. And what of the pension funds and financial institutions that still held Penn Central paper? Would the default affect their liquidity? For several hours it appeared that America might be headed for a serious financial crisis. The chance that this might occur ended when Federal Reserve Board Chairman Arthur Burns stepped in to announce that the Fed would provide necessary funds for any distressed company. The stock market did decline, however, over the hulk of the largest corporate failure it had ever seen.

The bankruptcy and subsequent reorganization wasn't really understood very well at the time. The Penn Central itself wasn't in bankruptcy, but only the Transportation Company. Nor was the Pennsylvania Company endangered; in fact, it was safer than before, since now its assets couldn't be used to bail out the railroad. Speculators soon recognized this to be an interesting situation. Perhaps the courts would separate the two entities, giving Penn Central's shareholders an interest in a defunct railroad whose properties were about to be taken over by the government (possibly at a high price) and in an interesting though badly shaken conglomerate. In 1970, however, neither railroading nor the conglomerate phenomenon attracted much interest. Penn Central stock fell to below 10, and remained there while the courts decided the next move. In time the Transportation Company would become part of Conrail, a government-sponsored attempt to rationalize several defunct operations. This left the Penn Central with the Pennsylvania Company and claims against the government for its railroad properties. This, and hopes of renewal sometime in the future. The outlook that June of 1970 wasn't particularly promising.

8

The Reaction

Each conglomerator reacted differently to the erosion of stock values and the antitrust assault. Here as in many other things, Ling proved the most innovative of the lot and took the lead in devising ways to come to terms with the new dispensation in Washington and the mood on Wall Street. Ironically, he was the only one of them who failed to survive the turning point.

More than the rest of the high fliers, Ling skated on the thin edge of insolvency. Traditionally LTV had a low ratio of assets to liabilities, a high long-term debt, and low reserves, while short-term obligations often ballooned in a fashion that would have panicked comptrollers and accountants at any other corporation. Ling was the master when it came to borrowing and financial manipulation, much of which involved sleight of hand and the imaginative use of techniques previously unknown or rarely practiced in corporate circles. At one time, when interest rates were low, money plentiful, and the price of his paper high, Ling could pirouette his way through acquisitions and divestitures with graceful ease, and if ever he stumbled, the markets were forgiving. There always was another takeover awaiting his touch, tempting him to strive for new heights.

The situation had changed drastically in 1969, as he was well aware. In the first place, the Jones & Laughlin acquisition was looking worse all the time. In April Ling thought the steel company might earn $38 million and pay LTV a large dividend, more than enough to cover interest and dividends on the paper distributed to acquire it. In fact, earnings that year would come to only $22 million, of which LTV's portion was $15.7 million, and this increased the flow of red ink at headquarters. Then there were problems at Braniff. At one time a rapidly growing airline and a formidable competitor, it was hit hard by a declining economy and the poor management of President Harding Lawrence, whose abilities failed to match his reputation. In April Lawrence had indicated that Braniff might earn around $25 million. He scaled down this figure several times to Ling's dismay. In the end Braniff would earn $6.2 million, of which LTV's share was $3.5 million. Okonite was also in trouble, as were several other LTV units, while the parent was strapped for cash, closer to insolvency than anyone except Ling knew at the time.

Then there was the antitrust suit. Ling was confident he could win it, but the case might drag on for years, draining resources, occupying his time, and casting a pall over the corporation. Ling still felt that J & L was worth having, that it would work out well once the economy recovered, at which time it might be carved up in another redeployment. Pride was also involved. Ling didn't want to admit that the J & L acquisition was as great a blunder as it then appeared. Just as Lyndon Johnson and then Richard Nixon slogged their ways through southeast Asia, Ling hoped to muddle along with his corporate miscalculation. He seemed to sense that this, more than anything else, was driving him on. "I think I can beat McLaren if I stick with it. But that could be just to satisfy my ego," he said in early June. "Is it—trying to look at it from a historic point of view like in Vietnam—a matter of getting so engaged in it to win my point that I might hurt other people, when there is really no other point in staying in the fight?"[1]

Ling's twists and turns in 1969–70 often were ingenious. He came up with a scheme, never implemented, whereby owners of badly depreciated 5 percent debentures might swap them for a lesser amount of 6½ percent face value debentures plus warrants, calculating that LTV would eliminate $400,000 of long-term debt and $11,000 of interest payments for every million dollars worth turned in. This would dress up the balance sheet nicely, with the only cost being the warrants. Then there was a scheme to sell LTV's interest in Braniff to Howard Hughes. Other conglomerators might have opted for a straight cash transaction, but not Ling, who always sought baroque solutions to simple problems. He wanted Hughes to make a tender offer for 2 million shares of LTV at $50 per share, while at the same time Ling would announce that Hughes was being granted an option to purchase the Braniff shares for around $230 million. This was the opening move in what Ling called "Project Home Run." The first step (or base) would be the exchange of those 2 million shares plus around $100–$130 million in cash for LTV's interest in Braniff, which would halve LTV's capitalization and provide it with funds to repay part of the short-term debt. This would have the effect of doubling LTV's per-share earnings (the second base) but eliminate Braniff's rather meager current contribution to earnings (base three). The home run would be completed with a sharp advance in LTV's price as the public, seeing the quantum leap in per-share earnings, would rush in to buy. This might also trigger the exercise of existing warrants, bringing in new money with which to service the debt.

◄ PRICES OF STOCKS OF LEADING CONGLOMERATES, 1968–1971

Stock	1968 Range	Price on November 29, 1968	1969 Range	1970 Range	1971 Range
Gulf + Western	64–38	59¾	50–17	20–9	31–19
ITT	63–45	61¾	60–46	60–31	67–45
Litton	90–53	79⅝	66–31	35–14	31–18
LTV	136–80	97¼	98–24	29–7	27–8
Textron	58–40	43¾	45–23	27–15	32–23

Source: *Moody's Industrials,* 1968–1971

Hughes was intrigued with the concept, perhaps because it appealed to his well-known sense of the bizarre. But in the end nothing came of it, and Ling had to turn to other ploys.

One of these was rather mundane by Ling standards. "Project Cutdown" involved slashing budgets in an attempt to boost earnings per share, but this amounted to more talk than anything else. Another scheme, "Master Game Plan," was more in his tradition. As indicated, Okonite was an ailing operation, demanding some kind of alteration, which Ling was prepared to provide. First he would bring in those Okonite shares still in the public's hands through an exchange offer, and then he would divide the corporation into two segments, one that owned all intangible assets (patents, trademarks, product lines, and the name) while the other would retain the physical plant and other tangible assets, and be provided with a different designation. Then Ling would attempt to find buyers for each. This rather farfetched plan soon was dropped, due as much to its implausibility as anything else.

Ling raised some ready cash by selling LTV's portion of Wilson Sporting Goods to Pepsico for $63 million, and came within a shade of disposing of his shares of Computer Technology, first to Prudential Insurance, and then to University Computing. He came close to luring David Mahoney of Norton Simon Inc., a rapidly growing conglomerate, into buying Braniff. When that failed Ling turned to Bluhdorn, perhaps figuring that the G + W executive might still have some interest in airlines having disposed of his Pan American shares. Bluhdorn rejected the notion out of hand, perhaps because he knew of Braniff's shaky condition, but also due to his growing interest in LTV itself. Earlier in the year he had purchased 10,000 LTV shares, a classic Bluhdorn step prior to making an unfriendly tender. Could it be that he was preparing to move in on Ling? There is no way of knowing, for Bluhdorn never took the second step. Indirectly, however, he may have contributed to the resolution of Ling's problems.

Less than two years earlier, when the Antitrust Division had questioned G + W's attempt to purchase Armour, there had been talk of a divestiture of South Puerto Rico Sugar and Consolidated Cigar in return for permission to acquire the meat packer, the theory being that by so doing Bluhdorn would have relinquished firms with revenues approximating those of Armour. That this wasn't actually the case mattered little, since Bluhdorn squashed the plan before it could be explored and evaluated in any detail. Moreover, it hardly was the kind of solution that would satisfy either antitrusters or defenders of conglomerates, and would have been a weak base upon which to erect guidelines for future action. The idea had been broached, however, and doubtless Ling knew of it.[2]

This then was the situation in late 1969. Ling was fighting off a serious antitrust challenge, and was seeking purchasers for Braniff and Okonite. J & L was in trouble, about to complete one of its worst years in terms of profit. Threatened with illiquidity, Ling was trying to locate buyers for all or part of J & L, and just about anything else that was lying about LTV.

Rumors of the extent of his troubles were bandied about Wall Street in early 1970, where the talk was that LTV might soon be obliged to renegotiate and roll over short-term loans or face what amounted to technical bankruptcy. Prices of the corporation's paper plummeted in January, setting off declines in those of other conglomerates and glamour issues. Several analysts were troubled about this situation, warning readers that an LTV failure could trigger a major panic in a market that had already been battered for more than a year. Democrats started comparing Nixon with Herbert Hoover, talking of "another 1929." There was a jittery situation in New York and Washington.

It was against this backdrop that McLaren and the LTV legal team met to discuss a settlement. One was finally reached and announced in March, to be completed three months later. Based upon what might be called "the Bluhdorn Model," its central clause contained an agreement by LTV either to divest itself of both Braniff and Okonite or to dispose of its shares in Jones & Laughlin. LTV pledged to refrain from reciprocity with J & L, but would be permitted to place members on the steel company's board. Finally, LTV and its subsidiaries would not be allowed to acquire companies with assets of over $100 million for the next ten years.

This was almost gratuitous. LTV common was selling for 12 and its bellwether 5-percent bonds maturing in 1988 going for 25, thus offering a 20-percent yield to speculators at a time when bonds of sound companies fetched around 6 to 7 percent. Rather than being able to seek out new takeovers, LTV was in danger of being acquired by some adventurous raider who, using Ling's approach, might carve it up and sell off the parts for more than they were selling for in the aggregate. Rumors persisted that Bluhdorn, the jackel of Wall Street, was planning just such a move.

News of the settlement was greeted by cheers from the investment community and a sharp attack from reformers. Ralph Nader charged the Antitrust Division with a sellout and called for an investigation. But he wasn't able to attract much of a following on this issue, for LTV clearly was an ailing corporation. Revenues for 1969 came to $3.8 billion, up by $1 billion from the previous year as a result of the J & L acquisition. But LTV had to report a loss of $38.3 million against 1968's profits of $29.4 million, which on a per-share basis came to a $10.59 per share 1968 loss. Doubts remained whether Ling would be able to service the corporation's enormous debt, which taken together came to $2.9 billion. The prices of LTV paper continued to slide, so that by mid-May the common stock was under ten and the fives of 88 could be had for 15, a sure sign that Wall Street expected a collapse.

For several months a number of outside directors had criticized Ling for having gotten LTV into such a mess. There had been talk of asking for his resignation. A number of prominent bondholders were urging a dissolution of the corporation, believing that they would get around 50 cents on the dollar, which was more than their paper was going for at the New York Stock Exchange. They held back until after the antitrust settlement, but when LTV's fortunes still failed to improve they went on the attack once more.

Ling knew what was happening but was powerless to do anything to stop it. On May 17, 1970, he was obliged to step down as chairman, though he would continue as president. Robert Stewart, head of the First National Bank of Dallas, was to assume the chairmanship. One of LTV's major creditors and a man who knew nothing about operating an industrial complex, Stewart was just what he appeared to be: a conservator of the bondholders' interests. LTV was close to collapse and would remain so for several years. In time it would revive, and even renew its interest in acquisitions (in October 1983 LTV's J & L announced plans to merge with the ailing Republic Steel), but LTV's conglomerate period seemed ended.

Gulf + Western had far fewer problems in these years, but Bluhdorn too had to adjust to a new role, that of manager rather than conglomerator. This was not due to antitrust problems or a liquidity crunch, though McLaren kept a weather eye on G + W and the corporation's net income declined from $72.1 million in 1969 to $44.8 million the following year.

Rather, like LTV, the G + W paper shrank in value, and Bluhdorn couldn't use it to pay for acquisitions. The common stock peaked at 64 in 1968 and was a fraction under 60 on November 29th of that year. At its bottom, in the spring of 1970, the shares were going for under ten. Yet the corporation was making money, its dividend had not been cut and was well covered, and management had made the transition to the new economic and political climate with as much grace as was possible.

G + W sold some of its holdings and abandoned whatever plans might have existed for raids on target firms. "We're out of the acquisitions business," Bluhdorn said, and in late 1970, when he had gone without a takeover for more than a year and a half, the statement was believable.[3] This did not mean he regretted having transformed an auto parts company into a conglomerate, or that there were to be major sell-offs and a return to basics. Bluhdorn defended his creation in reporting to stockholders that year, observing that while there had been setbacks due to the "trying economic environment" the corporation "performed well." "We were able to do this because of product and market diversification—the foundation on which Gulf + Western was built," he said. "Our performance was a positive answer to those who questioned the viability of the conglomerate form of free enterprise."

Thus, Bluhdorn would retrench but not retreat. His interest in show business and leisure-time activities remained, but while he may have flirted with the idea of taking over additional firms in these fields, Bluhdorn knew he hadn't the paper or cash to enter the marketplace. Instead, funds were diverted from several of G + W's less glamorous businesses and poured into Paramount, now the centerpiece of the corporation, whose interests occupied much of Bluhdorn's time, and for which he had shown considerable talent. Paramount would lead G + W back to prosperity, largely due to its spectacular success with two film releases, *Love Story* and *The Godfather*. Earnings recovered, coming in at $69.6 million in 1972, by which time G + W common stock was back to 44. The economy seemed stronger too, and McLaren's antitrust crusade was over.

Bluhdorn still denied that he intended to diversify further, and as though to demonstrate his sincerity there were additional small divestitures of poorly performing companies. But the following year he started circling A & P, still independent and ailing after Data Processing Financial & General proved incapable of swallowing it. A & P's board fought back, threatening antitrust action based upon Bluhdorn's continuing interest in Bohack. Bluhdorn backed away, in part because he wanted no trouble from the Justice Department, but even more due to a threat from another government agency, the Securities and Exchange Commission, which had initiated its own investigation of G + W's activities. A fine sense of timing had always been one of Bluhdorn's outstanding talents, and it didn't fail in the early 1970s. He knew he could wait it out with little difficulty. Then, when everything was in place, he would make his move, and return to the conglomerate wars.

Litton didn't perform nearly as well in the early 1970s. While continuing to grow, it did so at a far slower pace than before, due to the lack of takeovers and to difficulties in several subsidiaries, the most important of which was Ingalls. Revenues exceeded $2 billion for the first time in 1969, but earnings had plateaued by then and were starting to decline. From $82.3 million in that year they fell to $50 million in 1971, and in 1972, Litton reported a loss of $2.3 million on sales of $2.5 billion. The stock, which had pierced the 100 level in 1967, fell below ten in 1972.

By then the dream was over. Now Litton sold divisions, closed down inefficient operations, and tried its best to clean house. Just as Saunders and Bevan had done at the Penn Central, Thornton and Ash sold or in other ways divested themselves of properties so as to obtain funds to plow back into retained operations. But there was a crucial difference. The Litton high command rid itself of poorly performing units while beefing up the winners. Thus, even while posting a deficit, Litton was becoming a more viable, stronger corporation. Thornton proved as adept at divestitures as he once had been at acquisitions. During the late 1960s he had busied himself with many outside projects, leaving an increasing share of the actual management to Ash. Now he returned to headquarters on a full-time basis while Ash, in eclipse though hardly in disgrace, left the firm in early 1973 to assume the post of Director of Management and Budget in the Nixon administration.

Significantly, his replacement as chief operating officer was a man with no experience with takeovers, but who was thoroughly grounded in operations. Fred O'Green had come to Litton several years earlier to take charge of its important inertial guidance systems program. After putting together a successful record there he was advanced to Ingalls, which he had started to turn around when called upon to replace Ash. His promotion meant that in the future Litton would stress management far more than "numbers," which had been Ash's specialty.

O'Green planned to concentrate upon Litton's expertise in high technology, maintaining and broadening the base in military sales but expanding significantly into such areas as electric typewriters, copying machines, computers, and cash registers. Litton already had established beachheads in all four areas, but still lacked the financial muscle to fight with the likes of IBM, Xerox, Digital Equipment, and National Cash Register. Therefore, the divestitures had to continue. Eventually, even some of the more promising units had to go, with Thornton getting the best prices he could, but also undergoing the painful experience of seeing a dream cut up into chunks and sold. In March 1973, he announced that Stouffer, which at one time had been heralded as a major entry into an enormous and profitable industry, would be put on the block. "We thought there might be a razor-and-blade relationship between microwave ovens and frozen foods," said Thornton. "It was wishful thinking."[4]

In most respects ITT came out of this transitional period in better economic and financial shape than any other conglomerate, a striking demonstration of just how soundly Geneen had put his corporation together. Earnings advanced steadily from 1969 to 1973, and there were annual dividend increases. While the price of ITT common slumped badly in mid-1970, it recovered nicely soon after, and went on to a new all-time high the following year.

Geneen won most of his battles with the antitrusters, and although he had to make concessions on some points at least he was able to retain his most prized holdings. Considered the outstanding conglomerator and manager through the late 1960s, Geneen maintained his reputation on these scores until the early 1970s.

However, both his and ITT's reputations were tarnished beyond even those of Ling and LTV. This was not due to the way he ran the corporation, blunders in the business sphere, or even clashes with McLaren and others at the Justice Department. Rather, in the early 1970s Geneen became entangled with the Nixon White House in such ways as to cast doubt not only upon his judgment, but upon his business ethics as well. Geneen remained at the helm when it was all over, but he operated under a cloud during his last years at ITT.

ITT had become one of McLaren's chief targets, with challenges being made over the Grinnell, Canteen, and Hartford acquisitions. The corporation's formidable public relations and legal teams went into action even before the briefs had been filed, mounting a massive campaign to outflank the Antitrust Division. They lobbied the White House skillfully, claiming that the divestitures would harm ITT in ways that would disrupt its overseas operations, and so harm the U.S. balance-of-payments position. Geneen and others traveled regularly to Washington, meeting with Cabinet members and Nixon's closest advisors, claiming that McLaren had a vendetta against ITT, while Ned Gerrity, who headed the public relations operation, attempted to demonstrate that the Antitrust Division was operating at cross purposes with the president. "It was plain that McLaren's views were not consistent with those of the Attorney General and the White House," Gerrity observed to Vice President Spiro Agnew. "We are being pursued . . . not on law but on theory bordering on the fanatic." Thomas Casey, ITT's Director for Corporate Planning, spoke with White House insider Charles Colson, pointing out the differences between administration views and the Antitrust Division's actions. "If indeed the facts here are correct then we might be riding one horse and McLaren another," wrote Colson, who indeed thought that this might be the case. Soon after, John Ehrlichman, one of Nixon's closest aides, who was jockeying for position, started to speak against McLaren, perhaps hoping to use this matter as a means of driving a wedge between the president and Attorney General Mitchell. Such was the kind of Machiavellian scheming taking place in the Nixon White House. All would be revealed later. In 1970, however, ITT believed that it was engaged in a strong, blunt, but ordinary lobbying effort, and that it was succeeding in winning support from Nixon's inner circle.

It was against this backdrop that on December 31, 1970, the District Court for Connecticut found for ITT in the Grinnell case. Judge William Timbers issued a biting rebuke to McLaren, implying that the action was frivolous and never should have been brought. "The Court declines the government's invitation to indulge in an expanded reading of the statutory language and holds the statute means just what it says," wrote Timbers. "It proscribes only those mergers the effect of which 'may be substantially to lessen competition.'" In what sounded like an echo of Turner's views on the matter, he went on to say that if there were to be changes, they would have to come about through legislation, that "under our system of government . . . any decision to change the standard be made by the Congress, and not by the courts."[5]

For a few days Geneen hoped that the combination of the Timbers decision and the White House lobbying would deter McLaren from pressing ahead with the cases, but that wasn't to be. McLaren announced that he would ask Solicitor General Erwin Griswold to approve an appeal to the Supreme Court. As it turned out Griswold believed in the Turner approach to antitrust and was reluctant to make such a move. But in the end, with great reluctance, he filed the appeal, which led to an intensification of ITT's lobbying efforts.

Despite this, events were being set into motion that would result in an out-of-court settlement. The most important element was the developing power struggle within the White House, where Ehrlichman had outmaneuvered Mitchell and was forcing the Attorney General to back down. He seemingly had supported Geneen against McLaren as a means to gain position, but this wouldn't be deduced for several years. Then too, the growing realization both on Wall Street and in Washington was that the conglomerate movement had ended. The Penn Central collapse the previous June had completed the process begun in early 1969 with the stock market decline, and had squeezed the last bit of optimism out of merger-mania. Increasingly it appeared that McLaren was flogging a dead horse, and perhaps he was starting to realize this himself. There already was a formula for compromise, namely that used in the LTV settlement. Both sides agreed to take that route.

McLaren sent a memo to Kleindienst on June 17, 1971, proposing this switch in policy. "We have had a study made by financial experts and they substantially confirm ITT's claims as to the effects of a divestiture order. Such being the case, I fear that we must also anticipate that the impact upon ITT would have a ripple effect—in the stock market and the economy."[6] McLaren went on to sketch his terms: Hartford might be retained, but ITT would have to divest itself of businesses whose revenues were roughly equivalent to those of the insurance company.

Had the memo been written two months earlier—and had Geneen known of its existence—the matter could have been resolved in a week or so. There would have been charges of a sellout from Ralph Nader and other reformers, a day or two of headlines and business-page analyses, and that would have been it. Or if McLaren had decided to stand firm ITT might have won its cases, and come out of the litigation with barely a scratch. As it happened, the timing of McLaren's switch, combined with Geneen's acceptance of compromise, worked against the corporation.

For one thing, ITT was vindicated in the Canteen case, when on July 2nd (by which time Geneen had come to terms with the Antitrust Division) Judge Richard Austin decided that the government's case was without merit. Then Judge Joseph Blumenfeld was selected to hear both the Hartford case and the Grinnell appeal, and he was considered to be favorably disposed toward the ITT position. Thus, compromise really hadn't been necessary. Geneen could have retained everything had he waited only a few months.

More important—and damaging—was what in retrospect seemed a tainted attempt at further lobbying. On May 2nd, a month and a half prior to the sending of the McLaren memo, Geneen offered a substantial donation to the San Diego Convention and Visitors Bureau, to be used to get the Republican National Convention to that city. He and other ITT personnel later claimed that this was completely innocent and in the corporation's interests, since the GOP would be headquartered in a new Sheraton hotel then being constructed, and the publicity more than justified the donation. Testimony at a subsequent congressional investigation indicated that there was no direct relationship between the donation and the antitrust issues. Critics charged, however, that Geneen was really trying to bribe Nixon in this fashion, or at the very least place the president in ITT's debt. Whatever the truth, Geneen had been made to appear an amoral corrupter willing to use any means to attain his objectives.

None of this was known on July 31st, when McLaren announced the compromise out-of-court settlement. In return for keeping Hartford, ITT agreed to dispose of Avis, Levitt, Canteen, and part of Grinnell. Furthermore, the corporation agreed not to acquire any company with assets of more than $100 million during the next ten years. Thus, the ITT antitrust agreement was modeled after the LTV compromise of the previous year, and as anticipated evoked the same response from reformers: anger and charges of a sellout. McLaren responded with a claim to have stopped the conglomerate movement "dead in its tracks," but this really wasn't true. Even without the antitrust case Geneen would have had to halt or at the very least slow down his takeovers. The great burst of ITT acquisitions had to be digested. Troubles at Rayonier, Sheraton, and other newly arrived subsidiaries demanded his attention and required whatever funds ITT had or could raise on the capital markets—in a period of economic distress, with the stock market in a free-fall decline. ITT could no more have continued with diversification than could LTV, Litton, or G + W. Finally, its role as the chief villain on the American business scene was annealed by revelations that it had played a role in the overthrow of the left-wing Salvatore Allende government in Chile.

These and related problems seemed to have written the final chapter to the conglomerate movement. Certainly there was a slowdown in overall activity on the takeover front. In 1968, the peak year, there had been 207 mergers accounting for more than $13 billion in aggregate assets. There followed a sharp decline in activity, so that by 1972 only 70 mergers were reported, involving $2 billion in assets. By then autopsy reports were rife. Some credited (or blamed) McLaren for having stopped the conglomerate movement dead in its tracks, and he was quick to accept whatever applause might come his way for his actions, especially for the agreements with LTV and ITT. Others argued that the movement couldn't survive the stock market crash of 1969, which antedated McLaren's crusade (or vendetta, depending upon which side one was on). A few business observers believed that the major conglomerates would have had to slow down, even under the best of political and economic circumstances, if only to digest the 1968 takeovers.

John Burton, who was chief accountant for the Securities and Exchange Commission, believed the phenomenon to have been propelled by three forces: "the scientific manager, the psychedelic accountant, and the go-go fund." There was something to this—at least to the first two mentioned. The patina of technological marvels had become almost epidemic by the late 1960s, helping to boost the likes of Litton and Teledyne to new highs, while LTV, ITT, and G + W benefitted from imaginative and creative accounting techniques. As for the "go-go managers," they tended to deal in smaller fry, and their activities, while contributing greatly to the overall frenzy, had virtually no impact on the workings of the larger corporations. *Fortune* writer Lewis Beman believed "the most damaging result of the conglomerate merger era was the false legitimacy it seemed to confer on the pursuit of profits from financial manipulation rather than by producing something of genuine economic value." Yet even John Burton had to concede that in some cases mergermania produced sound and viable results. "It was like trying to build a house from the roof down," he said, "but sometimes the roof actually stayed up."

In any case, all of this was part of the unlamented past, since those managers, accountants, and go-go fund operators had been flushed out of the system. Beman concluded that the conjuncture of forces necessary for a revival of the movement "is unlikely to recur for years."[7]

But it really wasn't over—at least not for some of the survivors. Some would continue acquiring firms, though at a slower rate than before. Others would enter into a variant of what had happened at the Penn Central, namely turn away from diversification, but with a wholly different purpose: to preserve the core rather than feed the shell, and to transform themselves into more homogeneous and conventional firms. Finally, a small number of medium-sized corporations would attempt to expand by means of diversification and takeovers, though none of them were led by individuals who possessed the imagination of Ling, the rapaciousness of Bluhdorn, or the managerial skills of Geneen.

Yet, if the conglomerate movement had faded by the early 1970s the acquisitions mania had hardly ended. Rather, it was to reappear late in the decade in a new form, with a different cast of players. To some this mergermania represented a departure from the conglomerate drive, while to others it was a necessary and logical variant, which demonstrated that like all healthy movements, this one was capable of adjusting to new circumstances, and that the drive toward concentration was far from ended.

9

Nuclear War on the Corporate Battlefield

———————◦•◦———————

Money was dear in the 1970s. Toward the end of the decade, at a time when inflation was running in the double digits, investors were able to get as much as 20 percent with almost no risk from money market funds. It seemed then that there was little hope of a return to the halcyon days of the 1960s, when 4 to 5 percent inflation was considered a problem calling for the full resources of government to rectify.

Little wonder that investors avoided the securities markets. Those who were in equities in the late 1960s and early 1970s had for the most part done poorly. In the spring of 1980 the Dow-Jones Industrial Average bottomed at 730, which was where it had been in the spring of 1975, the summer of 1970, and November of 1963. That is to say that the market hadn't gone anywhere in the almost seventeen years following the assassination of John F. Kennedy.

But the situation was worse than that. The dollar had lost more than half its value in this period. By some estimates the Dow would have had to have gone to 1700 for it to have kept pace with inflation.

By almost any yardstick, the decade of the 1970s was one of the worst periods for equities in the twentieth century. Stocks that at one time had been considered "steals" at 20 to 30 times earnings were now in the single digit range with dividends in the double digits. It seemed that few wanted such securities, with the multitudes opting for liquid asset accounts offering much higher and more secure yields.

Their stocks devalued, conglomerates lacked the necessary currency to use in takeovers. No longer could corporate treasurers grind out high-priced stock and convertible debentures to exchange for the assets of acquired companies. Litton Industries, which once sold for more than 50 times earnings, rated a P/E of eight in late 1973, when its new president, Crosby Kelly, embarked upon a divestiture and cost-cutting program. The corporation's many divisions were demoralized; rumors spread about which subsidiary would be the next to go. "We made the mistake of saying we got rid of Stouffer Food because it didn't fit in with our mainstream," said Kelly. "Now people want to know what our mainstream is."

Meanwhile at Gulf + Western, Charles Bluhdorn preferred to talk about expansion at Paramount rather than about the performance of his stock portfolio or about forays into new areas. In the 1970s the corporation had acquired publisher Simon & Schuster, apparel manufacturer Kayser-Roth, and Marquette Co., a cement manufacturer. None had performed as hoped. True to his razzle-dazzle approach Bluhdorn purchased Madison Square Garden, which gave G + W control of a basketball and a hockey team. That neither team did particularly well in its league was an echo of the parent's performance at the N.Y.S.E.

By 1981 Bluhdorn seemed more concerned with ridding G + W of several disappointments than with acquiring new companies. Onto the block went New Jersey Zinc, Consolidated Cigar, and several other firms. Associates urged Bluhdorn to dispose of G + W's large stock portfolio and use the funds obtained from those sales to improve existing operations. But the chairman refused to abandon his long term ambitions to enlarge the corporation through acquisitions.

Then, on February 22, 1983, Bluhdorn died suddenly. A decade and a half earlier this would have resulted in consternation. Things were different in 1983. G + W common rose more than two points on the news, and continued upward when it appeared that the corporation would turn from diversification rapidly under new management.

Textron acquired a venture capital firm, American Research & Development, whose primary claim to fame was having purchased a large interest in the then-struggling Digital Equipment, which, when distributed to shareholders, was worth more than half a billion dollars. But President G. William Miller stressed the conservative nature of most Textron operations, the corporation's sound balance sheet, and its current concentration upon long-range planning rather than acquisitions. In addition he took pains to note that Textron never had been a voracious acquisitor, and in any case its period of diversification had ended. "The second generation manager . . . worried more about internal growth and credibility" than pyrotechnics, he said, while similar statements emanated from LTV, ITT, and the others.[1]

In this period, too, the Justice Department and the Federal Trade Commission proceeded against conglomerate mergers while congressional reformers continued their search for a viable method of containing the movement. The only major takeover in 1974 was Mobil's of Marcor, the giant retailing complex, while most others were challenged or investigated with renewed zeal. Nothing of consequence emerged from the Celler Committee's investigation of conglomerates, however. Senator Edward Kennedy (D–Mass.) attempted to stir interest by reviving the old idea of barring mergers of companies each of which had more than $500 million in assets, but he found few takers.

In a time when the nation suffered from stagflation there was little interest in legislation considered antibusiness, and in any case the need for such measures was hardly pressing, since the conglomerates were no longer making headlines. Merger activity was off by 16 percent in 1973 and by 30 percent the following year, with scarcely a stirring from the wheelers and dealers of the 1960s. That remained the situation until late in the decade. By then Harold Geneen, James Ling, and Charles Bluhdorn were looked upon as having been capable enough managers, but relics of an age gone by. Editors of business magazines no longer demanded articles on takeovers, and graduate school case studies of the companies were of more historical than contemporary interest. Few doubted that mergers and acquisitions would continue, but they were expected to be rarer, smaller, and less contentious. Conventional wisdom held that that would remain the case until and unless there was a revival on Wall Street, providing potential conglomerators with the means to bid for control of other companies.

But it didn't happen that way. Those who held to this view made the familiar error of supposing that history repeats itself. They also failed to appreciate that altered circumstances and values would lead the CEOs of major corporations to search out means of improving the performances of their existing enterprises. This resulted in the search for bargains and expanded empires.

There was a pickup in merger activity in 1976, during which 2,276 of them took place, with more than 40 in the $100 million range.[2] Perhaps the most interesting of these, and certainly the most significant, was Atlantic Richfield's purchase of Anaconda for $536 million—in cash.

Others would follow, as American business embarked upon this new chapter in the history of mergermania, one based upon the rapidly depreciating dollar rather than the constantly appreciating shares of the previous decade. Many of the takeovers of the period represented nothing more than a flight from currency into hard assets.

This movement was unlike the one that preceded it. For one thing, many of the takeovers weren't of the conglomerate variety, and for another there was no serious attempt to offer philosophical justification for the moves. A goodly number involved oil companies, either as acquirers or targets, and for obvious reasons. In 1973, when the Organization of Petroleum Exporting Countries increased its demands, the price of petroleum had been $3.39 a barrel; by 1981 it had risen to more than $22. In the same period proven reserves had declined from more than 36 billion barrels to under 27 billion. In 1981 most experts agreed that prices were bound to rise along with the costs of new discoveries. Therefore the petroleum companies attempted to diversify against the time when they assumed the price would be so high that oil would be uneconomical for many uses. At the same time, others tried to purchase those firms because the value of their reserves and other assets wasn't reflected in the price of their shares.

Battles for control of the takeover candidates were more common than they had been during the conglomerate period, often resembling outright warfare. During the 1950s conglomerators talked of the need for synergy, while Geneen, Little, and Thornton offered plausible rationales for their actions. Not so the new acquisitors who used terms like "white knight" (to whom a besieged firm would look to as a possible merger partner when courted by an unfriendly firm); "leveraged buy-out" (in which the suitor borrows money short term for the purchase, and then, when it is completed, sells off pieces of the property so as to obtain funds to repay part or all of the loans); and "discounted cash flow" (a method of measuring the return on capital invested, by which the potential acquisitor determined whether to make a bid for the target). By 1983, largely as a result of the three campaigns discussed below, several new terms appeared. There was the "Pac-Man" ploy, a term used to describe the situation when the pursued turns around and becomes the pursuer. In this case, the original takeover candidate makes a tender for shares of the company attempting to acquire it, the idea being that the best defense is a good offense. And unlike the traditional military sense of the term, when it is a tactic of the defender, in 1982 business practice a "scorched earth policy" referred to threats of dismissing entire management teams if they opposed the takeover. In order to balance the white knight there came a group of black knights, unwelcome predators who forced the search for a savior. More than one black knight earned the name "Jaws" from insiders at the assaulted company.

Yet there really was little new in all of this. Royal Little had been the quintessential white knight in his time. Many unwilling targets, the most prominent aimed at by G + W, searched for saviors in the 1960s. Harold Geneen had perfected the techniques of discounted cash flow. Francis White of American Woolen might have toyed with what later would become the Pac-Man strategy when combatting Textron's take-over three decades earlier. Scorched earth policies had been practiced by several conglomerators, Charles Bluhdorn in particular. But none of these men had the raw power employed in the late 1970s and early 1980s; that power led to the formulation of a new term. On Wall Street the gigantic struggles among the multi-billion-dollar corporations for control of one another was occasionally called "Nuclear War."

Among the acquisitors and their targets were some of the nation's largest, most easily recognized, and oldest companies. More comparable to elephants than gazelles in their movements, the hunters lumbered across the corporate landscape, slinging hundreds of millions of dollars in cash around with a sangfroid that astonished the most jaded Wall Streeters. Their actions were far removed from those of a young Jimmy Ling patching together a group of electrical contractors in the early days of Ling Electric or those of Tex Thornton scraping for money to purchase the firm upon which Litton Industries would be erected.

The leaders of the multi-billion-dollar giants who engaged in the takeover game during the late 1970s and early 1980s were managers rather than entrepreneurs, anonymous types who were creatures rather than creators of their corporate vehicles, without an imaginative or even clear-cut point of view. They were crude and obvious rather than innovative, and almost all were a decided cut below their counterparts of the 1960s. With a single exception—and that one embarrassing—they were colorless individuals, which was why the media rarely referred to them and failed to explore their outlooks.

The takeover battles of the current period were and are conducted by a different set of players, who have more chips but less panache and flare than their predecessors. And in three of the most spectacular power plays of 1981–82 they were interrelated in a curious and most revealing fashion.

Most of the leading corporate actors had familiar names. Du Pont, with 1980 revenues of $13.9 billion was in 15th place on the Fortune 500 roster that year. A gigantic chemical complex specializing in synthetics, Du Pont would either have to diversify out of petroleum-based chemicals or find a captive source of the feedstock. Chairman Edward Jefferson said, "We will combat the high price of oil by making more products that don't use it," but he also initiated the search for an acquisition among the small- and medium-sized producers that could provide Du Pont with an assured source of petroleum.

Though hardly a corporate pauper, Du Pont wasn't overly liquid. At the end of 1980 its balance sheet showed under $230 million in cash and equivalents, but its long-term debt was a mere $1 billion, giving the corporation plenty of room to maneuver when and if a comely target came into view. Du Pont was a potential white knight.

Then there was Seagram with 1980 revenues of $2.5 billion, which was cash rich and eager for action, destined for the role of black knight. The corporation was a leader in distilled spirits, but in 1981 it was earning more from the interest on its $4 billion in cash assets that had been held aside for a major takeover. Perhaps no one was driven to acquisitions as much as Edgar Bronfman, the chairman, chief executive officer, and inheritor of a successful operation, who was anxious to prove his own worth as a businessman.

Bronfman was the third generation in the field. His grandfather, a Polish Jew who had emigrated to Canada in 1889, had drifted toward hotel keeping, and the prime money earner there was a bar. One of his sons, Sam, began the liquor business, and in 1927 purchased Seagram & Sons, whose name he kept. The company did well during the American prohibition experiment and even better afterward. Though challenged by others it remained the largest factor in the American market, where it was represented by a subsidiary, Joseph E. Seagram & Sons. This was the legacy Sam left his son and successor.

There was more to the corporation than liquor, however. Seagram owned valuable parcels of real estate and Texas Pacific Oil, a relatively small producer of crude. Nor was Seagram the Bronfmans' only concern. Together with his brother Peter, Edgar owned Edper Investments, which controlled Brascan Ltd., an investment company, which in turn had a large position in Scott Paper and other interests. And both men had an unslaked ambition that couldn't be met by simply managing the inheritance and dabbling in investments. "Father always taught us to think in terms of generations," said Edgar. "He always expected each generation to surpass the previous generation." This was Edgar's expectation, too.

Bronfman began his move in 1980, when he sold Texas Pacific to Sun for $2.3 billion. Later he would dispose of some of the real estate, including the corporation's Park Avenue headquarters, in order to amass his $4 billion war chest. Then Seagram hired several consultants, headed by Arthur D. Little, to search out takeover candidates.

They came up with a prize: St. Joe Corp., a large mining complex whose assets weren't reflected in the price of its shares. Bronfman made a $2.13 billion offer for the corporation, which spurned his advances. The rejection was about as ugly as might have been expected; it seemed to some to have been tinged with anti-foreign sentiments, and reflections upon the "legitimacy" of the Bronfmans. "I don't hold it against him [Edgar Bronfman] that his father was a bootlegger," said St. Joe Chairman John Duncan, which translated into just the opposite. And as though to slap Bronfman in the face, he found a more suitable acquirer in Fluor Corp., a leading international contractor with major interests in the Arab countries; some thought Duncan believed that to be preferable to a corporation controlled by Canadian Jews.

Bronfman lost; all he had to show for his efforts was a profit of $10 million realized on the St. Joe shares he had accumulated before being forced to drop out. That would have satisfied a person like Charles Bluhdorn, who had been through several such experiences. But not Bronfman.

His appetite had been whetted, and he now took on additional advisors, indicating he would consider any large corporation in all fields except steel, forest products, and nuclear energy. At various times in early 1981 there were rumors that Seagram was preparing offers for such firms as General Foods, Bristol-Myers, Kellogg, and Revlon. Would Bronfman consider a petroleum company? The sale of Texas Pacific appeared to indicate that the answer was no. But Bronfman was eager to move, the oils offered good value, and as the year wore on Seagram started considering several of them.[3]

U. S. Steel (1980 revenues, $12.5 billion) was an unexpected player. It had been the world's largest industrial corporation in 1901, but eighty years later was only number 19 of the Fortune 500, ahead of Western Electric and Eastman Kodak but behind the likes of Tenneco and General Electric. U. S. Steel's leaders were eager to diversify out of its major product, probably for the same reason Bronfman rejected the idea of acquiring a company in that industry. Steel was an ailing if not dying industry in the United States. Unable to compete successfully against the Europeans and Japanese in many domestic markets and having to upgrade facilities merely to break even in most years, the corporation faced a bleak, uncertain future. Chairman David Roderick knew that the purchase of another business could alter the outlook dramatically. At the end of 1980, U. S. Steel had slightly more than $900 million in cash and equivalents and a long-term debt of close to a quarter of a billion dollars. The corporation would be hard put to raise the kind of funds needed for a major acquisition, but under the circumstances Roderick had little choice but to try for the part of white knight.

Mobil Corporation, with $59.5 billion in revenues, was the nation's second largest industrial corporation (behind Exxon), and the quintessential black knight. In order to appreciate its size, consider that Mobil had more sales than Ford and Chrysler combined and twice those of International Business Machines. Its profits of $2.8 billion were greater than the total revenues of such corporations as Merck, Singer, and Gillette. Entities like Mobil are more empires than corporations, their power positively awesome.

So were their problems. Although it had spent $4.3 billion on domestic exploration during the preceding five years, Mobil's reserves had dipped by 10 percent. Moreover, like most large internationals, the corporation was eager to expand its domestic reserves against the possibility of future expropriations. Mobil obtained nearly half its crude from Saudi

Arabia, a relationship symbolized by the presence on the board of Suliman Olayan, a Saudi businessman who presumably reported to and spoke for his government. Mobil meant to cut back on this dependence through the takeover of a sizeable North American corporation.

In 1980 Mobil's proven domestic reserves stood at 890 million barrels, below that of many of the medium-sized companies, which Mobil was eyeing so hungrily. None of the majors had searched for merger partners more avidly than Mobil, and few had been so frustrated.

The search began in earnest in 1979, after the second "oil shock." Chairman Rawleigh Warner and President William Tavoulareas looked at the list of independents and initiated discussions to little avail. First there was Belridge Oil, which slipped away when Shell won a bidding war at $3.6 billion. Mobil had wanted to purchase Texas Pacific Oil from Seagram, only to lose it to Sun. For a total of $1.5 billion it had purchased General Crude and TransOcean, but these firms merely slowed Mobil's reserve shrinkage. "At our size we can't consistently replace production with discovery," said Warner in the summer of 1981. "That's why you see these [takeover] attempts."[4]

But Mobil was not as liquid as some of the other players. At the end of 1980 it had $1.9 billion in cash and marketable securities. More important, however, Mobil's existing and potential lines of credit came to several times that amount. Having been frustrated in their earlier attempts at landing a major prize, Warner and Tavoulareas had become more eager than ever and more prepared to throw their weight around than might otherwise have been the case. Especially Tavoulareas, a rugged, blunt man who managed the tender offers, and who was the original corporate "Jaws."

When petroleum industry insiders referred to medium-sized companies they usually meant those with less than around $10 billion in revenues. Many were deemed takeover candidates, and the list included Union, Cities Service, Getty, Kerr-McGee, and Pennzoil. Even Sun, which had revenues of close to $15 billion, was deemed a proper target for one of the truly large corporations.

Conoco Inc. (until 1979 known as Continental Oil) was also a potential target. In 1980 Conoco was the nation's twelfth largest corporation, with revenues of $13 billion. A good deal of its holdings were in North America, and Conoco had a majority interest in the Canadian firm of Hudson's Bay Oil & Gas. Hudson's Bay owned drilling rights on valuable, untapped acreage in Alberta; it also was participating in some promising projects in other parts of the world. The corporation had proven reserves of more than 2 billion barrels, but according to industry estimates the unexplored areas, especially those in Canada, contained at least half again as much. Hudson's Bay also had reserves of nearly 8 trillion cubic feet of natural gas. Little wonder that Conoco was considered a near-ideal marriage partner.

In addition to its producing properties Conoco owned marginally profitable plastics and chemical operations, and a number of well-situated pipelines. Its most interesting nonpetroleum subsidiary was Consolidation Coal, acquired in 1966 when that industry was depressed. The role Consolidation played in Conoco was evidenced by the fact that the corporation's chairman, Ralph Bailey, had been an executive there before the takeover, and he still believed that a large part of Conoco's future would be in coal.

The price of coal had shot upward as a result of the oil shock, so Consolidation was a most valuable property; whose worth wasn't fully reflected in Conoco's market price. How much was Conoco worth? While such estimates must necessarily be approximate, it appeared that $150 per share on a breakup basis was reasonable. Since Conoco was then selling in the 50s it seemed a prime candidate for a leveraged buy-out. A would-be acquirer might offer a premium price for the stock, raise the funds on a short-term basis, and then sell off parts of the enterprise—first to go would be Consolidation—and use the funds obtained from the sale to pay off all or a large part of the loan.

Like Conoco, Marathon Oil (*Fortune*'s number 39 corporation on sales of $8.2 billion) was deemed by the investment community a probable takeover candidate. Known as the Ohio Oil Company when it was part of the Standard Oil empire, it changed its name in 1962, and around that time expanded into pipelines and distribution while also purchasing crude producers at what proved to be low prices. Marathon had sizable domestic reserves (682 million barrels) as well as large holdings in the Middle East and Indonesia, with some promising areas in the North Sea as well. The company had a half interest in the Yates field in west Texas, considered the most exciting and potentially most valuable find in the lower 48 states since the end of World War II. Estimates varied of just how much petroleum existed in Yates, but the figure generally was believed to be in the billion barrel range. In addition, Marathon had new production coming on stream from the Brae field in the North Sea.

Industry insiders considered Marathon even more promising than Conoco, perhaps the most undervalued oil stock on the New York Stock Exchange, with a breakup value of around $200 a share, or approximately four times its price in early 1981. The company was a distinct favorite among accountants armed with information about discounted cash flows and those concerned with leveraged buy-outs. Recognizing this, Marathon's President Harold Hoopman and his board arranged for a

$5 billion line of credit, to be used to ward off prowling would-be acquisitors. The word was that the company was resigned to being devoured, however, and was actively searching for a friendly suitor, a white knight.

Martin Marietta, whose $2.6 billion in revenues earned it a place in the 149th slot, was hardly as attractive. A conglomerate of sorts, this firm had been formed from a union of the old Martin aviation interests and American Marietta, whose jumble of chemicals, cement, aluminum, and household products at one time had earned it the reputation of a "junior Du Pont," one which it hadn't lived up to in the early 1950s. Under Chairman Thomas Pownall Martin Marietta was a well-run if unexciting corporation, where tradition was strong and surprises unwelcome. Although none of its major businesses were performing outstandingly, the corporation did have a good research and development facility which, if teamed up with the proper production operations, might be worth more than its stock valuation indicated.

United Technologies was the only true conglomerate in the pack. Harry Gray, who was the number three at Litton behind Tex Thornton and Roy Ash, had taken over at what then had been United Aircraft in 1971. The corporation was large but flabby, having just posted a loss of $92.5 million on sales of $2 billion. Its most important products, aircraft engines and helicopters, were deemed technologically advanced, but the profit margins on them were low due to poor bidding and lax controls. Moreover, the Vietnam War was coming to an end, which would result in lower orders. As for the commercial aviation market, that too was overcrowded; General Electric and Rolls Royce had just won major competitions against United's Pratt & Whitney subsidiary. Given his proclivities and experience, it was natural for Gray to consider conglomerating out of trouble.

Soon thereafter, United Aircraft embarked upon a dramatic but calculated acquisitions campaign. For the most part, Gray utilized common stock, and into the renamed United Technologies came such established, medium-sized firms as Otis Elevators, Carrier Corporation, Ambac, and Essex International, along with young high-technology outfits such as Dynell and Mostek. For 1980 United Technologies reported revenues of $12.3 billion, placing it 21st on the Fortune 500.

Gray paused the following year, and few expected him to make a major bid of any kind. For one thing several of his more recent acquisitions required large amounts of capital (Mostek and Otis alone had taken $621 million in cash), and for another the corporation was short of research and development capital. United Technologies was in fact cash poor, with liquid assets of less than $150 million. Still, Gray was prepared to listen if the right deal presented itself. Like dozens of other leaders of large corporations, he was in the mood to merge.

The former Allied Chemical (revenues $6.4 billion, *Fortune* 500 rank 59), was rechristened Allied Corporation in 1981 to reflect its new opera-tions and aspirations. Under Chairman Edward Hennessy Allied had become a prime acquisitor itself, having recently gobbled ELTRA (a conglomerate with a wide variety of products from storage batteries to sneakers), ailing electronics complex Bunker-Ramo, Fisher Scientific, and Apollo Lasers, while at the same time developing a considerable interest in petroleum, especially the North Sea fields. All of this sapped Allied's resources. By the end of 1980 Allied had cash and equivalents of only $189 million and a long-term debt of $650 million. The corporation had room to borrow, and Hennessy remained on the merger trail, only too interested in hearing about attractive opportunities, and quite willing to play the role of corporate savior. Especially if by so doing he could embarrass Harry Gray.

Before he arrived at Allied Hennessy had been senior vice-president for finance and later executive vice-president at United Technologies, second in command to Gray and for a while considered his likely succes-sor. The two men were quite similar in temperament, and often clashed. Moreover Hennessy, a prominent Catholic layman, made little attempt to disguise his disapproval of Gray's having been twice divorced and recently married for the third time. Taking a plum from anyone else would have been pleasant, but to do so to Gray would be an absolute delight.

Bendix Corporation (1980 revenues, $3.8 billion; *Fortune* ranking 87) was headed by erratic and quirky young chairman William Agee; he also had a bundle of cash and was eager to wheel and deal. One analyst thought him "a very volatile trading-oriented type of person." Another, purportedly an admirer, said Agee was "a very tough asset manager. He has no loyalty to businesses. If it can't be shaped up in five years, out it goes." Later he would be called the loose cannon on the deck of American big business; that sobriquet seemed justifiable by his activities in 1972–73. In the late 1970s, however, he was more concerned with remak-ing Bendix in his own image.[5]

Under the guidance of former board chairman W. Michael Blum-enthal, Bendix had acquired firms and grown internally to the point where it was a major factor in such diverse areas as automotive goods, aerospace, industrial machinery, and forest products. When Blumenthal left in 1976 to accept the post of Secretary of the Treasury in the incoming Jimmy Carter administration, Agee, then 39 years old, suc-ceeded to the chairmanship. Showing clear disdain for the core opera-tions, he told reporters of his yearning to transform Bendix into a high-technology corporation. Agee was quite eclectic, however, willing to buy anything of value assuming it could be had for a proper price. It was with this in mind that in 1978 he purchased 20 percent of ASARCO, a mining company, for $127 million, and two years later bought a controlling interest in machine tool manufacturer Warner & Swasey for slightly more than $130 million. But Agee's divestitures, made in order to obtain cash for a major takeover, were far more significant. In January 1981, Agee disposed of Bendix Forest Products for $425 million in cash. A year later the ASARCO holdings were dropped for $336 million. Other sales—Bass & Co., Modern Materials, United Geophysical, and Caradco—brought in another $130 million. Portions of these funds were used to pay off short-term indebtedness and clean the Bendix books in preparation for any new borrowings that might be necessary to finance a takeover, and the rest was placed in a war chest for that same purpose. By September 1981, Agee had $1.4 billion in cash, and he was earnestly searching for a candidate.

It seemed almost everyone else was doing the same in those days.

These were the prime participants and their backgrounds. If they have been presented in a manner similar to that of the cast of characters in an Agatha Christie mystery it is because the machinations in which they engaged during 1981-82 seemed to fall more into the realm of fiction than fact. That isn't to suggest that their activities during this period were at all mysterious, though perhaps at times they were a trifle bizarre.

If the Atlantic Richfield-Anaconda merger can be said to have opened the new era and provided clues to how the deals would be financed, the struggle over Conoco offered a taste of the ways the more spectacular of the struggles would be waged.

The explosives were in place, and they were triggered in late October 1980, when the Canadian government announced its intention to take control of the country's petroleum and natural gas assets by the end of the decade. This caused the price of shares for those companies with extensive Canadian operations to decline sharply, putting them on the bargain counter.

Dome Petroleum, an aggressive Canadian petroleum company, now singled out Conoco as a target, and on May 6, 1981 announced a $65 per share tender offer for 14 million shares. Did Dome really expect to achieve control of Conoco? Probably not, but the Calgary-based company shrewdly guessed that its campaign would attract other sharks to the area with bids of their own. Meanwhile Dome would sit on the sidelines, watching the contest, and in the end use its Conoco shares as a means with which to obtain what it really wanted—Conoco's increasingly valuable shares of Hudson's Bay.

Conoco's Bailey started making calls, seeking his crucial white knight. The ploy worked. On May 29th Edgar Bronfman contacted Bailey, offering to purchase enough shares to ward off a Dome takeover. At first it appeared that something might come of this, but Bailey wanted to sound out other potential candidates before making any commitment to Seagram. A week later he initiated discussions with Cities Service, itself being wooed by several suitors; Cities Service hoped to avoid them through a union with another reluctant potential bride, such as Conoco.

Soon thereafter Bronfman and his group presented Bailey with a firm offer: Seagram would purchase 35 percent of Conoco's treasury shares at around $70 per share, which would provide the petroleum company with a massive cash infusion, the money to be used to expand exploration and reduce the long-term debt and at the same time discourage Dome. Since Seagram was a Canadian corporation the government there wouldn't attempt to force the sale of holdings in that country. Bronfman suggested that Seagram wouldn't expect to take a hand in Conoco's management initially, but might want to do so after a predetermined period.

Bailey and the Conoco board rejected this as too low an offer while opposing any Seagram influence, even after a fifteen year hiatus. And with this negotiations broke down, everyone knowing that Seagram would go ahead with an unfriendly tender.

So as to clear the decks for the coming struggle Conoco came to terms with Dome. The Canadian company got what it wanted on June 1, but the price was high. In exchange for the 22 million Conoco shares it had gathered plus $245 million in cash Dome received Conoco's interest in Hudson's Bay. Thus the first act in the drama ended, with Dome exiting from the stage.

Now Bailey conferred with Conoco's investment banker, Morgan Stanley, to uncover a possible white knight. Into the computer went the relevant information: which company could afford to pay $3 billion or more—the price Bailey thought reasonable—40 percent in cash, the rest in stock? The readout consisted of 25 companies, among them such industrial giants as Eastman Kodak, Union Pacific, General Electric, Du Pont, and Merck, along with several petroleum companies: Exxon, Gulf (Canada), Shell, Superior, and Standard Oil of Indiana. There was no shortage of firms to be approached, and Conoco spoke with several.

Knowing nothing of this but suspecting what was happening, Bronfman pressed on, offering several packages to Conoco's board in the hope of obtaining an agreeable settlement. None was forthcoming; now that Hudson's Bay was gone Conoco had no need of a Canadian partner. So on June 23rd Seagram began purchasing shares on the open market, the first step in an unfriendly buyout. Three days later the corporation posted an open tender offer for 41 percent of Conoco at $73, the bill for which would have been in excess of $2.5 billion.

Its negotiations with Cities Service stalled and time running out, Conoco next approached Du Pont, the largest American chemicals concern, which on July 6th agreed to purchase 40 percent of the outstanding shares for $87.50 each and the rest for Du Pont common shares. Du Pont didn't have that kind of money, however, and the expectation was that the company would borrow heavily short term in the capital markets and then sell off some of the Conoco holdings—led by Consolidation Coal—to obtain the rest. That would have been a classic leveraged buy-out.

The Conoco board was satisfied with this arrangement. A takeover by the Bronfmans would have meant a loss of Conoco's independence as well as probable control by Seagram, while Du Pont assured management that it would be content to leave things in place so long as it obtained cooperation in the matter of feedstocks.

In early July it appeared that the deal would be concluded on this basis; Seagram would be left disappointed but with a sizeable profit from its holdings. Once more Bronfman had engaged in a transaction that Charles Bluhdorn might have envied. Why worry about liquor and petroleum, he might have thought. A failure like that once every six months or so and Seagram might emerge as one of the most profitable corporations on the N.Y.S.E.

At this point a new force entered the picture. Quite knowledgeable regarding Conoco's reserves, Mobil came up with a bid for 51 percent of the corporation at $90 and $90 worth of its common stock for the rest.

It was a bold and unexpected move. Everyone knew that Mobil had the money, but assumed that it had held back because of near-certain antitrust action. The Justice Department might have tolerated the takeover of a small or medium-sized reserve-rich firm, but surely it would act to block this deal, even if Mobil would agree to divest itself of all noncrude operations should the marriage take place. "[Mobil] could have gone to $125 or even $130 and still [have] lost," thought one knowledgeable onlooker. "You just can't cross a credibility gap that wide with a bridge made of money."[6]

Taking no chances, Seagram upped the ante to $92 a share, or $4.1 billion in cash, for 51 percent of the common. Mobil countered by going to $105, obliging Du Pont to raise the amount of shares to be acquired with cash from 40 percent to 45 percent. Almost immediately Mobil raised its bid to $115, while Du Pont and Conoco moved closer to completing their deal. Sensing this, Mobil went to $120, too late however for by then the final arrangements for the merger were being hammered together.

On August 4th Du Pont sweetened the pot by raising the cash portion of its offer to $98. Mobil tried to obtain a temporary restraining order to buy time while preparing yet another bid, but this ploy failed. Du Pont had won the prize.

Du Pont had paid $7.2 billion—almost half of which was in cash—for Conoco. In contrast, Dome's $1.4 billion for its share of Conoco seemed almost piddling. By adding Conoco's long-term debt to its own and adding the $3.9 billion it had to borrow to finance the merger Du Pont quadrupled its debt from $1.9 billion to $7.4 billion—interest alone was to cost the corporation $739 million in 1982, paid for in part through the sale of 10 percent of Conoco's proven reserves. This increased debt cost Du Pont its AAA bond rating, and assured that the corporation's first order of business for the rest of the decade would be to clean up its balance sheet. Had the takeover been as fortuitous as Du Pont had expected? Given the oil glut of 1982–83, the answer would have to be no.[7]

Seagram had given $2.5 billion for what came to a third of the Conoco stock. Later, in a separate deal, it would exchange this holding for 20 percent of Du Pont. Thus, while Du Pont acquired Conoco, Seagram became the chemical company's largest though not controlling shareholder. Was Seagram pleased with this? Hardly, for its treasury had been drained, and all it had to show for it was a minority interest in the chemical company. Within months rumors surfaced that Seagram was seeking a buyer for its holdings.

What would Bluhdorn have done in this situation? After all, it wasn't that different from several he had faced in the 1960s. One suspects that he would have finessed it better than did the clumsy Edgar Bronfman—he had a daring and a sophistication almost wholly missing in Bronfman, who in comparison was a blundering novice at such games. Bluhdorn surely wouldn't have settled for a minority position at Du Pont, whose dividends were only a fraction of what Seagram could have earned from so large an amount in liquid assets. Given Du Pont's past record there wasn't much hope of substantial capital gains either. Some thought it pleased Edgar Bronfman's ego to be associated with Du Pont, but this seems to have been a large price to pay for status. In time Bronfman would try to dispose of his Du Pont holdings, but he couldn't find a taker willing to accept so large a block without a substantial discount.

Mobil made a profit on its transactions by tendering its Conoco shares, but management was emotionally desolate. Yet another prize had eluded their grasp. Undeterred however, the corporation sought another large candidate.[8]

There had been much maneuvering and one could understand how confusing all of this seemed to bystanders—and how the various bids perplexed Conoco's stockholders. But it was mostly an exercise of raw, brute financial muscle, compared to which James Ling's manipulations appeared almost elegant.

The Du Pont-Conoco-Mobil-Seagram-Dome fandango focused attention on other crude-rich medium-sized corporations; their stocks bubbled on Wall Street as rumors were started and spread about which would be the next to go. Marathon was considered a plum, and management there prepared for an assault by arranging a $5 billion line of credit. Then, on July 13, 1981, at a time when the duel for Conoco was close to its conclusion, Marathon announced that there had been a special meeting of its board "to discuss merger activity in the oil industry." Did this mean that Marathon considered itself a target and was preparing for the assault? Or was this a proclamation that it intended to start out on the takeover trail itself? At the time the latter interpretation seemed quite plausible. Marathon purchased a share in Indonesian offshore properties and initiated negotiations to purchase Husky Oil's American subsidiary for $650 million in cash. The company announced that this was part of a strategy to leave Canada before being forced to do so. (Husky, a Canadian firm, wanted the money to make bids for the holdings of American firms in that country.) And in late September it was learned that the corporation had taken on additional outside legal muscle to assist should an "unfriendly" approach be made.

Management was correct in its belief that an assault was on the way, but who would have guessed from where it was to begin? On October 1st it was learned that Sedco, a $385 million Texas-based drilling company, had acquired 4.8 percent of Marathon; three days later Sedco said it had upped the figure to 5.5 percent. Subsequently the company revealed that it had been making purchases since December, and intended to add to its holdings.

Toward the end of the month the newspapers carried reports that a group of Texas operations, headed by Bass Brothers Enterprises, had made open-market purchases of 5.1 percent of Marathon. One of the wealthiest families in a state known for its centi-millionaires, the Basses attempted to stay out of the public eye. But it was known that their Texas holdings alone pumped out 300,000 barrels of oil per month, worth some $118 million a year at then current prices. Even so, the Basses and their allies lacked the resources to make a concerted effort for so large a company as Marathon.

What all of this meant wasn't clear; it certainly raised all sorts of questions. Were Sedco and Bass Brothers working separately or together in this matter? Did they mean to make overtures to Marathon? And if so, where would they get the kind of money to play in so big a game? Might it be that they hoped to duplicate the deal that Dome had made with Conoco regarding Hudson's Bay, namely exchange their shares for a prized property—perhaps Marathon's interest in Yates? Or could it be that they were establishing positions in anticipation of a takeover bid from some more plausible suitor?

Whatever their rationale, the last option was the one that came about. Rumors which were heard in the financial district for weeks turned out to have a basis in fact when, on October 30, Mobil announced that it would make a cash bid for two-thirds of Marathon common at $85 a share (the stock had been selling in the mid-50s the previous week), which worked out to $5.1 billion. As expected, Marathon President Hoopman accused Mobil of "high-handed arrogance" and said that the price was "grossly inadequate." Both statements contained elements of truth. Mobil had long had the reputation of being ham-fisted in such matters, as the takeover duel for Conoco had shown. And Marathon certainly was worth more than $85 if calculated purely on an asset basis.

That Marathon had prepared carefully for such an attack soon became evident. Hoopman asked for a federal court ruling on the legality of the offer.[9] Then he obtained a restraining order preventing Mobil from taking any further action in regard to the tender. Mobil appealed the ruling, but was turned aside by a federal judge. Meanwhile the Justice Department agreed to permit the Federal Trade Commission to review the bid, with an eye toward determining whether violations of the antitrust statutes were involved. Marathon helped organize rallies in its headquarters city of Findlay, Ohio, where the mayor predicted a massive slump if Mobil took command and moved operations from there. And Hoopman began to seek a white knight, contacting Pennzoil and Standard Oil of California initially and others afterward.

In Washington, Republican Congressman Clarence Brown, who represented the area in which Marathon was based, introduced legislation that would have imposed a nine-month moratorium on takeovers by large oil companies, while Ohio's Democratic Senator Howard Metzenbaum sponsored similar legislation in the upper chamber. Governor James Rhodes signed into law a measure that would bar acquisitions of corporations domiciled in that state if the acquisition would lessen competition in the oil business. Both this and the proposed federal legislation were of dubious constitutionality, but they certainly placed the pressure on Mobil. Clearly Marathon had laid its plans carefully, as was shown in this, the initial stage of the battle.[10]

On October 10th, while Hoopman passed out cards saying "I'm sorry, I can't talk about Mobil" at a convention, Mobil received the court's permission to proceed with its tender. Encouraged, it petitioned the FTC for permission to acquire Marathon prior to the settlement of the antitrust matters, with the understanding that it would divest itself of the holding if ordered to do so. This move was denied, but Mobil proceeded nonetheless. And all the while Hoopman ran down the roster of white knights. When Pennzoil and SoCal turned him down he went to Texaco, and was rebuffed there as well. It wasn't that these firms didn't recognize the merits of a merger, but rather they feared getting into the ring with the likes of Mobil. To further complicate matters Sedco began purchasing shares in the open market, told reporters that it once had planned a million share tender, and hinted that the plan was being revived.

Aid finally came from a most unlikely source. On November 19 Marathon announced that it would be willing to unite with United States Steel, which on that date entered the bidding with an offer of cash and stock that came to $6.4 billion.

Why had this aged, somnolent giant made this move? The mix did not make much sense, and until then steel companies were more often the acquisitioned than the acquisitor. But there was a rationale to it all. U. S. Steel felt the need to diversify out of an ailing industry into one with more promise. But was this the way to go about it? If all went well—and given Mobil's attitude this was questionable—the new company would be burdened by a huge debt that, unless oil prices firmed and the steel business improved, might well cause it to collapse into receivership. The talk was that U. S. Steel's Chairman David Roderick probably would sell off his railroads and some of the corporation's real estate along with several of Marathon's subsidiaries, using the money thus obtained to pay off at least part of the new debt. Even so, was it worth the while?[11]

The answer came on November 30th, when Roderick conceded that he had been reluctant at first to enter the bidding war with Mobil. But Marathon had pressed him hard, and made an offer that couldn't easily be refused: in order to obtain U. S. Steel's cooperation, Marathon gave it an option to purchase its share of the Yates field and an option to purchase 10 million Marathon shares at $90 each. This had been a clever move. Should the Yates option be exercised Mobil might think twice about the takeover, and if the stock option were acted upon it would be all the more difficult to obtain control of Marathon.

This came on the same day that Allied Corporation revealed that it too had considered making an offer for Marathon, while General Electric had had some preliminary negotiations toward that end. Doubtless other firms on the Morgan Stanley list had conferred with the Marathon team before deciding not to enter the arena. The very fact that Allied and GE had gone as far as they had is a commentary on the mergermania of the period, when most of the nation's giant corporations, if not on the prowl for such deals, were at least willing to discuss them.

The contest proceeded swiftly, as U. S. Steel and Mobil fought each other on the proxy front and through newspaper ads. Mobil failed to obtain control that first week, which heartened the Steel-Marathon forces. As Marathon had earlier, Steel obtained a $5 billion line of credit for use in the contest, making certain that the news was widely disseminated so as to be known at Mobil. But if Roderick was prepared to put more chips on the table a now frustrated and angry Mobil was more than willing to make a suitable response.

Imitating the strategy that Dome had used in the initial act of the Conoco drama, and perhaps planning the kind of switch that Seagram had pulled on Du Pont, Mobil started buying U. S. Steel shares on the open market, and on November 24th announced that it had obtained approximately $15 million of the shares and was prepared to take on more. Mobil and Steel would continue to raise the ante during the next month, and all the while Mobil's open-market purchases of its rival's shares continued. By late December Mobil had some half a million of them, worth more than $800 million, and hadn't stopped this second-front campaign.

The strategy seemed obvious. If Steel were to control Marathon, then Mobil would take over at Steel, doing with that corporation what it wished, and in a scorched earth policy presumably oust Roderick and others who were leading the campaign. Or it might be that Mobil would exchange its Steel shares, along with a sizable amount of cash, for the Yates interest. Either way it would have that valuable prize, and presumably in a way so as not to arouse the ire of the FTC.

Mobil's ambitions were thwarted when the courts issued a preliminary injunction blocking its tender for Marathon, while Marathon announced that it was calling off its $650 million bid to purchase Husky Oil's American properties, and that it would use the money instead to purchase its own shares as part of the defense against Mobil. Mobil now revealed just how far it was willing to go to obtain control of Marathon by announcing that if its takeover were permitted it would sell that company's refining, distribution, and transportation interests to yet another player, Amerada Hess, and in order to make this possible would lend Amerada the funds necessary to make the purchase.

The situation was more complicated and embarrassing than had been the contest for Conoco. U. S. Steel and Mobil staggered along during this last phase, with Steel being attacked by unions for an apparent abandonment of its primary interest and Mobil an obvious pariah, the unwanted guest at the wedding, who persisted nonetheless to press his attentions upon the disdainful bride-to-be.

The Mobil appeal reached the Supreme Court by the end of the year, and Chief Justice Warren Burger made it clear that he wanted as little as possible to do with the case. He refused to hear it on procedural grounds, stating that the matter first would have to go through the lower courts. Mobil objected in vain that any delay would work in the interests of U. S. Steel, but Burger held firm. Nor would he consider an appeal to halt the U. S. Steel tender until matters were resolved. It appeared that Mobil once again had lost out in a bid for a major acquisition.

There followed a series of appeals, counterappeals, writs, and other legal paraphernalia issuing from the offices of Mobil's attorneys, who attempted to win through the courts what the corporation couldn't in the board rooms. They were thwarted at every turn. Not only was Mobil unable to obtain a review of the case, but in mid-January the FTC issued a temporary injunction against Mobil's accumulation of additional Steel shares.

In the end Mobil simply threw in the towel; unlike Seagram during the tail end of the Du Pont-Conoco merger it rejected the notion of using those Marathon shares in its portfolio to acquire control of U. S. Steel or try to pry loose some promising properties. Rather, as it had done in the Conoco situation Mobil turned in its holdings under terms of the tender offer, took its profits, and started seeking other potential takeover candidates.

Which might these be? The betting on Wall Street was that Mobil might make a pass at Getty, Cities Service, or Superior. Or—as one analyst suggested—all three simultaneously, with the hope of getting one if the others eluded its grasp. That comment wasn't meant to be taken seriously, but the prices for all three advanced in late January and early February.

It was that kind of atmosphere.

The next important and dramatic move in the merger wars wouldn't come from or even involve Mobil, though it would involve other participants and near-players in the earlier contests. Rather, it began at Bendix, where the chairman, young William Agee, was finally ready to wheel and deal.

In late 1981 Agee was sitting on close to $2 billion in cash and searching out a possible takeover candidate, one that would fit in with his vision of Bendix as a high-technology operation. But that wasn't all he was doing, as the press had been observing for the preceding year. In September 1980, he had ousted President William Panny and accepted the resignation of Executive Vice-President for Strategic Planning Jerome Jacobson. Panny went because his thinking didn't coincide with that of Agee, while Jacobson left to make a place at the top for 29-year-old Mary Cunningham, who little more than a year earlier had graduated from Harvard Business School and had become Agee's executive assistant. A few months later she was named vice-president for corporate and public affairs.

That Agee's relationship with Cunningham transcended business was obvious to all at the company, as it was to Mrs. Agee, who a month before the Panny-Jacobson departures and after 23 years of marriage was divorced from her husband. In fact her leaving cleared the decks for Agee personally just as that of the others did professionally.

Was this a case of male menopause, true love, the beginning of an ideal personal-business relationship, or the surfacing of the real William

Agee? Whatever the answer it was obvious this wasn't simply coinciden- tal, and the business press, unaccustomed to such raw meat, had a field day. "Bill and Mary" were plastered over the society and front pages while the story was covered in the business section, to the irritation and embarrassment of the board and others at Bendix. In time several members resigned in protest. Clearly such a situation couldn't be allowed to continue; either Agee or Cunningham would have to leave. Or both.

Cunningham resigned in October. She later emerged as a vice- president at Seagram and, shortly thereafter, she and Agee were married.

By then a substantial number of Wall Streeters had concluded that Cunningham was behind Agee's merger cravings, masterminding the action from her perch at Seagram, which of course was no stranger to such activities. Just how much of what next transpired was her doing and what originated from Agee remains a matter of contention, not only among business analysts, but feminists as well. Whenever it appeared that Bendix was on the verge of success several spokespersons would proclaim Cunningham's role saying that it proved just how able women could be in the corporate world; they remained on the sideline when Agee started to fumble.

In early March 1982, Agee announced that Bendix had purchased a 5 percent interest in RCA, this "for investment only," by then a cliché usually meaning just the opposite. He later indicated that RCA's man- agement knew of his interest, and that the accumulation had begun the previous September, after a discussion with the RCA board.

The RCA of this period was a troubled, accident-prone corporation, which in the preceding decade had tried its hand at diversification without much success. In 1982 it owned such diverse firms as Hertz, CIT Financial, Coronet Industries (a large manufacturer of carpets), and a grab bag of other companies. Thornton Bradshaw, who had recently taken over as CEO, was attempting to sell some of these to reduce RCA's long-term debt and to have funds to concentrate upon the original core businesses—telecommunications and broadcasting. This was another firm whose parts were worth more than the whole, a prime candidate for a leveraged buy-out.

But not an unfriendly one, for RCA was also the parent of National Broadcasting, and any takeover would have to be approved by the Fed- eral Communications Commission. In his day Harold Geneen had failed to acquire ABC-Paramount when a minority of the commission opposed the merger with a conglomerate, and not much had changed at the FTC by 1982.

Was Agee really prepared to don the armor of a black knight? Or might it be that he anticipated opposition from Bradshaw, who then would advertise for a white knight, after which Bendix would tender those shares obtained earlier and pocket a nice profit? Charles Bluhdorn had shown the way in the 1960s; Agee would have been only one of many, led by Edgar Bronfman, who imitated the Gulf + Western ploy.

James Magid, an analyst for the investment banking house of L. F. Rothschild, Unterberg Towbin, offered a different analysis. Bendix might secure a beachhead, struggle for a while with whatever white knight came along, and then divide the spoils with it. "Just as the hyena grabs a zebra's leg and waits for another hyena to grab another, Bendix can wait for someone else to come along. Then the two hyenas can dismember RCA and run off with whatever they can get away with."[12]

Magid turned out to be remarkably prescient, though even he couldn't have imagined just how bizarre the developments would be, and how difficult it would be to tell the zebras from the hyenas.

Thornton Bradshaw, an urbane, sophisticated businessman known as one of the subtlest executives in America, had only recently come to RCA from the presidency of Atlantic Richfield, where he had worked in tandem with Robert Anderson, a man equally at home in the classics as with drilling and refining. Bradshaw could hardly relish the idea of any form of relationship with the mercurial, trendy Agee—it would have been a marriage of Mozart and the Beach Boys. Nor did Bradshaw think much of the Agee-Cunningham notoriety. "Mr. Agee has not demonstrated the ability to manage his own affairs," he sniffed, "let alone someone else's." Without his cooperation nothing could be done, and so Agee went fishing in other waters.

Agee's hunting expedition was reported by television technicians present at the mid-August taping of an interview of Cunningham by Barbara Walters. Cunningham was vivacious and talkative, and during a break in the discussion referred to "The Strategy," advising the crew to keep a sharp watch on the newspapers for something quite interesting regarding Bendix.[13]

The Strategy was put into action on August 25, when Bendix announced that it already had purchased 1.6 million shares of Martin Marietta on the open market for slightly less than $40 million. Bendix also announced that it was making a tender for an additional 15.8 million at $43, which would cost another $680 million. All told, that would give it slightly less than a majority of the common. (Marietta common had closed at 33⅛, up 2½, the previous day.)

Immediately Marietta's stock shot higher, with Wall Street assuming that this was a fairly conventional leveraged buy-out. Bendix had ample funds in its treasury to handle the purchase, and more if obliged to up the offer due to the appearance of a rival. Then, with the prize in hand, it would merge its Martin Marietta Aerospace into Bendix Aerospace-Electronics and sell off the cement, aggregates, chemicals, and aluminum businesses, which accounted for approximately 40 percent of sales and an equal share of profits. Aerospace had recently been awarded several desirable missile contracts, while Marietta had invested more than $1.7 billion in the other parts of the corporation during the previous five years, and all would do well in the economic upturn that many were predicting was on the way.

Under the best of circumstances, Bendix might recover almost all the cash laid out for the tender, thus obtaining Aerospace for practically nothing. If all fell apart due to the arrival of a powerful white knight Agee might be obliged to withdraw, but only after reaping rewards from the higher price that his Marietta shares would fetch—especially the 1.6 million purchased prior to the tender. It had happened that way before, and given the rules of the game, it would appear that Agee had little to fear.

Several analysts observed that Marietta was unlikely to roll over and play dead, and they were right. The corporation's management team, led by Chairman J. Donald Rauth and President Thomas Pownall, had been expecting such a move, and even suspected that it might come from Bendix. Rauth was nearing retirement age, with Pownall preparing to assume the post of CEO—an office he wouldn't get if the Bendix takeover came to pass. So he had much at stake in this contest.

Along with an increasing number of corporate leaders Pownall had been appalled at Agee's personal and business activities, and would have nothing to do with him. Agee made repeated efforts to meet with Pownall and the Martin Marietta board during the next few weeks and each time was rebuffed or simply ignored. "I can find no useful purpose to be served by a prompt meeting with you" was a typical Pownall response, an indication of just how far he was prepared to go in order to avoid a takeover.

Under Pownall's direction a shrewd counterstrategy had been developed, the aforementioned Pac-Man defense. After a *pro forma* meeting to discuss the Bendix offer, Marietta's management rejected the overtures out of hand. Then, after arranging for a $1 billion line of credit at several banks, the corporation retaliated with a tender to purchase 11.9 million (which was a majority) of Bendix shares at $75, for a total of $892 million. But while Pownall refused to meet with Agee, there was an olive branch in the offer. Marietta would withdraw its bid for Bendix if Bendix abandoned its acquisition effort. Agee refused to respond, and so the offer continued.[14]

Trading in Bendix was halted at 57, as the NYSE's specialists and interested arbitrageurs attempted to fathom the next step in the drama.

Agee promptly sought an injunction to block the Martin Marietta tender, asserting that since it had a head start Bendix would win the competition. Indeed, by September 7th it appeared that more than a majority of Marietta's stock had been tendered. But what could be granted might be taken away. If a better offer came their way the tenderers might withdraw their tender in order to accept the new one, or simply stand aside while the contestants battled for their favor.

After being informed of a shareholders' suit demanding that he accept the Bendix offer, Pownall judged that the shareholders of both companies would be better served by supporting his proposal than that of Bendix.

All of this delighted occasional readers of the business pages. The spectacle of each company controlling the other—which seemed a likely outcome of the contest at the time—was akin to two snakes in a zoo each trying to gobble the other by grasping its tail. Simple logic might dictate that each would consume the other, so that both would either disappear—or be larger than before. It troubled executives at both firms, however, for at each turn of the screw the prize paradoxically became both more and less valuable.

Consider the following scenario, for example: Bendix finally manages to win full control of Marietta, after going deeply into debt to finance a sharply upward ratcheting takeover contest. What would it have? That valuable aerospace business already discussed, plus the other divisions that would be on the block. Moreover Bendix would have a large amount of its own shares that had been accumulated by Marietta; those could be retired, thus lowering the corporation's outstanding equity, increasing book value and earnings per share. But there would also be the debt accumulated to purchase the Bendix shares, many of which would have come in at highly inflated prices, and far more than could be retired through the sale of subsidiaries. A Bendix in this shape would be so debt-ridden that it would be close to financial paralysis, especially if short-term interest rates rose, causing Bendix's interest payments to climb.

On the other hand, Bendix couldn't afford to abandon its quest for Marietta, since to do so would make it a subsidiary of its former target. Subsequently, the Bendix management, led by Agee, would be likely victims of a scorched earth policy engineered by Pownall, after which Marietta would be burdened with debt and probably in serious financial trouble. So neither company could afford to lose the contest—or to win it.

Agee and Cunningham had planned a simple, conventional, low-risk, leveraged buy-out. Instead Bendix and Marietta were mired in a messy situation, one that soon was to become still more complicated. Both Pownall and Agee appreciated this. After it was all over Agee told reporters, "I wanted to avoid that ultimate chicken game. You could potentially destroy both companies, and that's the last thing a CEO should do. I told Mr. Pownall that."[15]

Nuclear war on the corporate battlefield may not result in wholesale deaths but, as Agee indicated, its impact was comparable to the real thing, as was the rhetoric.

The next surprise came on September 8th, the day following Agee's announcement that he had tenders for more than half the Marietta shares. Pownall had found his desperately needed ally in Harry Gray of United Technologies (whom Wall Street promptly dubbed the "Gray Knight"), which set its own $75 cash and stock tender for Bendix shares. At the time it seemed that United Technologies wasn't attempting a takeover, but only supporting Marietta in its defense. Agee was shocked at the appearance of this contender, which was larger than Bendix and Marietta combined; it was as though the neighborhood bully had picked on someone smaller than himself only to find himself contending with the victim's big brother.

The motives of Agee and Pownall might be easily understood at this juncture. But what was it that Gray had in mind?

It soon was learned that he and Pownall had arranged to split Bendix down the middle if their combined offers carried the day. Each would get a desired chunk of the aggressor-turned-victim, while Marietta would also receive its shares then in the Bendix treasury. And of course Agee and his crew would be dismissed out of hand. Moving quickly to guard his flanks, Agee arranged for long-term salary guarantees for himself and fifteen other Bendix officers, so as to make certain that they would not suffer financially in case they failed. (This too had a name in the rapidly expanding parlance of the game: golden parachutes.)

And what was there in it for Gray should the deal fall through? Under the arrangement United Technologies was to receive $2.5 million in cash from Marietta for its services. Agee yelled foul, but the Justice Department could find nothing in the statutes forbidding such an arrangement. Thus it seemed that once again Pownall had euchred the hapless Agee. "It looks to me like Bill might have blown it," said a business acquaintance. "I'm not sure if there is anything in his experience that would give him an edge in a situation like this."[16]

It now appeared that Pownall was home free. Under the best of circumstances he would wind up with his company intact, own prime parts of Bendix, and have an enlarged debt. And in case Agee won control of

Marietta, Pownall had hope United Technologies would counter by taking over at Bendix, liberating Agee only after he agreed to regurgitate Marietta.

That was pretty much what happened. On September 5, after Agee won a series of court rulings that gave him an edge in the bidding, Gray entered the lists with a tender for a majority of Bendix stock, upping the price to $85.

Now there were three $1.5 billion tenders on the table, and the only clear winners seemed to be the newspapers, which carried full-page ads from each, exhorting Marietta and Bendix shareholders to do the right thing. And of course those fortunate enough to have owned shares in Bendix or Marietta, and who now realized they were in for a windfall—if only they could keep their nerve, and the players straight.

As of September 22 Marietta owned 42.4 percent of Bendix under terms of its $75 a share tender. Bendix had 70 percent of Marietta through its $48 a share offer. And United Technologies was attempting to purchase 50.3 percent of Bendix.

On that date yet another player came onto the field. Allied Corporation's Edward Hennessy, acting as a Bendix ally, offered to purchase all of that company for cash and securities estimated to be worth $80 a share, and in addition he offered to buy all the Marietta shares not in the Bendix treasury. The total Allied offer came to $2.3 billion.

Allied's rationale was clear and direct. Bendix and Marietta's aerospace interests would provide Allied with its much-desired high technology component. But there was more to it. Hennessy had been frustrated in several takeover bids, the latest being that for Marathon, and like the leaders at Mobil he fairly itched for a significant success. Then too, the idea of snatching a prize from Harry Gray must have had strong appeal to him. What his ultimate plans for Agee were couldn't be fathomed, but it was clear that Hennessy would have no use for him. Nonetheless, Agee was to remain at the helm of Bendix and become vice-chairman at Allied. However, no one at either corporation expected him to remain long once the battle was over.

Add another term to the takeover lexicon. Now Agee, Pownall, Gray, and Hennessy were known on Wall Street as "The Four Horsemen of the Apocalypse."

This third round in the battle further confused the situation while troubling the original participants. Had they known what would happen Agee and Pownall might have come to some kind of agreement earlier in the game. Now it appeared that the struggle might end with Bendix a part of Allied while United Technologies might become Marietta's parent. In the beginning both executives had fought for both power and independence; now it appeared that they might lose on all counts.

Nonetheless the situation settled down somewhat shortly thereafter. Allied approached Marietta with what amounted to an olive branch. Under the terms of Hennessy's proposal Marietta would exchange its Bendix holdings for most of its own shares in the possession of Bendix. Agee balked at this but Hennessy was firm. He wanted to purchase a company, not an embroglio, and he was eager to see the contest end. Agee did make one final stab at winning Pownall, but couldn't have been too surprised when he was once again rebuffed.

So it ended there, abruptly. Of the four horsemen, only Gray came out of the experience with dignity and clear profits. Marietta had retained its independence, but Allied now owned 39 percent of its common (though Hennessy promised not to interfere in company business and to dispose of the holdings as quickly as possible). Marietta's short-term debt had swollen by almost $900 million as a result of the contest, and Pownall conceded that it would take the corporation at least seven years to straighten out its finances. Bendix was now an Allied subsidiary, with Agee's future in doubt. In fact he left Allied on June 1, 1983. Agee's dreams of business power had been shattered by the experience, but there was some balm for his troubles—his golden parachute was valued at over $4 million.

How much had all of this cost? Approximately $4 billion—in cash—had been borrowed to finance the duels.[17] Bendix had spent $1.2 billion in cash to purchase 70 percent of Marietta, and the latter corporation had spent $900 million for half of Bendix. Allied was larger and had a new big acquisition, but due to its price and the interest charges on its increased debt, would suffer through an earnings shrinkage; for the next few years it too would have to husband cash and sell off subsidiaries.

Allied had paid $1.8 billion for its control of Bendix (which included 39 percent of Marietta). Slightly less than $900 had been borrowed, $450 million was in Allied common shares, and another $294 million was of a fourth issue of callable preferred due in three years, with $159 million coming from two intermediate-term notes. For that Allied received a company that had earned $137 million after taxes the previous year, some $300 million worth of Marietta common, and other securities valued at around $200 million. As Hennessy saw it Bendix by itself had taken $1.3 billion. Trying to put the deal in the best light, the Allied chairman claimed that he was fortunate in having obtained so fine a corporation for around ten times earnings. Under the circumstances there wasn't much else he could say.[18]

Of course, those stockholders of Bendix and Marietta who had the foresight and luck to hold out for the top price came out in excellent shape. They were the only true winners of the three act contest in which the prices of securities were bid far beyond their original market prices.

On September 27th, attempting to draw some kind of moral or lesson from the struggle, *The Wall Street Journal* reflected:

> But there is obviously something amiss in an economy where corporate assets look more attractive to the investment strategists of other corporations than to ordinary investors. The reasons why are fairly complex but inflation has been at the heart of the problem. Not only has it discouraged personal savings and thus stretched very thin the supply of capital, but it also has attracted the available supply of capital to high-yielding debt rather than equities. Corporate assets have been on the bargain counter for anyone who might be able to put them to more profitable use.

Perhaps so, but surely there was more to it than that. The drive for power, the axiom that "big is better," the yearning for instant greatness, and simple egomania—all were present.

And what had Bill Agee derived from this experience beside the aforementioned golden parachute and the expected dismissal from Bendix? The marriage to Mary Cunningham, of course; the knowledge that he had a place (albeit not a particularly honored one) in modern corporate history; and a partnership with his wife in a new operation. During an interview with *Fortune* conducted after the contest had ended, the two spoke of their hopes in tones that dismayed old timers who recalled the ingenuity of Jimmy Ling, the sheer intelligence of Harold Geneen, the vision of Tex Thornton, and even the cheeky brashness of Charles Bluhdorn.

> Bill: Our dream is this. Mary formed a little corporation called Semper—a Delaware corporation—and heads it up. I'm the second principal officer. We have a team bank account. You ought to mention what Semper means, honey.
> Mary: It means always. It has a very broad charter. It can do virtually anything—be a holding company for consulting services of supply venture capital. To be specific, our long term dream is to work together. Many people don't understand the dynamism, excitement, and energy that can be generated by two people who are totally supportive.[19]

Except for cleaning up the debris—no small matter since this will take all participants through the 1980s—it had ended. Hennessy wrote the epitaph for this most recent stage of the conglomerate movement: "It was a very sorry spectacle for American business."

As might have been anticipated the takeover spree of 1982–83 prompted renewed calls to curb if not halt such spectacles. Ralph Nader charged that the mergers in petroleum added not a barrel to reserves and that the companies should be required to find new supplies by drilling and not engaging in tenders. A saddened businessman, observing the Bendix-Martin Marietta duel, thought that "maybe there is something wrong with our system . . . companies line up large amounts of money in order to purchase stock, when it doesn't help build one factory, buy one more piece of equipment, or provide even one more job."[20] To which a Mobil spokesman shot back that if oil could be had by acquisition at a fraction of the cost of exploration and drilling it would be foolish to act otherwise.

In fact this form of struggle did carry out the classic function of the marketplace, namely the allocation of capital. What Nader and others didn't take into consideration was that those billions of dollars would end up not in some dark hole but in the hands of the former shareholders, some of whom used the funds to make purchases; other proceeds were placed in savings institutions, while other dollars returned to the securities market to purchase shares in other enterprises. In each case they assisted in creating both products and job opportunities. But no one except the most naive would claim that this was what Bill Agee and the others had in mind.

In 1983 the Securities and Exchange Commission established a panel to study the matter, and this body (whose members included Edward Hennessy of Allied) heard an assistant attorney general from the Anti-Trust Division testify that mergers could be "a very socially beneficial mechanism," which were healthy for the economy.[21]

Nonetheless the panel came out with a report suggesting new curbs on takeover contests, including a recommendation to prevent any would-be black knight from acquiring more than 15 percent of a target's shares unless it had the cooperation of the latter's management. Carl Icahn, who had engaged in several contests, claimed that this would have a stultifying effect. "Corporate heads can now breathe a sigh of relief," he predicted when it appeared that the measure might have wide support. "Especially the mediocre managements," Icahn added, "and we have plenty of them in this country."[22]

Despite the heat and concern, nothing of substance passed into legislation. It now seems fairly certain that given a buoyant stock market America will see the conglomerators return, seeking to exchange their paper for assets and earnings, while a depressed market will prompt black knights to offer cash for undervalued properties. This is the nature of the system. Critics consider such phenomena among the chief disgraces of capitalism; defenders respond that it is part of the process of renewal.

Selected Bibliography

Invaluable for a work of this nature have been the popular press and business magazines, the most important being *The Wall Street Journal*, *The New York Times*, *Business Week*, *Fortune*, *Barron's*, *Forbes*, *The Economist* and to a lesser extent, *Newsweek*, *Time*, and *U.S. News and World Report*. In addition I have mined relevant government documents and issues dealing with conglomerates in several law journals. The books listed below are meant as a guide to future research; the list is by no means exhaustive.

Adams, Walter, ed. *The Structure of American Industry*. 5th ed. New York: Macmillan, 1977.

Aguilar, Francis. *Scanning the Business Environment*. New York: Macmillan, 1967.

Albers, William and Segall, Joel, eds. *The Corporate Merger*. Chicago: University of Chicago, 1966.

American Enterprise Institute. *Recent Proposals to Restrict Conglomerate Mergers*. Washington: American Enterprise Institute, 1981.

Asnoff, H. Igor. *Corporate Strategy*. New York: McGraw-Hill, 1965.

———. et al. *Acquisition Behavior of U.S. Manufacturing Firms, 1946-1965*. Nashville: Vanderbilt University, 1971.

Bagley, Edward. *Beyond the Conglomerates*. New York: Americom, 1975.

Bain, Joe. *Barriers to New Competition*. Cambridge: Harvard University, 1956.

———. *Industrial Organization*. New York: Wiley, 1968.

Barmash, Isadore. *Welcome to Our Conglomerate: You're Fired!*. New York: Delacorte, 1971.

Benston, George. *Conglomerate Mergers: Causes, Consequences, and Remedies*. Washington: American Enterprise Institute, 1980.

Bork, Robert. *The Antitrust Paradox: A Policy at War With Itself*. New York: Basic Books, 1978.

Boyle, Stanley and Jaynes, Philip. *Conglomerate Merger Performance: An Empirical Analysis of Nine Corporations.* Washington: Federal Trade Commission, 1972.

Brown, Stanley. *Ling.* New York: Atheneum, 1972.

Carleton, Willard; Harris, Robert; and Stewart, John. *An Empirical Study of Merger Movements.* Washington: Federal Trade Commission, 1980.

Chandler, Alfred. *Strategy and Structure.* Cambridge: MIT, 1962.

Cheit, Earl, ed. *The Business Establishment.* New York: Wiley, 1964.

Demsetz, Harold. *The Market Concentration Doctrine.* Washington: American Enterprise Institute, 1973.

Dory, John. *The Domestic Diversifying Acquisitions Decision.* New York: Research, 1978.

Doughen, Joseph and Binzen, Peter. *The Wreck of the Penn Central.* Boston: Little, Brown, 1971.

Galbraith, John. *The New Industrial State.* Boston: Houghton Mifflin, 1967.

Gilbert, Charles, ed. *The Making of a Conglomerate.* Hempstead, N.Y.: Hofstra University, 1972.

Green, Mark. *The Closed Enterprise System.* New York: Grossman, 1972.

Hutchison, G. Scott. *The Business of Acquisitions and Mergers.* New York: Presidents Publishing, 1968.

Kaysen, Carl and Turner, Donald. *Antitrust Policy.* Cambridge: Harvard University, 1965.

Lay, Beirne, Jr. *Someone Has to Make it Happen: The Tex Thornton Story.* Englewood Cliffs: Prentice Hall, 1969.

Letwin, William. *Law and Economic Policy in America.* New York: Random House, 1965.

Lynch, Harry. *Financial Performance of Conglomerates.* Cambridge: Harvard University, 1971.

Mace, Myles and Montgomery, George. *Management Problems of Corporate Acquisitions.* Cambridge: Harvard Graduate School of Business, 1962.

McQuown, Judith. *Playing the Takeover Market.* New York: Seaview, 1982.

Markham, Jesse. *Conglomerate Enterprise and Public Policy.* Boston: Harvard Graduate School of Business Administration, 1973.

Martin, David. *Mergers and the Clayton Act.* Berkeley: University of California, 1959.

Miller, Stanley. *Management Problems of Diversification.* New York: Wiley, 1963.

Morris, Charles. *The Cost of Good Intentions.* New York: Norton, 1980.

Nader, Ralph and Green, Mark. *Taming the Giant Corporation.* New York: Norton, 1976.

Narver, John. *Conglomerate Mergers and Market Competition.* Berkeley: University of California, 1967.

Nelson, Ralph. *Merger Movements in American History, 1895-1956.* Princeton: Princeton University, 1959.

Reid, Samuel. *Mergers, Managers, and the Economy.* New York: McGraw-Hill, 1968.

Salisbury, Stephen. *No Way to Run a Railroad: The Untold Story of the Penn Central Crisis.* New York: McGraw-Hill, 1982.

Saunders, Richard. *The Railroad Mergers and the Coming of Conrail.* Westport: Greenwood, 1978.

Scherer, F. M. *Industrial Market Structure and Economic Performance.* Chicago: Rand McNally, 1980.

Sobel, Robert. *The Entrepreneurs.* Weybright & Talley: New York, 1974.

———. *ITT: The Management of Opportunity.* Timesbooks: New York, 1982.

———. *The Money Manias.* New York: Weybright & Talley, 1973.

Solomon, Robert. *The International Monetary System, 1945-1981.* New York: Harper & Row, 1982.

Spruill, Charles. *Conglomerates and the Evolution of Capitalism.* Carbondale: Southern Illinois University, 1982.

Sullivan, Lawrence. *Antitrust.* St. Paul: West Publishing, 1977.

Winslow, John. *Conglomerates Unlimited: The Failure of Regulation.* Bloomington: Indiana University, 1973.

Notes

1. Origins

1. U. S., Federal Trade Commission, *Report of the Federal Trade Commission on the Merger Movement* (Washington, D.C.: Government Printing Office, 1948), pp. 46–59 ff.
2. The classic statement of this position is Richard Hofstadter, *The Age of Reform* (New York: Knopf, 1955). Also see Ellis Hawley, *The New Deal and the Problem of Monopoly* (Princeton: Princeton University Press, 1966).

2. Royal Little: The Pioneer

1. Royal Little, *How to Lose $100,000,000 and Other Valuable Advice* (Boston: Little, Brown, 1979), p. 14.
2. The name clearly is a variant of Lustron. According to his own account, Little asked the advertising firm of J. Walter Thompson to select a new name for his company, "something that says textile products made of synthetics," and Thompson came up with Textron. "Textron Inc." *Fortune,* May 1947, pp. 160–61.
3. *The Royal Little Story* (Boston: Textron Inc., 1966), p. 133.
4. "Whose Mistake at Nashua?" *Fortune,* November 1948, p. 98; Little, *How to Lose $100,000,000,* pp. 89-98 ff.
5. "Royal Little Looks at Conglomerates," *Dun's Review,* May 1948, p. 27.
6. Royal Little, "Why Companies Sell Out," *Fortune,* February 1956, p. 117.
7. Little, *How to Lose $100,000,000,* p. 113.
8. "Can Three Losers Make a Winner?" *Business Week,* December 4, 1954, p. 86.
9. Stanley Brown, "How to Manage a Conglomerate Making Many Products," *Fortune,* April 1964, p. 157; *The New York Times,* February 18, 1955.
10. *Business Week,* December 10, 1955.

11. D. Saunders, "Stormiest Merger Yet—Textron-Robbins-American Woolen Merger," *Fortune*, April 1955, p. 171.
12. Little, *How to Lose $100,000,000*, pp. 119-20.
13. "Closing a Deal," *Business Week*, November 5, 1955, p. 140.
14. "As They See It," *Forbes*, December 15, 1970, p. 41.
15. *Ibid.*, p. 42.
16. "Textron: An Orderly Conglomerate," *Magazine of Wall Street*, December 24, 1966, p. 352.
17. "How to Manage a Conglomerate," p. 157; Little, *How to Lose $100,000,000*, p. 192; "Profitable Diversification," *Financial World*, June 29, 1966, p. 8; "Textron: Phase II," *Forbes*, March 15, 1962, p. 25.

3. Tex Thornton: The Illusionist

1. John Wall, "Want to Get Rich Quick? An Expert Gives Some Friendly Advice on Conglomerates," *Barron's*, February 5, 1968, p. 19.
2. This and other biographical information regarding Thornton's youth comes from Beirne Lay, Jr., *Someone Had to Make It Happen: The Inside Story of Tex Thornton, the Man Who Built Litton Industries* (Englewood Cliffs: Prentice Hall, 1969). This work, more a eulogy than a biography, seems to have been written as a commissioned work (Lay's other books were in the field of popular aviation romance, and several were made into motion pictures), and most of the material probably came from Thornton himself.
3. *Time*, September 15, 1958, p. 84.
4. Lay, *Someone Had to Make It Happen*, pp. 110-11.
5. Charles J. V. Murphy, "The Blowup at Hughes," *Fortune*, February 1954, pp. 116–18.
6. In order to obtain capital, Ramo-Wooldridge sold a minority interest to Thompson Industries, a manufacturer of automobile parts. Later the two merged to form Thompson Ramo Wooldridge, which today is known as TRW, a major conglomerate itself.
7. *The New York Times*, November 26, 1981.
8. Among the more prominent Lidos, were Henry Singleton of Teledyne, William McKenna of Hunt Foods & Industries, George Scharffenberger of City Investing, Russel McFall of Western Union, Frank Moothart of Republic Corporation, and Fred Sullivan of Walter J. Kidde. Robert Sobel, *Money Manias* (New York: Weybright & Talley, 1973), p. 326.
9. For example, in a popular book of the time, *Investing in American Industries* (New York: Harper & Brothers, 1960), p. 98, Litton is classified as a "Business Machine and Electronic Data Processing" company.
10. "Litton's Shattered Image," *Forbes*, December 1, 1969, p. 64.

11. For Thornton's public views on Litton at the close of the 1960s, see U. S. Congress, House, Committee on the Judiciary, Antitrust Subcommittee, *Investigation of Conglomerate Corporations,* 91st Cong., 1st sess., 1970, Part 5 (Litton Industries) pp. 40-51.
12. *The Wall Street Journal,* March 2, 1959.
13. Carl Rieser, "When the Crowd Goes One Way Litton Goes the Other," *Fortune,* May 1963, p. 220.
14. Ibid.
15. "A Calculated Risk at Pasagoula," *Fortune,* August 1970, p. 31.
16. *Fortune,* April 1968, p. 139.
17. For a study of the situation at Ingalls, see U. S. Congress, House, Committee on Armed Services, *Hearings on Military Posture,* 92nd Cong., 2nd sess., 1972 and U. S. Congress, House, Joint Economic Committee, *Controls Over Shipyard Costs and Procurement Practice of Litton Industries, Inc., Pasaguola, Mississippi,* 92nd Cong., 2nd sess., 1972.
18. *Investigation of Conglomerate Corporations,* pp. 630-731, passim.
19. "Litton's Shattered Image," pp. 64-66.
20. *Investigation of Conglomerate Corporations,* pp. 1063-1383, passim.
21. One should note, however, that Litton wasn't alone in failing to make the grade as a publisher after demonstrating expertise in other fields. None of the high technology firms which entered this industry, from IBM on down, was able to infuse new vitality into their holdings.
22. Daniel Seligman and Tom Wise, "How Litton Keeps It Up," *Fortune,* September 1966, p. 154.
23. "Twilight on Olympus," *Forbes,* December 1, 1969, p. 70.
24. William Rukeyser, "Litton Down to Earth," *Fortune,* April 1968, p. 186.

4. James Ling: The Magician

1. These and other details regarding Ling's upbringing are drawn from Stanley Brown, *Ling: The Rise, Fall, and Return of a Texas Titan* (New York: Atheneum, 1972), pp. 43-51.
2. John McDonald, "Some Candid Answers from James J. Ling, Part II," *Fortune,* September 1969, pp. 136-37.
3. Brown, *Ling,* p. 52.
4. *Moody's Industrial Index,* 1958, p. 1528; 1959, p. 2882.
5. James Ling, "A Dialogue on Conglomerate Mergers," *Kentucky Law Journal* 57 (1969): 391-92.
6. Ibid., p. 392.
7. James Ling, "The Conglomerate and Anti-Trust," *The Business Lawyer,* January, 1970, p. 571.

8. Ibid., pp. 571-72.
9. Robert Sobel, *Money Manias,* pp. 343-44.
10. *Investigation of Conglomerate Mergers,* Part 6 (Ling-Temco-Vought), pp. 614-16.
11. Brown, *Ling,* pp. 221-22.
12. "Some Candid Answers from James J. Ling, Part I," August 1, 1969, p. 95.

5. Charles Bluhdorn: The Manipulator

1. Ted Stanton, "Gulf & Western's Head Led It to Big Time Using a 'Locomotive' Built of Auto Parts," *The Wall Street Journal,* July 6, 1966.
2. "Some Glitter is Gone at Gulf and Western," *Business Week,* July 5, 1969, p. 38.
3. United States, 91st Congress, 1st Session, House of Representatives, Committee on the Judiciary, Antitrust Subcommittee (Washington, USGPO, 1970), *Hearings on Conglomerate Corporations, Conglomerate Investigation Report,* Part 1, p. 204.
4. Ibid., p. 774.
5. Chris Welles, "Multimillion Dollar Reach of Wall Street's 'Mad Austrian,'" *Life,* March 10, 1967, p. 37.
6. Ibid, p. 34.
7. "Gulf and Western Sells Muskegon Shares to Toledo Firm," *The Wall Street Journal,* June 20, 1964.
8. William S. Rukeyser, "Gulf and Western's Rambunctious 'Conservatism,'" *Fortune,* March 1968, p. 124.
9. *Hearings on Conglomerate Corporations,* p. 340.
10. Ibid., p. 37.
11. Ibid., p. 47.
12. Ibid., p. 123.
13. Ibid., p. 71.
14. Ibid., p. 81.
15. Welles, "Multimillion Dollar Reach of Wall Street's 'Mad Austrian,'" p. 48.
16. Ibid., pp. 48-49.
17. *Hearings on Conglomerate Corporations,* p. 481.
18. Welles, "Multimillion Dollar Reach of Wall Street's 'Mad Austrian,'" p. 56.
19. "Some Glitter is Gone at Gulf and Western," *Business Week,* July 5, 1969, p. 35.
20. *Hearings on Conglomerate Corporations,* p. 728.
21. Ibid., p. 110.
22. Ibid., pp. 681-705, passim.
23. Ibid., p. 110.

6. Harold Geneen: The Master

1. *The New York Times,* December 23, 1977; *Business Week,* May 4, 1963, p. 81; *Vision,* September 1971, p. 56.
2. Otto Scott, *The Creative Ordeal: The Story of Raytheon* (New York: Atheneum, 1974), pp. 266–67 ff.
3. *Fortune,* February 1961, p. 112.
4. *ITT Annual Report,* 1959, p. 7.
5. *ITT Annual Report,* 1963, p. 5.
6. Walter Guzzardi, Jr. "I.T.T. Gets the Message," *Fortune,* February 1961, p. 115.
7. ITT, "Acquisitions Policy, March 11, 1963," in *Investigation of Conglomerate Corporations,* Part 3, p. 249.
8. Al Kroeger, "Merger Machine in High Gear," *Television Magazine,* July 1966, p. 7; Harvey Levin, "Broadcasting Structure; Technology, and the ABC-ITT Merger Decision," *Law and Contemporary Problems,* Summer 1969, pp. 452–84.
9. Richard Howe, "Harold Geneen: The Man at the Top of the ITT Pole," *Vision,* September, 1971, p. 54.
10. Robert Goolrick, *Public Policy Toward Corporate Growth: The ITT Cases* (Port Washington: Kennikat Press, 1978), p. 42.
11. *The Wall Street Journal,* December 22, 1966; Anthony Sampson, *The Sovereign State of ITT* (New York: Stein & Day, 1972), p. 90.
12. *The Wall Street Journal,* March 17, 1967.
13. *The Wall Street Journal,* April 20, 1967.
14. "ITT: The View from the Inside," *Business Week,* November 3, 1973, p. 53.
15. Carol J. Loomis, "How I.T.T. Got Lost in a Big Bad Forest," *Fortune,* December 17, 1979, pp. 42–45.
16. U.S. Congress, Senate, Committee on the Judiciary, *Hearings on the Nomination of Richard G. Kleindienst of Arizona to be Attorney General,* 92nd Cong., 2nd sess., 1972, p. 1651.
17. Goolrick, *The ITT Merger Cases,* p. 70.

7. Antitrust and the Penn Central Fiasco

1. U.S., Federal Trade Commission, Staff Report of the Federal Trade Commission, *Economic Report on Corporate Mergers* (Washington, D.C., Government Printing Office, 1969), p. 63.
2. Robert Sobel, *Money Manias,* p. 149.
3. Goolrich, *The ITT Merger Cases,* p. 42.

4. Senate, *Kleindienst Hearings,* pp. 116–18.
5. Goolrick, *The ITT Merger Cases,* pp. 50–51.
6. *Business Week,* August 2, 1969, pp. 27–28.
7. Goolrick, *The ITT Merger Cases,* pp. 60, 63.
8. Brown, *Ling,* pp. 169–70 ff.
9. Goolrick, *The ITT Merger Cases,* pp. 98–100.
10. Brown, *Ling,* p. 205.
11. Ibid., p. 216 ff.
12. Gulf + Western, *1970 Annual Report,* p. 2.
13. *The New York Times,* October 11, 1970.
14. Joseph Daughen and Peter Binzen, *The Wreck of the Penn Central* (Boston: Little, Brown, 1971), p. 85.
15. The failure and its impact upon the nation have been documented in several books and investigated fully by congressional committees. See U.S., Congress, House, Committee on Interstate and Foreign Commerce, *The Financial Collapse of the Penn Central,* 92nd Cong., 1st sess., 1972; U.S., Congress, House, *Staff Report of the Committee on Banking and Currency: The Penn Central Failure and the Role of Financial Institutions, 92nd Cong., 1st sess., 1972;* Daughen and Binzen, *The Wreck of the Penn Central;* Stephen Salisbury, *No Way to Run a Railroad: The Untold Story of the Penn Central Crisis* (New York: McGraw Hill, 1982); Richard Saunders, *The Railroad Mergers and the Coming of Conrail* (Westport, Conn.: Greenwood Press, 1978), chapter 13; and Robert Sobel, *The Fallen Colossus* (New York: Weybright & Talley, 1977).
16. Salisbury, *No Way to Run a Railroad,* p. 160.
17. Ibid., pp. 70–71.

8. The Reaction

1. Brown, *Ling,* p. 205.
2. *Time,* March 7, 1969, p. 76.
3. Isadore Barmash, "Bluhdorn Discusses Retrenching Program," *The New York Times,* October 22, 1970.
4. "Model Conglomerate Tries to be an Operating Company," *Business Week,* December 1, 1973, p. 69.
5. Goolrick, *The ITT Merger Cases,* pp. 98–100.
6. *Kleindienst Hearings,* pt. 2; pp. 103–10.
7. Lewis Beman, "What We Learned from the Great Merger Frenzy," *Fortune,* April 1973, pp. 70–144.

9. Nuclear War on the Corporate Battlefield

1. "2 + 2 = ?," *Forbes,* September 15, 1973, pp. 45–54.
2. *The Wall Street Journal,* March 10, 1977.
3. "What Edgar Bronfman Wants at Seagram," *Business Week,* April 27, 1981, pp. 138–40.
4. In addition, Mobil purchased W. F. Hall Printing for $50.5 million in cash, little more than pocket money for such a firm. Alexander Stuart, "What Makes Mobil Run," *Fortune,* December 14, 1981, p. 94.
5. *The New York Times,* September 10, 1982.
6. *The New York Times,* July 17, 1981.
7. "After the Merger Du Pont Still Likes Conoco," *Newsweek,* May 30, 1983, p. 73.
8. For a chronology of the contest, see Judith McQuown, *Playing the Takeover Game* (New York: Seaview, 1982), pp. 108–27.
9. Stuart, "What Makes Mobil Run," p. 93.
10. "Marathon Pumps Up Its Takeover Defense," *Business Week,* November 30, 1981, p. 52.
11. On November 22 Standard & Poor's announced it might have to revise downward U. S. Steel's bond rating if the merger took place. *The Wall Street Journal,* November 23, 1981.
12. *The Wall Street Journal,* March 10, 1982.
13. Roy Rowan and Thomas Moore, "The Bendix War," *Fortune,* October 18, 1982, p. 158.
14. Allan Sloan, *Three Plus One Equals Billions: The Bendix-Martin Marietta War* (New York: Arbor House, 1983), p. 176.
15. "Did Anyone Win the Bendix Game?" *Business Week,* October 11, 1982, p. 28.
16. *The New York Times,* September 9, 1982.
17. Sloan, *Three Plus One Equals Billions,* p. 22.
18. "The New Allied," *Barron's,* June 6, 1983, p. 55.
19. "Our Dream is to Work Together," *Fortune,* October 4, 1982, p. 165. "American Takeover Rules," *The Economist,* May 21, 1983, p. 80.
20. "American Takeover Rules," *The Economist,* May 21, 1983, p. 80.
21. For a survey of activities in the wake of the Bendix affair, see American Enterprise Institute, *Recent Proposals to Restrict Conglomerate Mergers* (Washington: American Enterprise Institute, 1981).
22. *The New York Times,* June 3, 1983.

Index